WAS IT SOMETHING I SAID?

WAS IT SOMETHING I SAID?

Everyday Etiquette to Avoid Awkward Moments in Relationships, Work, and Life

ALISON M. CHEPERDAK

W Publishing Group
An Imprint of Thomas Nelson

Was It Something I Said?

Published by W Publishing, an imprint of Thomas Nelson, 501 Nelson Place, Nashville, TN 37214, USA.

Thomas Nelson titles may be purchased in bulk for educational, business, fundraising, or sales promotional use. For information, please email SpecialMarkets@ThomasNelson.com.

ISBN 978-1-4003-5015-5 (audiobook)
ISBN 978-1-4003-5014-8 (ePub)
ISBN 978-1-4003-5012-4 (HC)

HarperCollins Publishers, Macken House, 39/40 Mayor Street Upper, Dublin 1, D01 C9W8, Ireland (https://www.harpercollins.com)

Library of Congress Control Number: 2025943808

Art Direction: Meg Schmidt
Cover Design: Thinkpen Design
Interior Design: Denise Froehlich

Printed in the United States of America

26 27 28 29 30 LBC 6 5 4 3 2

To Jason—my partner in everything. I love you.

CONTENTS

INTRODUCTION

BEFORE WE BEGIN, DON'T ASK IF SHE'S PREGNANT

If you learn nothing else from this book, do not under any circumstance ask a woman—unless you are absolutely, positively, beyond a shadow of a doubt certain—if she is expecting. I once wrongly jumped to this unfortunate conclusion when I was older than I'd care to admit and congratulated a friend I hadn't seen in a while on her pregnancy. I'd heard she was expecting, but my timing was regrettably very off. To my dismay, not only was she no longer expecting, but her sweet little one was already old enough to walk.

Thankfully, all things considered, my friend took it well, but my etiquette faux pas sticks with me as an important reminder that words matter, and they have the power to create or prevent awkward moments.

While the proper etiquette in one scenario may not be appropriate in another (e.g., a Taylor Swift concert versus a symphony orchestra, or a hockey game versus a golf tournament), every situation warrants some version of etiquette or social mores. In many respects, etiquette never stops. It's fine to take a day off from work or go on vacation, but we wouldn't admittedly take time off from having integrity or being honest and kind—and that's what etiquette is all about.

Prior to launching Elevate Etiquette, a modern etiquette consultancy where I teach and speak about modern manners for life, work, and love, I worked first as a television news reporter and anchor and then as an attorney. I had a role in every branch of the federal government, including the West Wing of the White House, as well as in a large corporate law firm and national nonprofit.

Throughout these varied roles, etiquette dilemmas were constant. I was asking myself: *How soon is too soon to follow up with an email for a job I'm really excited about?* What does one talk about in an informational coffee without seeming too forward? How do I tell my girlfriend I can't make it to her wedding because of final exams? Is it rude to put my AirPods in and not say hello to everyone I recognize on the Metro? If I order bacon for breakfast with my boss, is it weird if I eat it with my hands, or will it seem stuffy if I eat it with utensils?

These are just some of the many etiquette questions that would swirl through my head. Perhaps you can relate.

Over time, I got the hang of things, and I'm writing this book hoping to empower you with the etiquette and situational awareness you need to elegantly navigate those potential awkward moments with confidence and class.

Throughout my career, I've seen time and time again that while education and professional credentials are important, what truly makes people stand out are their soft skills. It's the way you treat the people who may not be in an obvious position to help, or the thank-you note that is sent immediately after a dinner party to express your gratitude. It's the little things, the small ways that we show we care, that we've prepared for a given moment, that we're giving someone our undivided attention.

Especially during my time as a law clerk on Capitol Hill and an attorney in the executive branch, meeting with many lobbyists and stakeholders on a vast array of issues, I got to see firsthand the styles of presentation and manners in meetings and in communication that worked—and those that didn't. I still remember specific public policy professionals who were so adept at respectful and effective negotiation and collaboration on typically controversial subjects.

Ultimately, it's people who are kind, respectful, enjoyable to be around, trustworthy, and hardworking—they are the ones who get the job, are recruited for new opportunities, are invited to social occasions, and are easier to celebrate because they're so gracious. It's the little etiquette details we can incorporate each and every day that make a dramatic and positive compounding impact over time.

Etiquette is about so much more than appearing polished. It is also an essential part of demonstrating respect and honoring relationships. While my etiquette knowledge certainly helped me better present my legal arguments, negotiate my compensation, and network effectively in pursuit of highly competitive positions, that knowledge is just as important in my personal life too.

How to Use This Book

This book was designed to be both a cozy front-to-back read and a handy resource you can return to when you're in need of a little guidance (or a gentle nudge). You may want to curl up with it and soak in the full journey, or you might prefer to dip in and out—flipping directly to the chapters or questions that apply to whatever situation you're experiencing in the moment.

There's no wrong way to read it. If you're preparing for a big interview, approaching a tricky social situation, or attending a funeral for the first time in a while, I encourage you to look those specific topics up. I've included a thoughtfully organized index to help you find what you need, quickly—whether it's how to gracefully decline an invitation, write a warm and timely thank-you note, or figure out if bacon is ever finger food (spoiler: it depends).

You'll also find Q&As woven throughout—real questions from real people who were wondering the very same things you might be now. These were selected to reflect the nuances, awkward moments, and "Is it just me?" etiquette scenarios we all encounter.

You may even come across a chapter that doesn't feel relevant to your life right now—and that's perfectly fine. Feel free to skip around. Etiquette is deeply personal and situational. What matters most is that you find what you need, when you need it.

Consider this book your trusted friend—here to help you move through meaningful moments with grace, ease, and self-awareness. With that, I cordially invite you to join me in learning the etiquette and soft skills you need to shine in relationships, work, and life.

What Etiquette Is and Why It Matters

Etiquette and manners are similar, but they are not the same. Manners are about demonstrating kindness, respect, and honesty more generally; etiquette tells us how to convey good manners in specific situations. While manners are behaviors that reflect a person's attitude or respect, etiquette, as defined by the Cambridge Dictionary, means "the set of rules or customs that control accepted behavior in particular social groups or social situations."[1] Etiquette varies from culture to culture, and even in different contexts within the same culture, but the deeper meaning behind manners generally remains the same.

Etiquette matters because it is how we demonstrate our manners. Abiding by etiquette powerfully honors other people, places, milestones, and occasions. It is also the foundation of our best relationships—because the highest form of human bond is grounded in respect. Respecting another person does not mean agreeing with every opinion they might hold, but rather recognizing that all people have inherent dignity and are worthy of respect, including you.

Learning etiquette undeniably has its benefits. With enhanced social-emotional intelligence and self-awareness, you will become more likable and capable in social and professional situations. Plus, in a competitive job market, though your technical skills may get you in the door, empathy, conflict resolution, and leadership will make you truly stand out. Each of these soft skills is rooted in etiquette and social graces.

Genuine etiquette, however, should not be confused with people-pleasing, a habit that is often born of insecurity, manipulation, or the desire to be liked at all costs. People-pleasing is about bending over backward for approval, often at the expense of one's own needs or values. Etiquette, by contrast, is about making others feel at ease without compromising oneself. It's a form of social intelligence—not self-erasure.

Then there's likability—a separate but often entangled concept that has become especially complicated for women. Women in politics, for instance, are often expected to be likable to win over voters, whereas men are more readily judged on competence alone. It's a double standard that suggests women must prove they're approachable and agreeable, while men aren't held to the same warmth test.

We've all seen how female government leaders—from former US secretary of state and presidential candidate Hillary Clinton to former prime minister of Great Britain Margaret Thatcher—have faced intense scrutiny over how likable they are, and have had their credibility questioned through the lens of likability.

It's tempting to tune out the noise entirely—and understandably so. But here's the truth: Likability does matter, to a point. It isn't the be-all and end-all, but it opens doors. It builds trust, and it helps people feel safe around you. But it should never come at the cost of your voice or your values.

That's where real etiquette comes in. Etiquette isn't about molding yourself into someone else's idea of who you should be. It's about showing respect, extending grace, and engaging in relationships in a way that honors both you and the people around you. It's not about being liked by everyone. It's about being thoughtful, clear, and kind—while staying firmly grounded in who you are.

You might be stressing out: How do I follow all these rules? But don't worry: The only hard-and-fast rule is that you must check any shame about what you don't already know or did "wrong" before. There will be no shaming for bad etiquette in this book. Whether you are here for a little refresher, or it's your first time learning about the subject and its long history, your interest is timely and worth pursuing—whether for your career or for your general quality of life. In fact, while universities, companies, and recruiters are investing more than ever in teaching everything from elevator chitchat to presentation skills, now is your moment to polish your presence and truly stand out.

I'd be remiss if I didn't acknowledge what may seem like the uninvited elephant in the room: Approaching etiquette in a transactional and exclusively self-promotional manner is not a great look. While it may work at times, others will ultimately see through it, and faking kindness for selfish gain is no way to live. That's not what this is about.

I encourage you to use the lessons from this book for good, to excel both professionally and personally, all while honoring and inspiring others with wisdom, magnanimity, and equanimity along the way.

CHAPTER 1

GREETINGS AND INTRODUCTIONS

Almost every semester and summer of law school, I served as a law clerk in offices across the federal government. This included four committees in the US Congress and in the Office of the Chairman of the Federal Communications Commission. I will spare you the details on everything I learned about tax and telecommunications policy, and how it prepared me to land my first job after graduation in the not-so-riveting but lucrative telephone-pole law specialty. But I will share what I learned about meeting people. Capitol Hill is a place where the friendly, extroverted, and socially savvy thrive.

What you won't learn from *Schoolhouse Rock!* about how things work on Capitol Hill is that any legislative victory typically involves lots and lots of meetings, with lots of different kinds of people—from others in government to constituents and beyond.

Some days, other than a break for lunch, my time would be filled with back-to-back meetings all on the same topic, with the same colleagues, in the same room, and the same duration. The only difference was the myriad guests who came to share their perspectives and recommendations. Some were lobbyists out of central casting—prepared, professional, smooth, solution-oriented, and effective. Others were late, oddly demanding, out-of-touch in the policy positions they were pushing, or not yet sufficiently informed on the issues.

Most were dressed in suits, others in flowy maxi dresses, and there was even one lobbyist from California wearing red suede shoes and no socks despite the rain, who handed out business cards with his first name only that were the size of coasters. I learned a lot about the power of making a lasting, positive first impression. There are so many details, from how you dress to how you enter a room to what you do with your hands during a meeting, that directly contribute to how you come across.

First Impressions

We don't get a second chance to make a strong first impression, whether it's professional or social. So why not prepare and learn how to wow everyone you meet right from the start? While we may like the idea of not judging a book by its cover, we make judgments about others upon meeting them within the first seven seconds.[1] It's a survival-motivated reaction that helps us quickly judge our perceived level of safety. That means you have seven seconds or less to convey the confident, calm, competent demeanor you want to display.

Q: *I get that first impressions are important, but I'm afraid I just made a terrible first impression on my new colleague. I lost my cool at the office when all our printers went down before a big meeting. Is it possible to recover?*

A: Yes. While strong first impressions are ideal, it's never too late to turn things around and overcome an underwhelming first impression. If you made a mistake or lost your temper or otherwise did something that warrants an apology, doing so should be your first order of business. Apologize to anyone you may have yelled at, been short with, or otherwise acted unkind toward. Show that you understand your behavior was inappropriate, and don't blame others or circumstances even if you could or feel like you should. Commit to correcting things in the future. Then, from that point forward, behave in ways consistent with the person you want to be, and don't lose hope. Mistakes happen to the best of us, and in apologizing appropriately, you will likely gain more respect.

Personal Appearance

While we may not be super proud of it, the truth is, before anyone listens to what we say, they have typically already made preliminary judgments based on the way we look. This includes what we wear. Your outfit is like a nonverbal introduction—it gives people a hint about you before you even say a word.

Whether you have put thought and intentionality into it before or not, you are a brand. Every choice you make regarding your outward appearance, communication style, body language, topics you do and do not discuss, how you handle conflict, your ability to solve problems—all of these qualities contribute to how you are perceived. There is only one you. Being intentional about your appearance is just as important as the way you speak, carry yourself, and handle challenges—and it's one of the most tangible ways to reflect the image you want to project.

As a starting point, visualize the person or persona you want to be. Is it calm and classy? Artistic and fun? Polished and professional? Timeless and chic? Comfortable and friendly? Confident and creative? You can begin taking steps to dress like this person today. This is the simplest kind of personal branding, which is often a layered process that takes time and conscious effort. As you are shopping, choosing outfits, and streamlining your wardrobe, ask yourself, *Does this piece visually support my personal brand?*

However, your appearance is more than what you are wearing.[2] At work, for instance, everything someone can see on your person, at your workspace, or in your office is part of your personal brand. So, if you are sporting a fabulously dapper suit, ensure that your shoes and bag are complementary and in mint condition. A messy bag or office space, unprofessional photos either in your work area or on your phone's lock or home screen, a notebook that is not well kept—all these details undermine a persona of competence, organization, and success.

Even if you don't work in a traditional office, the same idea applies. Whether you're working remotely, freelancing from coffee shops, leading a classroom, or running a household, your environment, tools, and digital presence all contribute to how others experience your professionalism. What people see around you still speaks volumes about who you are.

Standing Tall with Poise and Deliberate Deportment

Good posture is more than just standing tall; it's a statement of inner strength. It tells the world you're poised and self-assured.

Now, how do you convey this? Align your ears over your shoulders, keep your chin parallel to the floor, relax your shoulders, and let your spine remain neutral. It's all about balance and grace—being grounded without appearing rigid, lifted without looking stiff.

Good posture lends you an air of poise and is a key part of good deportment. What does that mean? Poise and deportment are often used interchangeably but actually describe complementary qualities.

Poise refers to your inner calm and outward composure. It's that serene self-possession that allows you to remain steady under pressure, speak with grace, and move with confidence even when a situation is unfamiliar or uncomfortable. Poise is quiet power—it's how you carry your presence.

Deportment, on the other hand, is about how you physically carry yourself—your posture, movement, and bearing. It includes the way you walk into a room, how you sit, how you gesture, and even how you exit a conversation. It's the outer expression of inner respect—for yourself and for those around you.

When poise and deportment work together, the result is magnetic. You come across not only as polished, but as grounded, gracious, and fully present.

The Power of the Chin: How Body Language Shapes Perception

Body language plays an essential role in how we're perceived by others, and the position of your chin can speak volumes. Let's break down how subtle shifts can make a big impact.

1. **Chin Pointed Above Parallel**

   If your chin is raised above parallel to the ground, you might be perceived as haughty or contemptuous, sending a message that you feel superior or detached from those around you. Research in nonverbal communication indicates that this posture can create a sense of arrogance or unapproachability. Studies in body language analysis by experts like Dr. Albert Mehrabian suggest that nonverbal cues heavily influence others' interpretations of our attitudes.[3]

2. **Chin Parallel to the Ground**

   A chin held parallel to the ground signals healthy pride and confidence. This posture projects a strong, assured presence that suggests you are comfortable in your own skin and attentive to your surroundings. Research has shown that confident, upright head positions contribute to perceptions of leadership and reliability.[4] This simple alignment reflects a more traditional understanding of confidence and assertiveness in body language.

3. **Neutral, Relaxed Chin**

   When your chin is neutral and relaxed, the message conveyed is one of calm and strength, though it may not exude the same level of confidence as the slightly raised position. This posture is often associated with approachability and trustworthiness. A study by Dr. Amy Cuddy at Harvard University found that open, relaxed body language can foster an impression of authenticity and reliability, though it may not carry the same power as more assertive poses.[5]

4. **Chin Slightly Below Parallel**

When the chin is dropped just below parallel, it can create an impression of concern or worry. People often drop their chins when experiencing negative thoughts or feelings of uncertainty. This subtle shift can signal that you are introspective, processing information, or feeling apprehensive.

5. **Chin Significantly Below Parallel**

A chin that dips well below parallel conveys sadness or feeling low. This posture occurs naturally when people are in emotional distress or feeling defeated. It's a protective stance that suggests retreating into oneself and can make a person appear disengaged or vulnerable. This downward tilt has been noted in psychological studies, such as those examining depression-related body language, which highlights the way postural changes mirror emotional states.[6]

In sum, chin position is an often-overlooked detail that can influence social interactions, public speaking, and even professional encounters. Mastering the subtle art of adjusting your chin can help project the exact image you want: poised, approachable, and confident.

Please, Have a Seat

What do Princess Mia Thermopolis, White House interns, and members of an orchestra have in common? They've all been taught how to sit—with intention, grace, and presence. Because whether you're on stage or simply seated at a dinner table, the way you sit says more than you think. Let's talk about how to do it.

The Duchess Slant

The Sussex Slant

The Queen's Pose

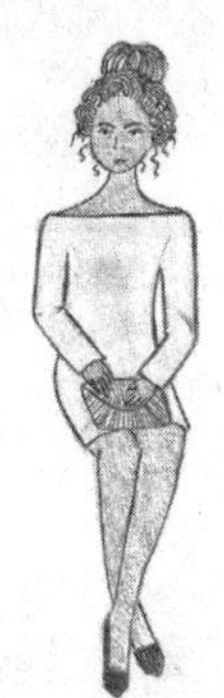
The Cambridge Cross

SEATING POSITIONS FOR DRESSES AND SKIRTS

The Duchess Slant

The "Duchess Slant" is a poised and elegant seating position made famous by etiquette expert Myka Meier. It's perfect for maintaining modesty when wearing skirts or dresses with hemlines above the knee. To achieve this, keep your knees and ankles together, then subtly angle your hips to the left or right, placing your feet neatly on the floor. The result is a graceful zigzag line from your thighs to your feet, ensuring both comfort and a polished look.

The Sussex Slant

The "Sussex Slant" is an elegant position in which, even when crossing your legs at the knees, your knees and ankles remain together, creating a graceful slant. This helps prevent any unintended foot shaking, which can sometimes signal nervousness, boredom, or annoyance. If you're wearing heels, be mindful to keep them tucked back to avoid any accidental nudges. It's all about maintaining that composed and polished look.

The Queen's Pose

Another option is to sit with your entire body facing forward, keeping your knees and ankles together. This is the simplest position to master and was a favorite of the late Queen Elizabeth II.

The Cambridge Cross

Another graceful option is crossing your legs at the ankles. With your body facing forward, place one ankle in front of the other and keep both heels resting on the floor.

Leg Cross

Upper Body Considerations

Feet Flat

SEATING POSITIONS FOR PANTS

Leg Cross Another comfortable and composed option for those wearing pants is crossing the legs. It's perfectly fine to do so, but try to keep your ankles close together to avoid a messy, upside-down V shape. Not everyone finds this comfortable, so it's a matter of personal preference.

Upper Body Considerations When it comes to your hands, keep them relaxed—tightly clasped hands can signal stress. Leaning back against the chair adds a casual touch, but it's best to avoid in formal settings.

Feet Flat A great position is sitting with both feet flat on the floor, knees slightly apart—think about the width of a golf ball. Hands can rest on your lap, either flat on your thighs or gently clasped in a relaxed, carefree manner.

Fragrance: Fabulous or a Faux Pas?

During my time ice dancing—a sport replete with dramatic costumes and fragrance choices—as part of my skating training, I worked out with a personal trainer at 7:00 a.m. every Saturday. Naturally, I'd show up with a full face of makeup and a spritz (or several) of my favorite perfume. Looking back, the thought of all that makeup at dawn makes me cringe—my poor skin! But at the time, it was a vibe.

That is, until my trainer told me other clients had trouble breathing in the gym after I left. Definitely not my finest moment! My perfume lingered in the air long after I was gone, and not in a "signature scent" kind of way. It was a wake-up call: Maybe not everyone shared my enthusiasm for eau de parfum. Years later, my sister, then in medical device sales, confirmed the lesson when she was formally told she couldn't wear perfume at hospitals in the operating room. Personal fragrance policies in professional settings exist for a reason, especially in industries like health care, where close proximity to others means extra sensitivity is required.

Reasonable minds may differ on wearing fragrance, but in general: When in doubt, less is more—or skip it altogether. If you work in an environment with a no-fragrance policy, respect it. And if your signature scent is causing someone you regularly encounter to feel unwell, the courteous thing to do is adjust when possible.

Now, if you do choose to wear a fragrance, consider narrowing it down to one or a few signature scents. Constantly switching can project indecisiveness, while a consistent scent becomes part of your personal brand—sophisticated, understated, and memorable. Because at the end of the day, the goal is to leave a lasting impression, not a lingering headache.

Q: *I love finding new fragrances and sharing them with friends and family. Is it appropriate to give fragrances as a gift?*

A: In general, a perfume or cologne worn on the body is very personal and can be considered romantic, sort of like a gift of red roses. For that reason, I don't recommend giving fragrances unless you are certain of the recipient's preferences. Even then, I would only give a fragrance to someone you are very close to. There are moments, however, when giving fragrances can be perfectly appropriate, such as replenishing a friend's or family member's fragrance that you know they enjoy using often or giving a gift to someone close to you who you know really appreciates fragrances and you are aware of their personal taste. Make sure to consider any cultural implications too. In some cultures, it is considered rude to give someone perfume or cologne because it can be interpreted as a sign that the recipient smells bad.

Mastering Deportment: How You Carry Yourself Matters

Coming across as the confident, likable person you aspire to be has everything to do with how you carry yourself—your walk, your posture, your presence. So let's discuss deportment, that aspect of physicality I mentioned earlier. Picture a celebrity commanding the red carpet with poise, a politician exuding authority during a tough Senate confirmation hearing, or that friend who walks into any room and immediately lights it up, even if she doesn't know a soul. They've mastered the art of how to carry themselves in a way that earns respect, attention, and authority.

If you've ever told yourself that you weren't born with the "it" factor, let me stop you right here. That belief is a limiting one—and it's time to let it go. Deportment isn't something you're born with; it's a skill. And like any skill, it can be learned and perfected with the right intention and practice.

Let's start with the basics of how to elevate your deportment, followed by common habits that might be working against you.

The Foundations of Dignified Deportment

Here are a few simple ways to project confidence and composure in any setting.

- **When You Enter a Room:** Smile, make eye contact, and if there's a door, close it behind you without turning your back to the people you're greeting. First impressions matter, so let yours exude warmth and respect.
- **The Handshake:** A Gesture of Assurance: Extend your right hand for a firm, but not crushing, handshake. It's a gesture that conveys assurance and approachability.
- **Stand Tall:** Maintain a neutral spine with your head aligned directly over your shoulders and hips. Keep your chin parallel to the ground—not too high (arrogance) or too low (timidity).
- **Sit Gracefully:** Sit with your back off the chair if possible, your knees and ankles together, and avoid leaning on armrests. No elbows on the table, though forearms are permissible in non-dining scenarios.

- **Mind Your Hands:** Keep them visible, especially when seated at a table. This small detail signals engagement, trustworthiness, and transparency.
- **Walk Well:**
  - In flats, walk with your feet hip-width apart for stability and natural movement.
  - In heels, place one foot directly in front of the other to elongate your stride.
  - Avoid excessive arm swinging or flailing bags and briefcases.

Habits That Might Be Undermining Your Deportment

Even small, seemingly innocent actions can chip away at your polished presence. Here are some habits to avoid:

- **Chewing Gum:** Practical as it may be, chewing gum—especially visibly or loudly—can make you appear less refined. Opt for mints instead.
- **Changing Shoes in Public:** Swapping flats for heels (or vice versa) in a hallway or on the street detracts from your composure. Find a discreet place, like a restroom or dressing area, for these adjustments.
- **Grooming in Public:** Fixing your hair or makeup in shared spaces, like at a table or in a meeting, is best avoided. Use the restroom for personal touch-ups.
- **Bringing Your Own Food or Drink to Meetings:** Unless you have a specific dietary need and have communicated it beforehand, arriving with your own snacks or beverages can seem out of place, especially in professional or refined settings.
- **Overloading on Accessories:** Jangling bracelets, oversized jewelry, or other noisy accessories can distract from your overall presence. Choose understated elegance.
- **Using Your Phone Constantly:** Checking your phone (even just glancing down at it intermittently) in meetings, conversations, or events signals disengagement. Be present with the people around you.
- **Talking Too Loudly:** Whether in conversation or on the phone, projecting your voice excessively can draw unwanted attention—and

unintentionally disrupt the people around you. If people in the next aisle, row, or table can clearly follow your story, chances are you're speaking too loudly for the setting.

Pay attention to subtle cues—if others are glancing over, shifting uncomfortably, or turning their heads, it may be time to lower your volume. And if you're in a public space where background noise suddenly drops (like an elevator or waiting room), bring your voice down with it. Being aware of your surroundings is half the battle.

- **Fidgeting:** Playing with your hair, tapping your pen, or bouncing your leg can undermine your composed appearance.
- **Eating While Walking:** Rushing down the street with a sandwich in hand feels far from polished. Plan time to eat in a calm setting instead.
- **Slurping from a To-Go Cup:** There's nothing wrong with carrying a to-go coffee or tea as you're out and about, running errands, or heading to your next stop—it's part of modern life. But if you're going to a meeting or an appointment, leave the personal beverage behind unless you've offered to bring one for the others you're meeting. Arriving with a latte while the other person sits empty-handed can feel unintentionally self-focused. It's a small detail, but one that signals consideration and awareness. And no matter what, don't show up late with a to-go cup. It communicates that getting your drink was more important to you than respecting others' time.

Why It Matters

Deportment is about more than just appearances; it's about how you make others feel in your presence. It's carrying yourself with poise—that graceful calm you maintain in your posture, expression, and movement, even under pressure. It's the balance of composure and presence that makes others feel at ease around you. Small tweaks to your posture, habits, and demeanor can elevate the way you're perceived, whether you're walking into a boardroom, attending a cocktail party, or simply crossing the street.

Ultimately, deportment is less about rules and more about moving through the world with thoughtfulness, conviction, and care.

Q: *I thought putting your elbows on the table was a good thing as long as you're not dining because it shows attentiveness and transparency. Is that right?*

A: Reasonable minds may differ on this, but I recommend keeping elbows off the table whether or not food is served. It is true that we are perceived as more competent, confident, attentive, and trustworthy when others can see our hands. Imagine watching someone on stage giving a presentation with her hands clasped behind her back the entire time. You would probably find it odd and wonder if she was hiding something.

The perception of trustworthiness that results from seeing someone's hands is quite primitive. It goes back centuries to when it was more common to carry weapons. Both shaking hands and keeping hands visible were ways of demonstrating that you came in peace. Today, some recommend putting elbows on the table because it allows you to lean in and really demonstrate your engagement in meetings and conversation. While I appreciate that point, you don't need to put your elbows on the table to demonstrate respect and focus. I recommend simply placing your forearms on the edge of the table and showing your attentiveness through nodding, smiling, taking notes (if applicable), and contributing to the conversation.

Q: *I tend to fidget when I'm nervous, especially during meetings. How can I practice sitting and moving with more poise, even when I'm feeling anxious?*

A: Practicing stillness and deliberate movement can help you project calmness, even if you're feeling a bit jittery inside. Start by anchoring your feet flat on the floor, which gives you stability and helps prevent fidgeting. Try to rest your hands gently on your lap or on the table in front of you, and make a habit of returning them there whenever you feel a fidget coming on.

Your Digital First Impression

I didn't use social media at all in middle school, high school, or college. I'm not proud to admit it, but the reason was less noble than you might think. It wasn't about staying grounded or focusing on "real life." No, it was because I was worried that what I perceived to be the small universe of people who thought I was cool would stumble upon my digital presence and realize I was not, in fact, that cool at all. I feared exposure—not in the dangerous, oversharing way, but in the what-if-they-find-out-I'm-just-regular kind of way. Imposter syndrome: party of one.

Thankfully, my relationship with myself—and with the internet—has evolved. Today, while I'm still human (and yes, the occasional mean comment still stings), I share a lot of my life, personality, hopes, and dreams online. I've been an early and active user of LinkedIn since my college days (firstborn, type A, recovering-perfectionist energy), but I didn't really venture into the rest of the social media world until I had to—as part of my job as an on-air TV reporter. Even then, it felt like I was putting on a digital costume rather than showing up as my full, multifaceted self.

All that to say, even if social media doesn't feel like your thing today, that doesn't mean it won't someday become a life-giving, dynamic, and even joyful part of your daily rhythm. Whether you're an all-in content creator, a lurker with a soft spot for birthday shout-outs, or somewhere in between, a bit of intentionality can help you make a great digital first impression—and a meaningful one over time.

And here's why it matters: A 2018 CareerBuilder survey found that 66 percent of employers research candidates online, and 57 percent have chosen not to hire someone based on what they found.[7] But beyond the job search, your digital presence can influence everything from professional opportunities to personal connections to how others perceive your values, voice, and credibility.

Your online presence—whether polished, playful, or still evolving—isn't just personal. It's also public. And powerful.

The good news? You don't need to be an influencer. You just need to be intentional. Because in today's world, your digital footprint often walks into the room before you do—and sometimes, it speaks on your behalf.

We've already talked about creating a personal brand in person—it applies to how you conduct yourself online too. To craft a brand that feels authentic, start with three questions about your online posts:

1. What are my core values?
2. How do I want people to feel when they interact with me online?
3. What's the balance between professional and personal I'm comfortable with?

Your personal brand should feel like the best version of you—approachable yet polished, authentic yet intentional. And remember, you're allowed to evolve. The you from five years ago doesn't have to be the you of today.

Social Media Audit: Cleaning Up Your Digital Closet

Perhaps you haven't given much thought to the impression you're making online. Maybe it's time to clean it up. A social media audit is like Marie Kondo-ing your online life. Does that tagged photo from spring break ten-plus years ago spark joy? Probably not.

Start with your main platforms and look at them as if you're a stranger. Ask yourself:

- Is this aligned with how I want to be seen?
- Would I be comfortable with a boss, mentor, or future partner seeing this?
- Does my content reflect my current goals and values?

And don't forget privacy settings. Studies suggest that more than half of American social media users have posted and deleted something they regret.[8] If in doubt, archive, delete, or change to "only me" view. And while you're at it, you might consider updating bios and profile photos to match your current vibe. Although it's perfectly fine to treat your social media like a scrapbook that encapsulates your prior eras and personal growth, use your best judgment on what is and is not appropriate for a long-term position on the grid to share with the world.

Q: *Is it better to have public or private social media profiles as a professional? I've heard mixed things. I used to think it was better to keep all social media private, but I've also heard that some employers prefer job candidates or employees have public profiles because it shows that nothing nefarious is being hidden, and it provides a fuller sense of your life and values.*

A: There is nothing wrong with not being on social media, taking a break, or spending less time on various apps if that is your preference. Reasonable minds may differ on this, but I don't think you need to announce taking a different approach to your personal time online. As for whether there is a professional advantage to having a public or private social media account, again, I think that's a matter of personal choice and career goals. If you want to work in a personal brand–driven industry, such as sports, media, art, entertainment, or entrepreneurship, I recommend having a strong presence on social media, but that doesn't mean you need to include or divulge personal details beyond what you're comfortable sharing.

Making Introductions

So, you've made a great first impression—your entrance was poised and deliberate, and now it's time to say hello. If you're introducing yourself, keep it simple and confident: Make eye contact, offer your name clearly, and add a touch of warmth with a smile or a handshake, depending on the setting.

Introducing others can be a bit trickier, especially in unfamiliar or formal contexts. Thankfully, there's a simple formula for getting it right.

First, make sure you know how to pronounce everyone's names and honor their preferences. If you're unsure, asking ahead—"How do you like to be introduced?"—is thoughtful and effective. It's also essential to respect how people prefer to be addressed. Just because you've called your childhood friend "Ellie" for years doesn't mean it's appropriate to introduce her that way if she now goes by "Eloise" in professional or social settings. Thoughtful introductions show care—for both the person being introduced and the one you're introducing them to.

Here is sample language for some of the most common introduction situations when a little professionalism and formality are in order:

State the name of the person you want to honor most, first.	"Ms. VIP Guest, may I please introduce Mr. Friend?"
Lower-ranking employees are introduced to more senior employees. In a professional context, seniority is determined by position, not age, gender, or length of time at an organization.	"Mr. Managing Partner, may I introduce Ms. Intern?"
Colleagues are introduced to clients.	"Ms. Client, may I introduce Mr. Colleague?"
Vendors/suppliers are introduced to clients.	"Mr. Client, may I introduce Ms. Vendor?"
Colleagues are introduced to vendors/suppliers.	"Ms. Vendor, may I introduce Mr. Colleague?"

When making introductions, titles and honorifics should be mirrored. So if you're using Ms. or Mr., or stating job titles, make sure you do the same thing for everyone. When possible, full names are best (unless you're introducing a child, in which case you would use a first name only for the child, but not the adult).

Introductions also don't stop with the name. It's important to provide those you are introducing with something to talk about, such as making them aware of shared interests or providing topics well suited for discussion. For example, "Dr. Melissa Kennedy, may I please introduce Mrs. Maria Garcia? Maria is also an avid gardener, and I'm sure she would love to hear about what you have been planting lately." This is helpful in both formal situations and casual get-togethers.

On a First-Name Basis

We live in an era when first-name-basis interactions are the norm, but don't get too comfortable just yet. While many people prefer being addressed informally, there are still situations—and cultures—where sticking to the formal route shows respect and saves you from an accidental faux pas.

In informal or semiformal settings, it's better to err on the side of formality until invited to do otherwise. This is especially true in Eastern cultures, such as those in Asia, India, and Southeast Asia, where addressing someone by first name, particularly if they are older, can be considered disrespectful.

For children, teaching them to use honorifics (Mr., Mrs., etc.) and last names for their friends' parents until told otherwise sets a respectful tone and helps establish boundaries. It's a tradition that continues to matter—for good reason.

The Nickname Dilemma

Nicknames can be a minefield of unintended offense. Just because you hear someone else calling your colleague "Bobby" or "Red" doesn't mean you should jump on board. Ask yourself:

- Does the person use the nickname themselves?
- Is the nickname tied to an incident or identity they'd rather not relive?

If you're unsure, don't assume. It's perfectly fine to ask, "I've heard others call you [nickname]. Do you prefer that, or would you rather I stick with your full name?" It's thoughtful and shows you care about getting it right.

When introducing someone with a nickname, check with them first. Many people prefer their full name in formal or professional settings, even if they're "Katie" to friends.

Pronunciation Etiquette

Names are not just what people call us—they're a huge part of our identity. And yet, getting someone's name wrong happens all the time. Speaking from experience, it's awkward for everyone when someone mispronounces your name—especially if you've known each other for years.

My last name is Cheperdak (pronounced like "shepherd"), and trust me, I know it's not the easiest to say. Back when I worked in television, I actually went by my maiden name, Carey, in part because I figured Cheperdak didn't exactly roll off the tongue for nightly-news introductions. Yet I always feel cared for when people bother to ask how to say it. No matter how complex or simple a name is, saying it correctly is about showing care and respect.

So, whether you're meeting someone new or reintroducing yourself to an old acquaintance, taking a moment to get their name right—and helping them with yours—is a small act that leaves a lasting impression.

Q: *My name is spelled unconventionally, and people are always mispronouncing it. I'm never sure exactly what to say. Do I just let it go? Do I correct them immediately? Do I smile awkwardly and hope they never say it again? What is a kind way to correct them, if ever?*

A: If someone mispronounces your name, it's absolutely appropriate to gently correct them—it's your name, and it deserves to be said correctly! Addressing it right away is not only kind to yourself but also to them, as it prevents the mistake from being repeated when they introduce you to others.

Here's how to handle it with grace:

- As soon as you notice the error, respond in a warm, friendly tone: "Actually, my name is pronounced [correct pronunciation]." Keep it lighthearted to ensure they don't feel embarrassed.
- If it feels right, you might even make a small joke about how often people mispronounce your name—it can help ease the moment. Something like, "It happens all the time; I've lost track of the variations people come up with!"
- For those who seem to struggle with remembering, consider offering a quick mnemonic device or tip to make it easier for them: "Think of it like 'Reena,' as in 'ballerina.'"

The key is to stay calm and approachable, ensuring the correction feels like a natural part of the conversation. You're helping them get it right, and that's a win for both of you!

Q: *I'm terrible at remembering names. Do you have any tips to help make it easier? And what should I do when I want to introduce someone, but can't for the life of me recall their first or last name?*

A: First, when a person introduces themselves, ensure that you heard them well enough. If you didn't quite catch their name, politely ask them to repeat it. If the name is potentially challenging to pronounce, you might ask how it is spelled, but do so gently. It is generally rude to point out someone's otherness, similar to how it can be rude to ask where someone is from on the basis of difficulties with a foreign language.

Second, use the person's name throughout your conversation. Saying the name aloud will make it easier for you to remember.

Third, link the new name with something you already know—the sillier the better, as this will likely make it easier for you to remember.

As for what to do if you cannot remember someone's name, if you see them coming, and you are with someone, such as a friend, significant other, or colleague who has not met them before, pull them aside and ask them to introduce themselves to that person. This is a sneaky way of jogging your memory without the person ever knowing you forgot.

When you can't lean on a wing person to help, I recommend saying something graciously honest like, "Please forgive me. Can you remind me of your name?" Asking for a reminder is better and more positive than the common alternative "I forget your name," which can make people feel . . . forgettable. The awkwardness of forgetting a name can also be softened by sharing any information that indicates you remember your prior meeting, such as, "I so enjoyed our conversation about gardening at Melanie and Ben's Memorial Day weekend cookout, but please forgive me. Could you kindly remind me of your name?"

Q: *How do I introduce two friends or colleagues when I'm unsure how they might get along? I don't want to create an awkward moment if they don't click right away.*

A: When introducing two people who might be on different wavelengths, it's helpful to keep the introduction light and neutral, focusing on shared interests or traits that might bridge the gap. Try starting with something like, "Sam, this is Alex. Sam's a bit of a foodie, and I know you love finding new spots too!" This approach highlights their common ground without overselling it. Keep it brief, and give them a chance to connect naturally. If they don't hit it off immediately, don't feel the need to steer or direct the conversation—just introduce, smile, and let the rest flow. Sometimes, letting people find their own rhythm can lead to the best surprises.

Q: *A senior colleague keeps calling me Liz instead of my full name, Elizabeth. I don't think they mean anything by it, but it bothers me. How do I handle this without making it awkward?*

A: The nickname conundrum—where good intentions meet a pet peeve. When someone shortens your name without invitation, it can feel like they're editing you. And when it's a senior colleague, the stakes feel higher. But here's the good news: You can address it gracefully without causing a ripple in your dynamic.

Start by assuming positive intent—they likely think they're being friendly. The key is to redirect with a kind but clear nudge. Next time they use "Liz," smile and say something like, "Actually, I prefer Elizabeth. It just feels more like me." Short, sweet, and nonconfrontational.

If the habit persists, gently reinforce it the next time they address you. For example, "I know you've been calling me 'Liz,' but I really love my full name, Elizabeth. Would you mind using that instead?" Most people will get the hint and make the adjustment—no drama required.

And remember, you have every right to set boundaries around how you're addressed. Your name is part of your identity, and advocating for it isn't impolite—it's empowering. Bonus? It's a subtle reminder to others that respect starts with the little things.

Handshakes

Once a sign that two men came unarmed and in peace, handshakes continue to be the most common physical greeting in business and social scenarios, especially for initial introductions.

Qualities of an excellent handshake include:

- **Right Hand, Web-to-Web:** Regardless of whether someone is left- or right-hand dominant, the right hand is used, and the web of each person's hand should connect. This is the area between the index finger and thumb.

- **Strength:** The squeeze of a handshake involves approximately the same amount of force necessary to check a piece of fruit, like a nectarine, to determine whether it is ripe enough to enjoy. The appropriate amount of force for the shake is about the same amount needed to open a refrigerator door.
- **Length:** In the Western world, we shake twice in professional settings and three times socially. You can remember the two pumps for business because we are getting right down to business and not wasting any time, whereas social occasions can be more relaxed with three pumps.
- **Eye Contact:** Make eye contact with the other person during the entire handshake. If it feels awkward or uncomfortable, it may indicate that your handshake is too long.
- **Left Hand:** Your free left hand should remain beside you. It is not appropriate to place your left hand on top of the other person's hand. Although some may interpret this as an endearing sign of warmth in social settings, in professional and more formal scenarios, it can be seen as an act of aggression and trying to assert authority over the other. And aside from very casual scenarios among family and close friends, you do not want to use the left hand to touch the other person, since doing so can be perceived as too casual or otherwise inappropriate.

The Practice of a Perfect Handshake

Let me tell you about the most painful handshake of my life. It happened on the first day of my new job as a law clerk for a committee in the US Congress. I met a woman with a petite frame—she could have passed for a middle schooler, and I say that in the most loving way. Her wardrobe and office supplies? Think Elle Woods and add more glitter. Notebooks, tumblers, and pens that sparkled and shone like they were auditioning for a rom-com.

And then, the handshake. When she reached out to greet me, she squeezed so hard that the ring I was wearing dug into my fingers, leaving me wondering if she was a mean girl or trying to send some kind of message. It was jarring, to say the least.

Here's the twist: Over time, we became friends, and I realized that her handshake wasn't about dominance or malice. It was probably an overcorrection—a way of ensuring she didn't come across as too soft or too feminine in a world where gravitas can feel like a currency.

But that initial encounter taught me a valuable lesson: Finding the right balance in your handshake matters. Too soft, and it can seem disinterested; too firm, and you risk leaving a lasting (and painful) impression for all the wrong reasons. If you're unsure, practice with a friend or colleague. A good handshake is firm but not crushing, confident but not overpowering. It's a small but effective way to convey professionalism and set the tone for a positive interaction.

Because, as I learned that day, details count—even in a handshake.

Q: *I really don't like shaking hands or being touched by people I don't know. Is there a polite option for a non-touch greeting?*

A: Yes, there are plenty of kind and respectful ways to greet someone without physical contact—and the good news is, many cultures already do this beautifully. In some devout Muslim communities, for example, it's customary for men and women not to shake hands with the opposite gender. Instead, greetings are often exchanged with a warm smile, a slight nod, and a hand placed gently over one's heart—a gesture that feels deeply respectful and sincere.

If you're choosing a non-touch greeting, there are a few things to keep in mind.

First, aim for consistency. If you hug some people but pull back from others who extend their hand, it can unintentionally signal rejection. Your choice not to shake hands should come across as a personal preference—not a judgment of someone else's hygiene or intent.

Second, be clear and deliberate with your body language. Clasping your hands in front of or behind you can help avoid the awkward "are we shaking or not?" moment.

Third, your tone, eye contact, and verbal warmth become even more important. A sincere smile and a friendly "It's so nice to meet you" can instantly make someone feel acknowledged and welcomed.

And finally, you don't need to explain your choice unless you want to. If you do decide to share, keep it short and kind: "I'm not shaking hands right now, but I'm so glad to see you." Let your presence and poise speak for themselves.

Other Forms of Greeting: Kindness Without the Handshake

Greetings are more than a formality—they're a reflection of culture, context, and the nature of your relationship with the other person. Whether you're exchanging pleasantries at a business meeting or catching up with a friend, understanding the nuances of greetings can strengthen rapport from the very first moment. Here's how to approach common forms of greetings that go beyond a standard handshake.

The Air Kiss

In many parts of the world, air kisses—touching cheeks and kissing the air—are more than a gesture; they're a cultural ritual that speaks volumes about connection and respect. But like any good ritual, the details matter: How many kisses? Which cheek first? And is this a handshake moment instead? Don't worry—mastering the air kiss is easier than it seems.

HOW TO EXECUTE THE PERFECT AIR KISS

The mechanics of the air kiss are straightforward, but a dash of finesse makes it feel effortless.

1. **Lean In.** Start with your right cheek (unless you're in Italy or another region where left comes first; see more guidance below).

2. **Touch Cheeks.** Gently touch cheeks while making a soft kissing sound—skip the dramatic *mwah!*
3. **Add Extra Kisses if Needed.** If two or three kisses are customary, switch sides accordingly.
4. **What to Do With My Hands?** For close friends, a light hug is acceptable. For less familiar acquaintances, gently place your hands on their shoulders or lightly touch their upper arm with the hand opposite your starting cheek.

While some cultures embrace actual lip-to-cheek contact, it's safer to stick with the air kiss—especially in a post-pandemic world.

HOW MANY KISSES?

The number of kisses can vary by country, region, and even the person, so follow your host's lead. Here's a quick guide:

- **One Kiss:** Common in the US, Colombia, Argentina, Chile, Peru, and the Philippines.
- **Two Kisses:** Standard in Spain, Italy, Greece, and many parts of Latin America, as well as Germany, Hungary, and Croatia.
- **Three Kisses:** Expect this in Belgium, the Netherlands, Switzerland, and parts of Eastern Europe like Macedonia and Serbia. In Jordan, you start with one kiss on the left cheek, then move to multiple kisses on the right depending on the relationship.

WHICH CHEEK?

While most countries begin with the right cheek, there are exceptions—and knowing them can save you from an awkward misstep. One of my closest friends, who worked for a company headquartered in Brazil, learned this the hard way. Lean the wrong way, and you could accidentally land a kiss on your colleague's mouth.

- **Italy:** Italians often begin with the left cheek and lean to the right. Two kisses are the norm but are reserved for casual, social settings.

- **Southern Europe:** Many countries in Southern Europe start by leaning left and touching right cheeks.

If you're in doubt about the local customs, let the other person lead.

WHEN AND WHERE TO AIR KISS

- **Casual Social Settings:** Air kisses are perfect for friendly gatherings, casual dinners, or meeting acquaintances.
- **Professional or Formal Settings:** In these environments, a handshake is often more appropriate unless you know the local custom allows for kisses.
- **In Mixed-Gender Dynamics:** Air kisses are common between two women or a man and a woman. They're less frequent between men, though exceptions exist in places like Argentina, Southern Italy, and Serbia.

IF YOU'RE UNSURE

When in doubt, just as you would if you were seated at a dining table and unsure about your utensils, follow your host's lead or mirror what others are doing by paying attention to how others greet each other.

In some parts of the world, including parts of Europe, it's not just close friends who exchange kisses. You might air kiss friends of friends, colleagues of your spouse, or even distant family members you've never met. But if you aren't sure, a warm smile, steady eye contact, and a small step forward—with or without the kiss—usually communicates friendliness and goodwill.

PERSONAL BOUNDARIES

While air kisses are common, some people may prefer a handshake or wave. Read the room, and don't push a kiss if it doesn't feel right.

And if someone pushes a kiss on you? Stay composed and warm. A gentle turn of the cheek, a step back paired with a kind smile, or even extending your hand for a handshake can signal your preference without making the other person feel awkward. In most cases, people will quickly take the hint—and no harm is done. Etiquette is never about shaming someone; it's about protecting comfort and connection, including your own.

Air kisses are about more than the mechanics—they're a gesture of goodwill and respect. Even if you don't nail the exact number or sequence, the effort to engage will be appreciated. Lean in, smile, and let the cultural connection take it from there.

The Cheek Kiss

A cheek kiss is far more intimate and usually reserved for family. This is when your lips come into contact with the other person's cheek. Think of it as the kind of kiss a grandparent might give a grandchild. It's not a greeting you'd use in professional settings and is best kept within close personal relationships.

Hugs

Hugs are warm and friendly but are typically limited to social settings. They're perfect for family and close friends but are less common in business interactions. Always be mindful of cultural expectations and personal comfort levels when offering or receiving a hug.

Touch-Free Greetings

Not every situation calls for physical contact, and that's okay. Use body language to communicate your preference for a touch-free greeting. Clasping your hands in front of your chest with a polite nod or placing your hands behind your back while nodding can signal your intent clearly and respectfully.

The key to any greeting is to read the room and adapt to the context. By being mindful of cultural norms, personal relationships, and individual boundaries, you can create a warm and respectful interaction.

The Takeaway: Your Greeting Sets a Powerful Tone

When I think back to that glitter-filled office and the handshake that quite literally left an impression, I'm reminded of this: In the world of greetings and introductions, details matter. Your posture, your presence, the way you say your name or pronounce someone else's—all of it contributes to how you're received and remembered.

Introductions aren't just about where to place your feet or how to pronounce a difficult name. They're about how to show up—with self-assurance, with warmth, and with an awareness that even the smallest gestures can shape how others experience you. From the first glance to the final handshake, your manners are more than surface-level niceties—they are your calling card.

So whether you're walking into a job interview, attending a dinner party, or just saying hello online, carry yourself like it matters. Because it does.

CHAPTER 2

SMALL TALK, BIG IMPACT

If walking into a room where you don't know a soul sounds intimidating, you're not alone. For nearly half of adults, this is the making of a nightmare—the kind of scenario where you're checking your phone in the corner and pretending to be fascinated by a potted plant. But then there are those you know who seem like pros at this—the ones who breeze through introductions, always know what to say, and somehow make every conversation look easy. If you've ever planned a wedding or other large meal with a seating arrangement, these would be the kind of people you could put anywhere—next to your quirky aunt, at the table with your college friends, or even among colleagues who've never met—and they would fit right in with alacrity.

Are these people fabulously wealthy, ultra-educated, or just effortlessly charming? Maybe, but chances are, their real secret isn't fortune or luck—it's practice.

In this chapter, we're diving into the etiquette of everyday conversation: the dos, the don'ts, and the little tricks that can make connecting with people feel like second nature. From the perfect elevator pitch to small talk that doesn't make you cringe, you'll learn how to handle any social situation with style and self-assurance. Conversation may look like a natural talent, but it's a skill anyone can master—and with a little practice, you'll never have to hide behind that potted plant again.

Calling People by the Right Name

When I worked in the West Wing of the White House, I had lots of experience greeting important guests and diplomats whose names I either couldn't remember or was afraid to pronounce incorrectly. Ironic, since an important part of my role as assistant staff secretary to the president was ensuring his notes for meetings and prepared remarks for speeches were complete with phonetics, so he could easily pronounce names, places, and other tricky terms.

In a perfect world, we would use others' names with the same care journalists do when they use someone's full name before reverting to either *sir* or *ma'am*. But when you are in a pinch and are not sure what to say, honorifics can be a lifesaver. This is a tip I learned from a girlfriend who served in the West Wing as the receptionist of the United States, and I never forgot it. I will admit there is a cisnormative element to *sir* and *ma'am*, so it won't work in every situation, but generally speaking, whether a man is a stranger you encounter on the street, a client, CEO, senator, five-star general, or head of state, the term *sir* works well. The same is true of *ma'am*. If you are ever unsure of a person's title or name, a simple "Good morning, ma'am. It's wonderful to see you," can give the gracious cover you need.

For moments when you know someone's name but are not sure if they prefer to use a nickname or not, err on the side of formality and deference before getting too familiar. Every Madison doesn't go by Maddie, and someone you know as Teddy may prefer to go by Theodore in professional settings.

Q: *I was raised to say "sir" and "ma'am" as a sign of respect, but I've noticed that not everyone responds positively. What's the best way to handle this, given how differently people respond in various parts of the country?*

A: "Sir" and "ma'am" can feel like a warm sign of respect or a subtle reminder of age, depending on where you are and who you're speaking to. In the South, for instance, these terms are often second nature and considered polite. In other regions, though, people might feel they're a bit too formal or even distancing. To keep things respectful and adaptable, start by listening to how others address you or respond in conversation. If they respond warmly to "sir" or "ma'am," you're in the clear! But if you sense hesitation or prefer a safer route, go with a friendly "Mr." or "Ms." followed by their last name, or simply a kind greeting.

If someone directly mentions they're not a fan, don't sweat it; just take it as a cue to adjust. Showing flexibility with your language can be its own form of respect—and it's generally appreciated.

Small Talk

How would you fare if you had to take a pop culture quiz in front of your new colleagues on your first day on the job? I won't say I wasn't warned that this would be part of the onboarding as a new law clerk in the Office of the Chairman of the FCC, but my public performance was underwhelming. I had never heard of the tennis star they asked about, and the other questions are a blur to me now, but I do remember I got quite a laugh when I could only name one member of the band The Beatles. This little quiz was over lunch on the first day of my new job. It was all in good fun; I was never made to feel teased or bullied, and if anything, it made me feel more connected and like a member of the team, even as a law student among much more senior lawyers. The quiz was also about the staff laughing at themselves in feeling old when with each semester the law clerk hires would do worse and worse in recalling cultural icons from a bygone era.

This was a highly collegial and close-knit office that had lunch together nearly daily, and we covered just about everything in conversation—from political prognostication (it was Washington, after all!) to talking about shows and movies, books, family, travel, and overall life. In fact, most everything I know about scuba diving, I learned from an attorney who was a former competitive swimmer.

During this semester, I also had the privilege of meeting with some of the top executives and lobbyists in the telecommunications, media, and entertainment industries, and I got to see how my colleagues who were such a delight to have lunch with—excellent storytellers with range—could talk about everything from legislation to celebrity baby names. They knew how to be both professional and disarming, even in potentially acrimonious settings when talking about controversial policies. They knew how to break the ice and pepper in lighter topics to make others feel at ease, and they also knew how to remain professional and respectful of everyone's time.

Small talk isn't just for boardrooms and business meals and mixers. Working with those masters of small talk taught me the value of practicing conversation regularly—on all kinds of topics, with all kinds of people, in low-stakes settings. It's in those everyday interactions—at the coffee shop, in the elevator, at a dinner party—that we build the muscles for meaningful, confident conversation when it really counts.

Mastering the Art of Small Talk: The Ultimate Icebreaker

Small talk is like the appetizer of conversation—it's light, inviting, and sets the stage for something more meaningful. The secret? Keep it breezy, open-ended, and aimed at finding that shared moment of connection. Instead of grilling someone with direct or yes-or-no questions, make general comments and see where the conversation naturally flows. It's all about finding common ground, no matter how small.

Some cultures have truly mastered this art. The British and Arabs, for example, are small talk pros—they can chat effortlessly about almost anything. On the other hand, Germans and the Dutch often skip the chitchat or dive straight into the deep end, which can feel a little intense if you're not used to it.

When in doubt, stick to safe and universal topics. The weather? A classic. Your trip getting there or the room you're standing in? Perfect, because everyone shares that context. General news works too, but steer clear of anything heavy or controversial—this isn't the time for debates or tragic headlines. Mutual connections are another go-to: If you're at a party, "How do you know the host?" is a simple yet brilliant way to keep the conversation flowing.

If you're feeling bold, topics like children or sports can work, but tread carefully. In some cultures, talking about kids can feel too personal unless they bring it up first. And asking, "What do you do?" can come off as prying, so try something softer like, "How have you been spending your time?" or, "What are you really into these days?"

What to avoid? Anything that risks putting someone on edge: age, appearance, money, politics, religion, or relationship drama. And absolutely no gossip or complaints—you're there to connect, not critique.

Q: *If I'm in a group conversation and feel left out, is there a polite way to join in without seeming pushy?*

A: When you're standing on the edge of a group conversation, it can feel like everyone else has the secret handshake and you're left guessing. But here's a gentle way to slip in without feeling like you're forcing it: Find a natural pause, then chime in with something like, "I love what you're saying about [topic]—mind if I add a thought?" or simply nod along and laugh when everyone else does, showing you're engaged.

Another subtle move? Ask a quick question about the topic at hand: "That sounds interesting—can you tell me a bit more?" It's friendly and low-pressure, and before you know it, you're part of the flow without making waves. Conversations are like double Dutch—you just need to catch the rhythm, and soon you'll be right in sync.

**If the Answer Is a Number . . .
Pause Before You Ask**

Some questions seem harmless—but if the answer is a number, they might put someone on the spot. Before you ask, consider: Is it kind? Is it necessary? Is it any of your business?

Here are a few examples that often do more harm than good:

- How old are you?
- How much do you weigh?
- How tall are you?
- How many kids do you want to have?
- How much did that cost?
- How much money do you make?
- What did you score on the test?
- How many people have you dated?
- How many followers do you have?
- How long did it take you to get pregnant?
- When will you have kids?
- How long did it take you to finish that?
- How many square feet is your home?

Curiosity is natural, but etiquette means managing curiosity with care.

Starting and Sustaining Conversations Like a Pro

Once small talk opens the door, what comes next is where the real magic happens. This is where you move from polite pleasantries to genuine connection—without forcing it.

Opening a deeper conversation is like setting the tone for a great dinner party—get the greeting right, be warm and confident, and show genuine respect. Introduce yourself with a few curated highlights—something about you that sparks interest but doesn't hog the spotlight. You're not delivering a TED Talk, so keep it light and leave room for the other person to shine. Ask about their interests, because let's face it, we all love to talk about ourselves.

Maintaining eye contact is key—it says, "You have my full attention." Letting your eyes wander? That says, "I'd rather be anywhere else," and nobody wants that energy. To kick things off, ask thoughtful, open-ended questions and show real interest in their answers. You'll be surprised how quickly the conversation takes on a natural flow.

When you're in the middle of the chat, think of yourself as a thoughtful host—polite, approachable, and never pushy. Respect personal space, and unless you're in a culture where it's customary, keep your hands to yourself. The golden rule? Ask about them. Whether it's their career (if it's a professional setting) or their plans for the future, people love when you show interest in their story. Sprinkle their name into the conversation—just enough to build a connection, but not so much that it feels rehearsed. Hearing our own name triggers happy brain vibes, but moderation is key.[1]

Compliments? Absolutely—just keep them genuine and within appropriate boundaries. Start with easy questions, and really listen to the answers—they're your gateway to the next topic. Asking their opinion is another winning move—it shows you value their thoughts. If the setting provides a natural conversation starter, like a piece of art on the wall or a shared experience, use it! Discuss lighthearted, noncontroversial news or current events, and keep the mood fun and engaging.

And here's one of the most important principles of conversation: Never, ever make comments that insult or alienate others, especially regarding ethnic, political, or religious groups. Instead, lean into empathy. Show concern, enthusiasm, and curiosity. Reflect their words back to them by paraphrasing or asking clarifying questions, which builds rapport and shows you're tuned in. At its core, rapport is about creating that spark of mutual understanding, so keep your ears open for common ground.

And yes, it's okay to disagree. A little difference of opinion can keep things lively, but remember, you're not there to win a debate. Share your thoughts without crushing someone with facts or dominating the conversation. Keep it conversational, not combative. The goal is connection, not conquest.

At its core, a great conversation is about finding the balance between giving and receiving. Be curious, be kind, and above all, stay present. You've got this.

More on Discussing Sensitive Topics

Let's dig more into one of the most delicate aspects of striking up conversations with new people: sensitive topics. Avoiding topics like money, sex, politics, religion, or health doesn't magically create a utopian society of well-mannered conversation, as some might believe. Instead, it can lead to an atmosphere that feels more closed-off and ignorant than courteous. These subjects can be fascinating, insightful, and even connect us more deeply—but only in the right setting. Again, in those initial moments of getting to know someone, or when you're aiming to keep things light and welcoming, steering clear of these weightier topics often keeps the conversation more comfortable and open. But what to do when they come up?

In my experience, avoiding talk of sex, politics, and religion comes naturally to many people. It's those sticky conversations about money and health that can easily sneak up on us. There are myriad reasons why health is not a recommended go-to conversation starter—chief among them that many get squeamish learning about medical details. It's better to share, for example, that you had a tough bout of the flu rather than going into detail about every little side effect and symptom. Health refers not just to illnesses but diet, fitness, and wellness regimens too. Unless you're speaking with someone who appears genuinely interested in hearing more of your health journey, it's best to keep the granular details of your wellness routines to yourself. Health-related conversations can easily come across as preaching, showing off, or trying to convince others to convert to a different way of living.

Now to the topic of money . . .

Discussing your salary with colleagues can seem tempting, especially when it feels like everyone else is comparing notes. But here's a tip: Think like a manager, even if you're not one. From a manager's perspective, setting compensation is a complex process that considers many factors—experience, market rates, specialized skills, and contributions to the team. When employees openly share their personal compensation details, it can create challenges for managers and lead to misunderstandings among coworkers. Instead of fostering transparency, these conversations often stir up frustration, resentment, and unnecessary tension in the workplace.

The bottom line? Respecting boundaries around salary discussions with coworkers isn't the same as gatekeeping. It's about maintaining a professional environment and choosing the right context for financial conversations. When you want to dig deeper into compensation trends or wealth building, consider talking with mentors, financial advisors, or industry peers who offer a broader view.[2] Thoughtful financial transparency can be powerful—especially when it's approached with the long game in mind.

Q: *What do I do if someone brings up an awkward topic, like saying, "Can you believe how much weight Alex has gained?"*

A: Gossip disguised as small talk is like spilling red wine on a white tablecloth at someone's house. Uncomfortable, noticeable, and you can't just ignore it—but it's still fixable. The key is to gracefully pivot without feeding the drama.

You might say, "Oh, I hadn't heard, but I hope she's doing okay. Speaking of news, have you seen that new exhibit at the gallery downtown? It looks stunning!"

Think of it as conversational jujitsu: You're redirecting the energy toward something positive and steering clear of becoming part of the rumor mill. Because let's face it, your time is better spent sipping lattes than stirring tea.

Q: *How should I handle it if someone keeps asking about my plans for marriage or kids, and I'm not ready to share?*

A: When someone keeps pressing about marriage or kids, it can feel like they're flipping through the pages of your life story, searching for the next chapter before you're even ready to write it. The trick here? Keep it light, but keep it firm. Try something like, "Oh, I'm letting life surprise me!" or, "I'm still working on a few plot twists."

This way, you're sending a clear message that your plans are your own without actually laying them out. If they keep pushing? Feel free to steer the conversation right back to them—"But enough about me, tell me about that trip you're planning!" They'll get the hint, and you'll keep your storyline all to yourself, until you're ready to share.

How to Know When You've Lost Your Audience

Not every interaction will be a home run, but every attempt is a chance to practice connection. When a conversation starts to get awkward, it may be time to change the subject, and sometimes, the best conversational skill is knowing when to gracefully move on.

A great conversation is about finding the balance between giving and receiving.

Q: *I was telling a story at a party, and I got the vibe the other person wasn't really into it. How do I know for sure, and what should I do?*

A: First of all, let me say this—you're not the only one who's felt this way! We've all been mid-story, only to realize our audience is more interested in their cocktail or scanning the room than what we're saying. It's awkward, sure, but it's also not a reflection of your worth or conversational skills. Sometimes, people just aren't in the mood—or your story about your cat's social media fame wasn't the hit you thought it'd be (no judgment; I'd listen!).

Here are a few telltale signs that you've lost your audience.

- They're giving you short, polite responses like "Oh, really?" or "That's nice," without asking follow-up questions.
- Their eyes keep wandering, or they're looking at their watch or phone.
- They nod a little too much, like they're trying to wrap things up.

If you notice any of these, don't take it personally. It's not about you—it could be the topic, the timing, or simply that they're distracted. So maybe it's time to pivot.

Here's How to Pivot Like a Pro

- **Acknowledge the Vibe Shift and Redirect:** "Okay, enough about me! What's been going on with you?" Many people love talking about themselves, and this move shifts the spotlight without any awkwardness.
- **Wrap It Up and Gracefully Exit:** "It was great catching up! I'm going to grab another drink—let's chat later!" This keeps things light and gives you an out without anyone feeling weird.

- **Find a Fresh Audience:** If you're excited about your story, there's probably someone else at the party who'll appreciate it. Keep your energy up and find a more receptive audience—maybe the friend who just got a cat and is looking for social media posting tips!

And remember: Not every conversation is meant to be a showstopper. Parties are full of opportunities to connect, and if one chat fizzles, there are plenty more waiting to happen. Keep it fun, keep it light, and keep being your charming self.

Q: *How do I pivot a conversation when someone brings up a topic I'm uncomfortable with or know nothing about? I hate feeling out of the loop, but I also don't want to fake interest.*

A: We've all been there—someone dives into a topic that either bores you to tears or leaves you completely lost. The art here? The graceful pivot. Instead of faking enthusiasm, offer a smile and say something like, "You know, I'm not too familiar with that, but I'd love to hear about . . ." and redirect to a topic you both enjoy.

Or, if you're in the mood to be a little playful, say, "I'll need the CliffsNotes on that one!" It's light, it's honest, and it takes the pressure off pretending you're an expert in everything. The goal is to guide the conversation somewhere you're both comfortable with without feeling like you have to nod along to every detail. Conversation should be a two-way street, after all, not a one-sided lecture! There is no shame in not knowing everything about every conversational topic all the time, and pretending like you're following along when you actually aren't can lead to some unnecessarily awkward and embarrassing moments.

Q: *If a friend frequently interrupts or one-ups me in conversations, is there a way to address it gently? I don't want to create tension, but it's starting to wear on me.*

A: When a friend can't help but interrupt or play the one-up game, it can start to feel like a conversation competition, and let's face it—that's exhausting. One way to handle it without stirring up tension is to gently call it out with humor. Try something like, "Hold on, let me finish this story before it gets outdone!" Say it with a smile, and you're letting them know you notice without making it confrontational.

Or, if humor doesn't feel right, a simple, "I really want to share this with you—can I get to the end?" can work wonders. It's kind, clear, and lets them know you value being heard. Sometimes all it takes is a gentle nudge to remind them that conversations should be shared, not stacked.

Q: *How can I politely create space if someone is standing uncomfortably close to me?*

A: A close-talker can catch anyone off guard—but there's a polite and subtle way to create space without making it awkward. Try this: Take a small step back with one foot—whichever feels more natural—while keeping your other foot planted. This gentle shift moves your body just enough to create breathing room. The beauty of this trick is that the foot you leave in place acts as a quiet boundary most people instinctively won't cross. It's graceful, effective, and spares you from having to say a word.

You've reclaimed your space, all while keeping things polite and composed—no awkwardness, no drama, just a graceful pivot (literally). If they still don't get the hint? It's time to make a graceful exit.

Giving and Receiving Compliments

There's a little magic in a compliment, both in giving and receiving one. When you give a compliment in conversation, think of it as a small gift, something genuine and specific that shows you're paying attention. A well-placed "I love your sense of style" or "Your insight in that meeting was spot-on" can lift someone's day without feeling forced. And when it comes to receiving a compliment? Resist the urge to brush it off. Let it land! A simple "Thank you, that means a lot" shows grace and appreciation, giving the compliment—and the person offering it—the spotlight they deserve.

When it comes to compliments, context is key. In professional settings, keep compliments focused on skills, achievements, or specific efforts—"Your presentation was so engaging" or "You handled that meeting like a pro." Complimenting someone's personal appearance in a workplace, depending on the relationship, can feel too familiar or even uncomfortable unless it's something neutral, like "I love your jacket—it's great!"

In social settings, you can be a bit more personal, though it's still wise to avoid anything too intimate or appearance-based that might feel invasive. Comments like "You have such a warm presence" or "You're always so thoughtful" are both friendly and respectful. Save more personal compliments, especially about someone's body or lifestyle choices, for close relationships where you know the person well, ensuring your words will come across as genuine and considerate. And if you do choose to comment on someone's physique or lifestyle choice, know that you are treading into risky territory. What might be the highest compliment to one person could be negatively triggering for another.

Focus Compliments on the Receiver

A well-placed compliment centers on the person you're speaking to, not your own perspective. Shifting the focus from you to them makes the compliment feel more genuine and thoughtful. For example, instead of saying, "I love your dress," try, "You look really nice in that dress." The difference? The former is about the compliment giver's opinion of the dress itself, while the latter highlights how the person shines in it.

Here are more examples to help you make your compliments truly memorable:

- Instead of: "That color is stunning!"
    - Say: "That color looks incredible on you!"
- Instead of: "I love your kitchen!"
    - Say: "You've created such a warm, welcoming space here!"
- Instead of: "That's a great idea!"
    - Say: "Your idea is so creative—it really adds value to the conversation."
- Instead of: "I like your presentation style."
    - Say: "You presented that so clearly and confidently—it was really engaging!"

And remove qualifying phrases like "I think" that undermine the message. For example,

- Instead of: "I think your proposal is terrific."
    - Say: "Your proposal is terrific."

Want to compliment someone's car, or watch, or amazing chandelier in their front hall? A kind word about the things we've chosen to wear or display certainly can leave us glowing, but it's also worth considering the other side of the coin: Overindulging in praise for someone's material possessions can feel shallow or insincere. For some, excessive focus on the surface can even seem like an unspoken critique of their priorities.

When in doubt, aim for compliments that focus on the person rather than their things. "You have such a warm, inviting home" goes further than raving about the furniture. Compliment their creativity, their effort, or the way they make others feel. The most meaningful compliments are the ones that make someone feel truly seen—not just their possessions.

Avoid Reflex Compliments

It's easy to fall into the habit of reflexively responding to a compliment with, "Oh, I like yours too!" While it might feel polite in the moment, it can often come across as insincere—like you're deflecting rather than genuinely appreciating the kind words. A simple, gracious "Thank you" not only acknowledges the compliment but also allows the moment to feel authentic and meaningful.

For example, if someone says, "I love your dress!" and you instantly reply, "Thanks, I love your shoes!" it can feel like you're just trying to even the score rather than accepting their compliment. Instead, take a beat, smile, and say, "Thank you so much, that means a lot!" If you truly want to return the favor, save it for later when it feels more natural—"By the way, your shoes are amazing!" It's thoughtful, genuine, and leaves everyone feeling great.

Q: *How should one respond to backhanded compliments? I never know what to say!*

A: Backhanded compliments are those "compliments" that somehow leave you feeling worse than before. When someone says, "You look so put together today! I barely recognized you!" or "Wow, you're so brave to wear that," it's easy to feel thrown off, but the trick is to stay cool and decide how much energy this person's comment really deserves.

Here are a few ways to respond depending on your personality and the circumstance:

1. **Playfully turn it around.** Sometimes, a lighthearted approach disarms the backhanded nature of the compliment. You could respond with a smile, "Guess I'm full of surprises!" or "I'll take that as a compliment—thanks!"
2. **Accept only the positive.** Ignore the slight and accept the

compliment at face value. Respond with a simple, "Thanks! I like to switch it up now and then," or "Thank you, I appreciate that." This subtly suggests that you're not taking the bait for any underlying negativity.

3. **Call it out gently.** If this person regularly gives backhanded compliments, a gentle but direct response might help. Try, "Thank you! That was . . . an interesting way to put it." This might make them pause and consider the impact of their words without escalating the situation.

Remember, how you respond is up to you—pick the approach that feels most natural. The key is to stay composed and let the compliment land as lightly as possible, without letting it weigh you down.

Q: *What's the best way to respond if someone compliments me in a way that feels uncomfortable? I want to be kind but also set a boundary.*

A: Compliments can be wonderful when they land well, but if one feels uncomfortable or too personal, there's nothing rude about setting a clear boundary.

Start by assuming good intentions. Many people don't realize their words may come across as inappropriate or uncomfortable. A simple, polite acknowledgment can often shift the tone.

For example:

If someone says, "You look so much better than usual," you can respond with a kind but neutral, "Thank you," and steer the conversation elsewhere.

If the comment crosses a line, such as focusing too much on appearance, try, "I appreciate the compliment, but I'd prefer to focus on [the topic at hand]."

The goal is to redirect without escalating. Keep your tone calm and steady—it's about setting boundaries, not creating confrontation. If the person persists, you can be more direct while staying kind: "I know you mean well, but that comment makes me uncomfortable. I'd really appreciate it if we could leave it there."

Remember, you're allowed to protect your space and feelings, even in social or professional settings. The key is responding in a way that's firm but still leaves the other person with their dignity intact. It's a balancing act, but one that leaves you feeling empowered—and respected.

Disagreeing Without Being Disagreeable

The longer I've lived in the nation's capital, the more I've come to believe that being informed and holding space for different opinions—with kindness and compassion—is one of life's most underrated skills. In Washington, DC, where everyone either works in a political capacity or isn't too many steps removed from it, every conversation has the potential to get interesting fast. It's also a place where who someone works for can be a major tell about their political leanings.

But here's the thing: If I only embraced friends who agreed with me on everything, my dinner parties would be insufferably boring! I am not someone who wants to live in an echo chamber. Instead, I've learned to approach conversations with grace, knowing when to lean in and when to let go.

Disagreeing without being disagreeable is an art, and the secret is balance. Start by finding common ground: "I see where you're coming from, and you've got a point about X." Then, gently present your own perspective without bulldozing the other person's. Think of phrases like "Another way to look at it might be . . ." or "I see it a little differently because . . . ," which signal that you're bringing something to the table, not throwing it across the room. The goal isn't to "win," but to share ideas and maybe even learn something along the way. Disagreeing is like dancing; you're moving in your own way without stepping on anyone's toes.

Living in DC has taught me that conversations—whether they're about work, politics, or the best place for brunch—don't always need to end in agreement. Sometimes the real magic is in the listening, the laughing, and the ability to pivot when things don't land. Because at the end of the day, a great dinner party—or a great life—isn't about everyone seeing eye to eye; it's about everyone bringing something to the table.

Graceful Goodbyes: Ending Conversations with Ease

I'll admit it: I've absolutely been that person stuck in a conversation, nodding politely while mentally reciting my to-do list and wondering if it's possible to vanish like Elphaba in *Wicked*. But as I've learned (the awkward way), knowing how to end a conversation with ease is just as important as knowing how to begin one—whether you're at a social gathering, networking event, or just trying to get home before your mascara gives up.

Ending a conversation well is a learned skill, and when done right, it leaves people feeling seen—not sidelined. The key? Be fully present before you even think about exiting. There's nothing more disheartening than talking to someone who's clearly scanning the room for a better option. Focus on the person in front of you, and when it's time to go, exit with warmth, clarity, and just enough charm to be remembered. And whatever you do, don't lie. Don't say you are going to get a drink and be right back if you have every intention of exiting for good. People see through that.

For One-on-One Conversations

1. SIGNAL THE GOODBYE

Use a friendly cue like, "It's been so great catching up," or, "Let me give you a hug before I go." If appropriate, you can even stand up or subtly shift your posture to signal that you're preparing to leave.

2. MENTION SOMETHING SPECIFIC YOU DISCUSSED

This shows that you were engaged. Try:

"I can't wait to hear how that trip goes—send pictures!"

"You've inspired me to try that new place—thank you!"

"Keep me posted on that project—I'd love to hear how it turns out."

3. WRAP IT UP WITH A WARM CLOSING

Leave the door open for future connection:

"Enjoy the rest of your evening—I look forward to seeing you next week."

"Let's catch up again soon. It was really wonderful chatting."

If the situation calls for it, you can exchange contact info or business cards. And remember, be considerate of their experience too—don't leave someone standing alone if you can help it. If appropriate, introduce them to someone else before stepping away.

For Group Conversations

Leaving a group is a bit like leaving a party—you don't need to make a grand exit, but you do want to leave people feeling appreciated. The trick is timing and tone.

Look for a natural pause. Don't try to jump in mid-laugh or story. Instead, wait for a lull and then say something like, "I've really enjoyed chatting with you all, but I'm going to check in with [another guest/the host] before the night gets away from me."

If it's a more intimate group, you can personalize it:

"This has been such a fun conversation, but I see someone I need to catch up with. Let's connect again soon!"

Always close with a warm group acknowledgment:

"Enjoy the rest of your night—I hope to see you all again soon!"

"Have a great evening, everyone!"

Group exits are all about timing, kindness, and a little finesse. It's not about disappearing—it's about leaving others with a sense of connection, even as you step away.

The Takeaway: Speak with Intention, Listen with Care

Let me take you back to DC for a moment—to the glittery colleague I introduced in the previous chapter—the one with the painfully firm handshake. We did eventually become friends, yet that first impression taught me something I'll never forget: The smallest details in how we show up—how we sit, greet, speak, and say goodbye—can shape how others remember us, far more than we realize.

The same goes for all our efforts in conversation. It's about knowing that—just like a good handshake—a kind greeting, a well-placed compliment, or a thoughtful goodbye isn't fluff; it's the foundation of connection. It's how we show respect for ourselves and others, no matter who's in the room.

Whether you're on Capitol Hill or wherever, remember: The way you carry yourself matters, and your choice of words has real impact. The goal isn't to perform in conversations with others—it's to be present. Polished, yes. But always rooted in grace, warmth, and genuine human connection.

CHAPTER 3

MAIN CHARACTER ENERGY: JOB SEARCH EDITION

One of my law professors once told me that getting a job is like trying to become one of the chocolates selected off the conveyor belt in that iconic episode of *I Love Lucy*. You know the one: Lucy and Ethel are working at a candy factory, tasked with wrapping each chocolate as it passes by. At first, it's manageable. Then the belt speeds up, chaos ensues, and before long, Lucy's shoving truffles in her hat, her mouth, and down her shirt just to keep up.

That image has never left me—because at times, the job search (and let's be honest, professional life in general) can feel exactly like that: fast-paced, absurd, and a little sticky. You're trying to stand out while everything's whizzing by, hoping someone will pause, notice you, and pick you out of the lineup.

But here's the good news: We don't have to rely on panic and peanut clusters. If you are in the job market, there are ways to set yourself apart—gracefully, strategically, and with your dignity intact. Whether you're interviewing for your dream job, negotiating your worth, or learning to network without feeling like a used-car salesperson, this chapter is your guide for showing up with both polish and power.

Because even in a world that can move like a conveyor belt, you have the ability to step off, be intentional, and let your presence do the talking.

Crafting the Perfect Elevator Pitch: How to Introduce Yourself with Clarity and Ease

For those looking to make professional connections, an elevator pitch is your opportunity to make a lasting impression—in thirty seconds or less. It's all about introducing yourself in a way that's clear, confident, and compelling, whether you're meeting someone at a networking event, an interview, or even in, well, an elevator. Think of your pitch as a polished yet conversational answer to the question "What do you do?" It's not about delivering a memorized speech, but rather finding a way to express who you are and what you offer in a way that feels natural and authentic. Here's how to craft an elevator pitch that strikes the perfect balance between professional and approachable:

Step 1: Start with Who You Are and What You Do

Give a simple introduction: your name and your role or expertise. Keep it straightforward, but avoid jargon that might confuse someone outside your field. For example, instead of saying, "I'm a strategic communications consultant," you might say, "I help companies tell their stories in a way that attracts customers and builds their brand."

Step 2: Highlight What Makes You Unique

Next, share what sets you apart. What is your superpower, your edge, or your unique approach? This is your chance to add a personal touch that leaves the other person intrigued. Try something like, "I'm passionate about finding creative solutions to complex problems" or, "I focus on creating content that doesn't just sell, but resonates."

Step 3: Keep It Relevant to Your Audience

A great pitch isn't just about you; it's about how you connect with the person you're talking to. Adjust your pitch based on the context and who you're speaking to. If you're at a tech conference, highlight your experience in that industry. If you're meeting someone in a social setting, lead with a personal passion or recent project.

Step 4: End with a Call to Connection

Wrap up your pitch with an invitation for further conversation, without being too salesy or pushy. You could ask a question that opens the door for them to share more about themselves, like, "What's your experience with [relevant topic]?" or, "I'd love to hear about what you're working on—does it relate to what I do?"

Tips for Making Your Pitch Feel Natural

- **Practice, but don't memorize.** The goal is to sound conversational, not rehearsed. Practice with friends or in front of a mirror, but focus on flexibility so you can adjust based on the context.
- **Keep it short and sweet.** Aim for twenty to thirty seconds. The pitch should be a teaser that invites further conversation, not a monologue.
- **Use body language.** Make eye contact, smile, and use open body language. Remember, people trust you more when they can see your hands—so don't keep them hidden.
- **Be ready to adapt.** Every situation is different, so be ready to adjust based on the context. If the person seems pressed for time, keep it shorter. If they seem interested, expand on your story.

Common Elevator Pitch Pitfalls to Avoid

- **Being too formal:** An elevator pitch should be professional, but it should also feel approachable. Avoid overloading it with industry terms or titles.
- **Rambling:** If you try to say too much, your main points can get lost. Keep it concise and focus on the essentials.
- **Forgetting the why:** People want to know what drives you. Adding a sentence about why you do what you do can make your pitch more memorable.

Practice Makes Perfect

Creating a strong elevator pitch takes practice. Test your pitch in different settings, tweak it based on feedback, and pay attention to what works. The more comfortable you are delivering it, the more authentic and engaging it will feel. Your elevator pitch is essentially your introduction to the world—a confident snapshot of who you are and what you bring to the table. With a little practice and finesse, you'll be able to deliver it effortlessly, leaving a strong impression wherever you go.

Q: *How do I give a killer elevator pitch without sounding like I'm trying too hard?*

A: I hear you. You've got thirty seconds, an audience of one, and the stakes feel sky-high. The key to nailing your elevator pitch is striking the perfect balance between confidence and connection. Start with your name and a little sparkle about what you do. For example, "Hi, I'm Emily, and I help companies tell stories that make their audiences swoon." Then pivot to why it matters: "In today's noisy world, storytelling is how brands build relationships."

Now, here's the golden rule: Don't just talk—connect. End with something like, "What's been the most exciting project you've worked on recently?" It turns the spotlight on them and makes the conversation feel more like a two-way street than a monologue. Remember, the best pitches don't just sell; they start a relationship.

Résumé Recommendations: Making Your Paper Trail Work for You

If your elevator pitch is your polished opener, your résumé is the supporting document that's supposed to say, "Yes, I really am as impressive as I sound." The key is to present the facts in the light most favorable to you (think golden hour on your dream vacation!), but don't cross the line into fiction.

I'll never forget interviewing a seemingly successful government affairs professional who was being honored by his alma mater. He appeared smart and charming, and was in his mid-thirties—exactly the kind of person you'd expect to have a résumé full of real accomplishments. Without my even asking, he sent over his curriculum vitae, or CV, in advance. So far, so good.

But after the in-person interview, he emailed me asking if I could kindly ignore a few details, admitting there were "some inaccuracies and exaggerations." One of those? That he had played on a particular high school hockey team.

I remember thinking: *You've built a legitimate career—why are you fudging hockey stats from a decade and a half ago?* And more importantly: *If you're willing to bend the truth about something like that, what else might not be real?*

That moment stuck with me. Because your résumé isn't just a summary of your experience—it's a signal of your credibility. Confidence and clarity are persuasive. Embellishment? Not so much.

So yes, shine and showcase those strengths! But let's keep it grounded. In a world of big talkers, honesty is a quiet kind of power—and it leaves the most lasting impression.

More Résumé Dos and Don'ts

Your résumé isn't just a piece of paper—it's your first impression and list of curated greatest professional hits on paper. It's where you've been, what you've done, and what you're ready for next. But here's the secret: It's not just what you say—it's how you say it.

STICK TO ONE PAGE

Unless you're applying for a corporate-suite position or bringing decades of experience, aim for one page. Think of it as the little black dress of résumés—simple, classic, and always in style. Just make sure your font is easy to read (no one wants to squint at 8-point script).

KNOW WHAT TO INCLUDE AND WHAT TO CUT

Your header is prime real estate—use it accordingly. Name, phone number, and email should go right at the top. Objectives? You can skip them in most industries. Instead, focus on a structure that's timeless: education, experience, skills. Activities and interests are optional, but if you list them, be ready to share why you love long-distance running or French cooking.

BE HONEST ABOUT LANGUAGE SKILLS

Languages are a résumé wild card. List them, but be honest—just like you're being honest about everything on your résumé. Elementary reading skills in German? Own it. Pretending you're fluent when you're not? That's a hard no—and a recipe for being politely (or not-so-politely) caught.

AVOID PHOTOS

At the time of this writing, résumé headshots are generally unnecessary and, in many industries, discouraged. Save the professional image for your LinkedIn profile.

Remember, a résumé isn't just a snapshot of where you've been—it's your ticket to where you want to go. Make it shine, but keep it real. Your résumé isn't just a list of achievements—it's a reflection of your experience, your values, and your potential.

Q: *When is the right time to send someone my résumé, and how do I make sure I'm building a connection, not just making a big ask?*

A: Sending someone your résumé right away can feel a bit like showing up to a first date with a U-Haul—it's a lot to ask before you've built any trust. Instead, think of networking like cultivating a garden: Plant seeds first, water them with genuine interest, and let the relationship grow naturally.

Start by reaching out with a thoughtful message: "I admire your work in [industry/role], and I'd love to learn more about how you got started." Ask for a short call or coffee chat (more on "informational coffees" later) to get to know them and their journey. After the conversation, follow up with a thank-you email and an open-ended note: "I truly appreciate your time and insights. If you think of anyone I should connect with who may have advice for someone looking to break into this field, I'd be so grateful."

When the time feels right, you can introduce your ask—but always give them an out: "If it's not something you're able to help with, I understand. I so appreciate your time and guidance."

The goal is to build a relationship that's meaningful and mutual, not transactional. Because let's be honest: A strong network lasts longer than any single job posting.

Q: *What about cover letters? Do people still actually read them?*

A: It depends. Some do, some don't. The résumé typically gets the first look, but a strong cover letter can still tip the scales in your favor, especially in industries that value communication and presentation.

I think the term "cover letter" could use a bit of a rebrand. In many industries, it's not a formal attachment at all—it's the body of the email with your résumé attached. What matters most is that it's thoughtful, tailored, and communicates who you are and why you're a strong fit for the role.

Personally, I appreciate a cover letter that's short, to the point, professional, moderately conversational, and has just the right amount of moxie. It should feel like a confident introduction, not a formal essay or a copy-and-paste job from a template. Show that you understand the role, the company, and your own value—and do it all in about three crisp paragraphs.

How to Shine in Any Interview

You did it! You've landed the interview, and now they want to connect in person for the first time. Take a moment to congratulate yourself, and then settle in to brush up on your etiquette before the big day. Interviews can feel nerve-wracking, but with a little preparation and polish, you can leave a lasting impression. Here's how to put your best foot forward:

Be Prepared and Curious

- Research the role and the company ahead of time and come with thoughtful questions—it shows genuine interest.
- Be ready to talk about your background and experience in a way that reflects your strengths.
- Bring a few printed copies of your résumé to job interviews—yes, even in the digital age, it's still a pro move.
- Share your enthusiasm! Let them know what excites you about the role and the company.

Nonverbal Cues and Presence During Interviews

Your actions speak just as loudly as your words, so make sure you're sending the right signals:

- Proofread every email to ensure it's typo-free and polite.
- For phone interviews, choose a quiet spot and speak clearly.
- Arrive about ten minutes early for an in-person interview to settle in.
- For video interviews, find a clean, distraction-free background and ensure you're well-framed (head and shoulders visible, with good lighting).

Dress for the job you want—imagine what someone in that role would wear on an important day, and go with that vibe.

Q: *How much research should I do on a company before an interview? I want to seem polished and prepared, but not like I've been scrolling their Instagram so much I know the CEO's dog's name and am following all her relatives.*

A: Researching a company is like prepping for a first date—you want to show genuine interest without coming off as overly intense. The goal is to be informed, not invasive.

Start with the basics: Visit their website, read their mission statement, and skim through their latest news or blog posts. This gives you a sense of their values, goals, and recent achievements. Then, check out their LinkedIn page for updates and milestones. A light scroll through social media is fine too, but don't dive too deep—you're there to get a sense of their culture, not memorize what their VP had for lunch last week.

During the interview, naturally weave in what you've learned. Instead of saying, "I saw on Instagram that your office had a taco bar last Friday," go for, "I really admire how your company prioritizes employee wellness—like the events you've highlighted on social media." It's thoughtful, not overbearing.

If you're meeting with specific people, a quick LinkedIn glance is smart—just don't mention every career move they've ever made. Stick to something like, "I noticed you've been with the company for [X years]. I'd love to hear about your experience growing within the team."

Think of it this way: Your research should feel like a spark of curiosity, not a forensic investigation. Be informed, be personable, and let your enthusiasm for the role shine through.

Q: *During a job interview, if they ask me about a skill I don't have, how do I answer without looking unprepared?*

A: It's the dreaded "Do you know how to do *X*?" question—like being asked if you've read the hottest book club pick when it's still sitting on your nightstand. Here's how to handle it with poise.

Be honest, but pivot to your potential: "I haven't had direct experience with [specific skill], but I've tackled similar challenges, like [example]. I'm confident I can learn quickly and excel with some training." Then, add a sprinkle of enthusiasm: "I actually love opportunities to grow and stretch my abilities—it keeps work exciting!"

Think of it as showing them your plot twist. You're not just a candidate; you're a capable problem solver who doesn't shy away from learning new things.

Questions That Shouldn't Be Asked—and You Don't Have to Answer—in a Job Interview

Ideally, a job interview will be a space of mutual respect and professionalism. Some topics, however, are better left untouched—not just because they're inappropriate but often because they cross legal or ethical lines.

Even if you're caught off guard, it's possible to handle these questions gracefully while maintaining firm boundaries. Respond calmly and redirect the conversation back to your qualifications. For example: "I'm curious, how does this relate to the role? I'd love to focus on how my skills align with your needs."

This approach shifts the dialogue back to where it belongs and demonstrates your professionalism under pressure.

Here are some more specific responses to potential inappropriate or illegal questions:

1. "Are you married?" or "Do you have kids?"

   Legally, questions about your marital or parental status are off-limits because they can lead to discrimination. From an etiquette perspective, they're intrusive and irrelevant to your ability to perform the job.

How to respond: "I prefer to keep my personal life separate from work, but I'm very committed to my professional responsibilities."

2. "What's your religion?" or "Do you celebrate [holiday]?"

   Questions about religious beliefs are not only inappropriate but also illegal in most cases. They shift the focus from your qualifications to your personal life, which isn't the point of an interview.

   How to respond: "I believe in fostering an inclusive and respectful workplace for everyone."

3. "How old are you?"

   Age-related inquiries can hint at discrimination and are rarely acceptable in a professional setting.

   How to respond: "I'm confident my experience and energy are well-suited for this role."

4. "What's your health history?" or "Do you have any disabilities?"

   Unless you've disclosed a need for accommodations, these questions are invasive and often illegal.

   How to respond: "I'm fully capable of meeting the requirements of this position."

5. "What's your ethnic background?" or "Where are you really from?"

   These questions can feel offensive and tread into discriminatory territory. They also derail the interview's focus on your qualifications.

   How to respond: "I'm excited to bring my unique perspective and skills to this role."

Why Your Privacy Matters

Legally, questions like these can tread into discriminatory territory, violating federal laws such as the 1964 Civil Rights Act, the 1967 Age Discrimination in Employment Act, and the 1990 Americans with Disabilities Act.[1] They detract from the interview's purpose, which is to evaluate your fit for the role, not your personal life.

Interviews are already high-pressure situations without veering into unnecessary detours. You're there to shine, not to share your life story.

By recognizing and handling these no-go questions with poise, you ensure the conversation stays productive and focused on what truly matters: your ability to excel in the role.

And don't forget: Not only are you being interviewed, you're interviewing them too. Just as they're deciding whether you're the right fit for the role, you're gathering clues about whether this is a place where you'd actually want to spend your days (and let's be honest, in some jobs, your nights too).

My senior year of college, I flew across the country interviewing for TV reporter and anchor roles in mostly small markets—bright-eyed, broadcast-ready, and newly engaged. At one station, the news director started asking me about my ring. Was it a "real" diamond? He followed up with oddly specific questions about my fiancé, our wedding, even our honeymoon plans. I told myself maybe he was just quirky or trying to figure out scheduling with a scrappy team. But then the assistant news director chimed in with a string of "jokes" about my appearance that weren't jokes at all—they crossed the line into full-blown harassment.

They offered me the job. I didn't have anything else lined up, but I turned it down. Looking back, I think I dodged a bullet—and trusted my gut before I even knew how to name what was happening.

So if a question feels invasive, or if the vibe is off, don't brush that gut feeling aside. You're allowed to take note of red flags. You're allowed to walk away. Because the right role isn't just one that wants you—it's one that respects you too.

Yes, you're there to shine. But you're also there to see clearly. And sometimes, the most powerful thing you can say in an interview isn't "I accept"—it's "No, thank you."

The Power of the Follow-Up: Closing the Loop with Purpose and Professionalism

Let me tell you, I learned my lesson about asking about timing in interviews the hard way: If you don't ask, you may be left in the dark. After all that hard work, it's easy to get caught in a mental loop of, *When will I hear back? Today? Tomorrow? Next week?* But here's the thing: Some parts of the process are simply out of your control.

A good interviewer will usually give you a general sense of timing for when they plan to fill the role, but that's not always the case. It doesn't hurt to ask before you leave the room. A simple "Do you have a sense of the timing for next steps?" can save you a lot of uncertainty later.

Send a Thank-You Note

Before you even think about following up, make sure to send a thank-you note after the interview (more on thank-you notes on page 115). Email is often the best route, as hiring timelines can move quickly. If time permits, a handwritten note can be a lovely, personal touch, but don't let it delay your follow-up. Your thank-you message should express appreciation, reinforce your enthusiasm for the role, and reference something specific from your conversation to show you were engaged.

For example:

> "Thank you so much for taking the time to speak with me about the [Role Title] position. I really enjoyed learning about [specific topic discussed] and left feeling even more excited about the opportunity to contribute to your team. I appreciate your insights on [another specific point], and I look forward to hearing about next steps."

What If the Timeline Passes Without News?

Now, here's where it gets tricky. What if they say you'll hear back in two weeks, and two weeks come and go with nothing but radio silence? Don't panic. Hiring is hard. I've seen this play out from every angle—as a candidate, as an executive, and, most recently, as an employer. Even with full-time HR support or a fantastic hiring team, filling a role is a lot of work. And often, the people tasked with hiring are already spread thin, juggling their regular workload while trying to find the perfect candidate.

If you don't hear back within the expected time frame, give it a little grace. Follow up politely but confidently. For example:

"Hi [Interviewer's Name], I wanted to follow up on the [Role Title] position and see if there are any updates. I remain very excited about the opportunity and would love to contribute to your team. Thank you again for your time and consideration!"

Share Meaningful Updates

If you've recently achieved something noteworthy—a new certification, a professional milestone, or a big accomplishment—don't hesitate to use it as a thoughtful reason to follow up. It's a subtle but strategic way to stay on their radar while reinforcing your value.

You don't need to worry about checking in too soon when it comes to these kinds of meaningful, happy updates—so long as they're significant. Sharing a fresh win not only keeps the conversation going; it also shows that you're proactive, evolving, and genuinely excited about the opportunity.

The Big Picture: Be Patient, but Proactive

Here's my big advice: Don't lose too much sleep if it takes a while. I've come to see that the way someone handles their interview—and the follow-up—is often a preview of how they'll approach their role as an employee. When I look back at my own job applications and interviews, I realize those moments were opportunities to flex my entrepreneurial, main-character energy. They were my chance to advocate for myself in strategic, creative, and confident ways—even when I was pursuing a behind-the-scenes, team-oriented role, like working in the US Senate.

By showing gratitude, being proactive, and treating the process with grace and professionalism, you're setting the tone for how others will see you. Whether it's a quick hire or a slower process, you're proving you'd be a thoughtful, determined, and capable addition to the team. And when the right opportunity comes along, you'll be ready to shine.

Navigating Post-Interview Decisions: Enthusiasm with Intention

So, you've nailed the interview and they've sent you your offer. Congrats! But now you may be wondering how soon is too soon to respond with your decision—or how to avoid coming on too strong. Here's the balance:

- **Present your best, truthfully.** Don't overstate your enthusiasm for the role if you're still unsure it's the right fit or if you're considering it as leverage for another opportunity. Authenticity matters and will serve you better in the long run.

- **Be careful what you say (and how you say it).** Whether the offer comes over email, on the phone, or in person, your response matters. If you're not ready to accept on the spot, that's okay—but don't go radio silent. A simple, gracious response like, "Thank you so much—this means a lot. I'd love a day or two to review everything carefully before giving a final answer," helps keep communication clear and respectful, especially if you're going to negotiate the salary (more on that soon). Your words carry weight. If you accept an offer verbally, even casually, that still counts. Walking it back later can damage your credibility—or worse, your offer.
- **Wait until you're sure.** It's better to take a little extra time to ensure you're truly all in before accepting an offer. This way, when you do say yes, your commitment is clear and confident, which leaves a stronger impression.

The Polished Ask: Handling Salary Conversations Like a Pro

If you're in the offer stage, congratulations! Here's how to approach salary conversations prepared, composed, and ready to advocate for yourself:

- **Do your homework.** Research the salary range for your role in your location and industry. Use trusted sources online and credible data points that you've gathered from mentors and colleagues to back up your ask. Know your value—and be ready to explain it.
- **Know what to say—and how to say it.** If the number isn't quite where it should be, counter with kindness and clarity:

"Based on my research and experience, I was expecting something closer to [$X–$Y range]. I'm really excited about the role and would love to find a number that works for both of us."

Frame your ask in terms of value, not just desire. For instance, my compensation has gone up and down as I've taken roles in the private, public, and nonprofit sectors. As I pursued roles in traditionally less lucrative capacities, I didn't ask for more money because I had previously earned more or due to my lifestyle choices and expenses. Instead, I focused on the unique blend of experiences and skills that I would bring to benefit their team.

- **Yes, you can negotiate compensation over email.** For many roles, especially corporate or remote positions, email negotiations are completely appropriate. They give you time to think and keep a written record.

Just keep your tone positive, professional, and solution-focused. End with an invitation to continue the conversation:

"I'd be happy to talk more if it's helpful—just let me know what works best."

- **If you're lowballed, stay calm and redirect.** A disappointing offer isn't the end of the conversation. Try:

"Thank you for the offer. Based on the scope of the role and my experience, I was expecting something higher. Can we explore a range that's more aligned with market standards?"

It's okay to walk away if the offer truly doesn't meet your needs. You're not just negotiating a number—you're setting the tone for your future.

Know your industry norms. Some fields (like clerking for a federal judge) have strict customs—such as accepting their first offer. In others, negotiation is expected and it's acceptable to ask for a reasonable amount of time to weigh other offers. Do your research or ask mentors in your field what's typical.

Why It Matters

Negotiating your salary isn't greedy—it's professional. It shows you know your worth, and you're not afraid to advocate for yourself with respect and grace.

Done well, it's not just about the number—it's about building mutual trust from day one.

Etiquette and Professional Ambition: Building Real Connections

We all want to make connections that help us thrive. Say, for example, you take the plunge and invite a more experienced professional out to coffee to talk career advice. Well played. But let me tell you, as a firstborn, type A, recovering-perfectionist daughter (yes, that's a whole identity), I've approached my fair share of professional coffee chats leading with lots of ambition. While I may seem sweet on the outside, your girl is determined. More often than not, my highly prepared, slightly high-strung energy has worked in my favor. But there are moments—oh, there have been moments—when my swing-for-the-fences approach has landed more like a swing-and-a-miss.

Case in point: I once set up an informational coffee with an attorney at the FCC. We'd met through the bar association for telecommunications legal professionals. I saw that he was serving there in a volunteer leadership capacity, and thought, *He seems like the kind of helpful person who might make time to meet with me.* So I emailed him and asked him to get together to discuss my professional goals. (Side note: It is very normal for most informational coffees to be initiated by the one seeking mentorship—not the other way around. Don't be discouraged if your inbox isn't flooded with senior professionals trying to get on your calendar. Keep reaching out to new people thoughtfully, and don't take it personally if some don't reply—follow up as you see fit, but then move on with grace.) Once we finally met at a local café, I laid it all out there—my dream of landing a job in telecommunications at a large law firm straight out of school, despite missing the on-campus interviewing process (where nearly all those jobs are filled) and, well, not having the grades to make me the obvious choice. Ambitious? Yes. Realistic? Not in the eyes of the attorney I was meeting with.

I could sense he wasn't exactly inspired by my lofty plan. In fact, he began suggesting backup careers and plans B, C, and D that I found condescending. So, I pivoted. Instead of sticking with my planned agenda, I asked him about his involvement in the bar association of telecommunications lawyers. Suddenly, the energy shifted and the conversation found its rhythm. It became more about him—his expertise, his experiences—and not just my uphill battle.

Here's the thing: Not everyone you meet is going to want to mentor or sponsor you, and that's okay. It's not personal. Mentorship, sponsorship, and recognizing potential are skills, and not everyone has them—or the time or inclination to use them for you. That doesn't mean you stop trying. It just means you keep making connections until you find someone who sees your spark.

Informational Coffees

Unlike a traditional interview, which is focused on assessing your qualifications for a specific role, an informational interview or coffee is a more casual, low-pressure conversation where you get to ask the questions. It's your chance to learn more about someone's career path, industry, or company culture—without the stress of being evaluated. To set one up, start by reaching out to people in your network (or extended network) with a thoughtful message: Let them know you admire their work and would appreciate twenty minutes of their time to hear about their experience. You'll find that many professionals are flattered and happy to share their story—you just have to ask.

Thoughtfulness Comes First

Later in my career, I saw examples of other people who, like me, sometimes missed the mark—probably in the name of ambition. There was one intern at the White House who, I believe, eventually landed an entry-level job there. He connected with me on LinkedIn after he briefly stopped by my office in the West Wing to drop off some documents. We weren't introduced; I don't think we even spoke.

Now, some people will tell you that you need to have a meaningful connection before reaching out on LinkedIn, but I disagree. I love how the internet opens up possibilities for connection, and I didn't mind when he requested to connect on LinkedIn the same day. The fact that I got a notification within fifteen minutes or so of him dropping off the documents did strike me as odd, though.

What turned me off was what came next. The day after we connected, he asked by way of LinkedIn message if he could attend one of the White House press secretary's press conferences in the James S. Brady Press Briefing Room. Now, let me set the scene: This is a small, packed space filled with journalists and staffers who have very specific roles, and I didn't have the authority to easily grant his request even if I wanted to.

What bothered me wasn't the request itself; it was that there was no context or connection behind it. I didn't know him, his interests, or his goals. If he had said something like, "I'm really passionate about communications and want to learn as much as I can about political messaging," or even better, "Is there a way I could help support the team in pulling off the press conference?" I would have been much more inclined to help. His approach felt more like he wanted a backstage pass to a show than a genuine learning opportunity. It also was a strong reminder that before you make a big ask, put in the work to show your value—essentially earn the moment to ask. You will be taken more seriously, like a colleague adding meaningful value, not someone who is out of touch and treating the experience like a field trip.

Why "Can I Pick Your Brain?" Misses the Mark

Asking someone to "pick their brain" might seem friendly and casual, but it often comes across as vague—and, let's be honest, a little one-sided. Instead, frame your request in a way that's specific, professional, and shows you've done your homework.

Don't Say: "Can I pick your brain about your career?"
Do Say: "I really admire your work in [specific field], and I'd love to hear about how you navigated [specific challenge]. Would you be open to a twenty-minute coffee chat?"

This approach is thoughtful and clear. It also tells them exactly how they can help, which makes it easier for them to say yes.

The Big Picture: Thoughtfulness and Connection Over Perfection

Professional coffee chats and informational interviews aren't about being perfect—they're about being authentic, prepared, and thoughtful. Every interaction is an opportunity to learn, whether it's about the industry, the person you're speaking with, or even yourself.

And while it's okay to swing big—trust me, I've been there—it's even better to make sure your swing is grounded in genuine curiosity, a clear purpose, and a little effort to connect with the person sitting across from you. Because when you approach these moments with care, the connections you build aren't just helpful—they're lasting.

Q: *What should I do if someone gives me terrible advice during an informational coffee? I want to handle it gracefully without offending them.*

A: Getting bad advice in an informational coffee is like being served a mocha that's way too sweet—you appreciate the effort, but it's not quite what you hoped for. The key is to handle the moment with gratitude and tact while keeping your own judgment intact.

Start by acknowledging their input without committing to it. Say something like, "That's an interesting perspective—I hadn't considered it that way before. Thank you for sharing." This keeps the tone positive while giving you space to assess their advice on your own terms.

If the advice feels wildly off base, redirect the conversation. For example, "That's helpful to know. I'm curious—what strategies have worked best for you in [specific challenge or topic]?" This brings the focus back to their experience and away from the questionable suggestion.

Remember, you're not obligated to take every piece of advice you receive. Part of professional growth is learning to filter feedback and decide what aligns with your goals. Thank them sincerely for their time and insights, but trust yourself to decide what works for you.

Networking

Networking can feel like the ultimate challenge in making a real, face-to-face professional connection. Whether you're at a formal mixer with name tags and business cards or casually chatting at a work event that just happens to be full of decision-makers, it helps to know the dos and don'ts before you dive in. Because, when done well, networking isn't transactional—it's relational. And it can open doors you didn't even know existed.

First of all, if you ever see someone at an event all by themselves without someone to talk to, it's considerate to go out of your way to include them in your conversation. And if you are the person who doesn't know anyone, where you stand matters. Rather than standing around the edges of the room, which is a less social zone, it's better to position yourself near the host and/or by the end of a bar or buffet line. These are areas where people are generally relaxed and ready to mingle. Being somewhere the host can see you is helpful because they can introduce you to others or include you in their conversations. Since the host picked the guest list, they should have a good idea of who you would enjoy speaking with.

Digital Networking

Networking used to mean exchanging business cards. But now? Social media connections, DMs, and email intros all count.

To nail digital networking:

- Personalize every message. Start with a compliment or mention shared interests.
- Don't immediately ask for something. Instead, focus on building rapport.
- Follow up, but don't hound. A friendly nudge after two weeks is plenty.

Networking is like planting seeds—it takes time to grow. Be patient, be kind, and let relationships flourish naturally. I've learned from experience to be open-minded about mentorship and embrace a "board of advisors" approach to seeking counsel. There are mentors with fantastic business advice who I wouldn't talk to about my faith. There are peers who are in a similar season and can help me talk through my current decisions in granularity, and there are those I look up to for how they prioritize their families and marriage.

I once interviewed for a clerkship with a federal judge who I thought could be an excellent mentor for me based on what I knew about her résumé—but within a few minutes in the interview, it became clear she was much less excited about me. While I didn't get the job, I did learn that picking a good mentor can't be based only on a résumé. It's more like establishing a friendship, because having compatible personalities is key.

The Takeaway: There's a Sweet Spot Between Strategy and Grace

Maybe getting the job is a little like being picked off a conveyor belt of bonbons—but here's the twist: You're not just hoping to be chosen. You're choosing too.

With every handshake, elevator pitch, email follow-up, and negotiation, you're telling the world how you'd like to be seen—and who you're becoming in the process. Yes, it takes courage. And yes, it takes practice. But you don't need to shout to stand out. You don't need to be perfect to be memorable. You just need to show up with intention, kindness, and a clear sense of your own worth.

In a world full of noise, grace and thoughtfulness are power moves. And the right opportunities? They're not necessarily looking for the loudest candidate. They're looking for someone exactly like you.

CHAPTER 4

THE POLISHED PROFESSIONAL

I've worked in offices with sweeping views of breathtaking skylines, and in other historic offices that still give me goosebumps just remembering I worked there. I worked in a windowless basement of a US House of Representatives building—where the only "view" was a poster of a palm tree taped to a cinderblock wall. I've filed stories in snow pants from the back of a live TV truck in upstate New York, and I've spent many quiet, focused days immersed in research and writing on my couch.

I've been very behind-the-scenes before, and I've also briefed the president of the United States on Air Force One and in the Oval Office.

My career has taken me to incredibly different professional settings. And while the scenery—and dress code—has varied wildly, one thing has remained constant: Etiquette, kindness, and confidence always matter.

This chapter is all about understanding and owning your professional presence—whether you're sharing an office space, joining a meeting, sending an email, or hosting a work lunch. Because no matter what role you play or what job title you hold, how you show up shapes how people experience working with you in a powerful way.

Let's dive into the etiquette essentials that help you show up as the most polished, respectful, and effective version of yourself—wherever work takes you.

Office Etiquette Basics: When You're Sharing Physical Space

Your office is your personal space—but it's not your private space.

It's where you answer emails, take meetings, prep for presentations, and maybe even eat lunch at your desk with your mic accidentally unmuted. But it's also where colleagues drop by with questions, where clients might be hosted, and where your background lives forever on Zoom recordings. In short, your workspace reflects not just how you work, but how you show up.

Which brings me to the time I sat down for a meeting in the office of a senior partner at a large law firm. He was a rock collector. Not the polished, glass-case, museum-worthy kind—but loose dirt-covered rocks, strewn across his desk like geological confetti. There were rocks in bowls. Rocks on bookshelves. Rocks teetering atop stacks of paper. He was incredibly enthusiastic about where each one came from too—"This rock's from Sedona!"—as if that justified the fossilized chaos.

Spoiler: It did not.

Your office can (and should) reflect your personality—but it's also a space that signals how you show up in the workplace. A little care and intention show that you're organized, focused, and mindful of the shared environment we all work in.

So let's talk about the dos and don'ts of office life—the little habits that help you work well with others.

Dos

- **Dress for respect.** Your attire should be polished and appropriate for your workplace culture. A professional appearance shows respect for yourself, your role, and your colleagues.
- **Maintain impeccable hygiene.** Cleanliness isn't just about you—it's about creating a pleasant environment for everyone. Think fresh breath, clean hands, and a subtle touch of fragrance (or none at all).
- **Hold the elevator door.** If someone's rushing to catch the elevator, a quick hand to keep the door open is a simple act that contributes to a more considerate office culture.

- **Respect personal space.** Keep your conversations at a reasonable volume, and give colleagues the physical and mental space they need to work effectively.
- **Practice punctuality.** Arrive on time for meetings and deadlines. Being late says, "My time is more valuable than yours"—and that's never the message you want to send.
- **Keep shared spaces tidy.** Clean up after yourself in kitchens, conference rooms, and common areas. Your mess shouldn't be someone else's problem.
- **Show gratitude.** A simple "thank you" for a favor, feedback, or even someone holding the door can brighten their day.

Don'ts

- **Don't eat someone else's food.** The communal fridge is not a buffet. If it's not yours, leave it alone—it's as simple as that.
- **Don't blast audio.** Whether it's a viral video or your favorite playlist, use headphones or earbuds in open workspaces. Respect the collective need for focus.
- **Don't gossip.** Office chatter can be tempting, but talking behind a colleague's back can quickly damage trust and morale.
- **Don't linger on personal devices.** Scrolling through social media during work hours or meetings? Not a good look. Save personal tech time for your breaks.
- **Don't bring strong odors into the office.** From overly fragrant lunches to heavy perfumes, be mindful of scents that might overwhelm others.
- **Don't assume everyone's availability.** Just because you're working late doesn't mean everyone else is. Respect boundaries and after-hours communication preferences.

Remember, good office etiquette is about balance: being mindful of others while maintaining your own professionalism. It's less about rigid rules and more about creating an environment where everyone feels respected and valued. Because at the end of the day, isn't that what we all want?

Understanding Corporate Structure: Knowing Who's Who

Everyone—and I mean everyone—you work with deserves your respect, no matter their title. That's nonnegotiable. But there are moments when understanding the hierarchy matters.

Early in my career, when I was a law clerk in the US House of Representatives, I learned this the very first week. Before I could fully settle into my desk, I was given a quiz—yes, a quiz—to name every single member of Congress who sat on the committee I was supporting. It was a little intimidating, but I passed (thankfully). I've always suspected the quiz was a response to an intern who had a "Do you know who I am?" moment with a less-than-amused member of Congress, and no one wanted that to happen again.

That experience highlighted just how important it is to understand the structure around you. It's not simply about status—it's about reading the room. When you know who's who, you're better equipped to communicate thoughtfully, show respect in the right moments, and avoid unintentionally making things awkward. It's a quiet kind of professionalism that speaks volumes.

Here are a few subtle ways hierarchy shows up in everyday etiquette:

- **Introductions:** Typically, you introduce the more junior person to the more senior one (e.g., Ms. CEO, I'd like to introduce Mr. Intern).
- **Emails:** Those expected to act go in the "To:" field; those being kept in the loop go in the "CC" field with names listed according to seniority and, if applicable, the team they belong to.
- **Listing Names:** In both writing and speech, it's customary to list the most senior person first.
- **Seating Arrangements:** Guests of honor or senior leaders are usually seated to the host's sense of the setup.
- **Whom to Approach with Questions:** Understanding the chain of command helps you direct questions or concerns to the appropriate person—ideally starting with your direct supervisor or team lead before escalating upward.

Depending on where you work, it may not be realistic or possible to memorize everyone's title—but being mindful of structure, whether formal or informal, helps you move through your professional world with thoughtfulness and quiet confidence. And trust me: It's far better than being the reason someone institutes a quiz.

And if no one hands you an organizational chart? Ask for one. Seriously. It's not only a smart move—it's a professional one. Whether you're new to a company or joining a new project team, asking for a basic overview of roles and reporting lines shows that you're thoughtful about how you work with others.

Manners for Meetings: Whether You're Leading or Listening

When Seth Phillips—aka the man behind the viral Dude with Sign Instagram account—held up a cardboard sign that read "This could have been an email," the internet nodded in collective agreement. It became one of his most viral posts of all time, because it struck a nerve. People have feelings about meetings—especially the ones that are chaotic, unproductive, or clearly created by someone who just wanted to hear themselves talk.

But meetings aren't going anywhere. And when they're done well, they're actually kind of magical. Decisions get made. Teams feel aligned. People leave thinking, *Wow, it was actually worth putting on real pants for that.*

Whether you're leading the meeting, taking notes, asking the questions, or just trying to remember what the meeting was about, manners matter. How you show up—on time, prepared, and present—makes a difference, no matter where you sit at the table (or on the screen).

Let's talk about how to make meetings feel less like a meme and more like a positive moment.

In this section, we'll cover best practices for both meeting leaders and participants, because everyone benefits when meetings are respectful, focused, and worth showing up for.

Best Practices for Well-Run Meetings

Whether you're leading the meeting or simply attending a meeting, here are some ways to make them count:

FOR MEETING LEADERS: YOUR ROLE IS TO DIRECT THE FLOW

Have a purpose and a plan. Appoint someone to lead, create a clear agenda, and send it out in advance so attendees come prepared—not improvising.

Start and end on time. Respect people's calendars. Don't wait for late arrivals, and don't let the conversation drag.

Invite the right people. Only include those who truly need to be there. Too many voices can muddle the mission.

Stick to the script (mostly). Keep discussions focused. If new topics emerge, take note for follow-up—don't derail the meeting.

Watch the room (or screen). If someone looks like they're ready to contribute, invite them in. Equal airtime matters.

Wrap it up well. Recap key takeaways and next steps. If needed, schedule a follow-up instead of dragging the meeting out.

FOR ATTENDEES: HOW TO SHOW UP WELL

Be present and prepared. Read the agenda, arrive on time, and bring what you need to participate fully.

Contribute meaningfully. Speak up when it's relevant. A simple "May I add something here?" can help you join the conversation respectfully.

Use body language. Lean in when engaged, nod to show agreement, and lean back once you've made your point—it signals that you're listening.

Read the room. If the discussion is heating up, keep your cool. If you disagree, do so with professionalism: "I see it differently, and here's why . . ."

Support others. A smile, a nod, or a quick "That's a great idea" can build trust and boost the energy in the room.

Virtual tip: If you're meeting online, turn your camera on, stay on mute when appropriate, and engage in the typed chat if you're not ready to speak aloud.

Q: *What if I'm running late?*

A: Let someone know right away. When you arrive, offer a brief, gracious apology and then ease into the conversation without derailing the flow.

Q: *How do I end a meeting that's going long?*

A: Say something like, "This has been really productive. Let's quickly recap action items and wrap up to stay mindful of everyone's time."

Q: *How do I stand out in virtual meetings?*

A: Keep your camera on, nod or smile to show you're engaged, and contribute—whether by speaking up or adding thoughtful comments in the typed chat. In virtual meetings, silence doesn't make a positive impression—participation does.

Hosting Clients and Colleagues at a Restaurant: A Guide to Graceful Business Meals

Business meals are a unique combination of meeting and social event. So of course they present their own etiquette challenges. While they're a great chance to relax with colleagues and enjoy some good food, just because you're dining outside the office doesn't mean your polished presence goes on PTO. A successful business meal starts with a clear purpose: Are you celebrating a milestone, building rapport, or getting to know a new client? Define the why before you consider the venue.

Choosing the Right Spot

As the host, your job is to choose a restaurant that's been vetted—not one you've always meant to try. Think: great food, thoughtful service, and a quiet enough setting to have an actual conversation. If the client hosted you recently, consider the tone they set and aim to reciprocate—generously, but within your budget and any company policies.

If they suggest a venue that feels too casual, it's okay to gently steer the conversation:

"That sounds fun! I was thinking of [insert place]—it's a little quieter, and I find it's great for focused conversation. Would that work for you?"

Reservations and Invitations

Reserve under your name, not theirs. If you know of any dietary restrictions, share those with the restaurant ahead of time—it's a small detail that makes a big difference. An emailed calendar invite works just fine, but if it's a special occasion, a handwritten card adds a lovely touch. Include the usuals: time, address, dress code, and a link to the menu if helpful.

Who Sits Where (and Why)

In seating, comfort comes first. Think about the whole picture: airflow, noise, and accessibility. And yes, while seating a left-handed guest at a corner spot may avoid the elbow shuffle, the real art is balancing comfort with connection. At its best, hosting is a blend of intention, warmth, and the ability to adapt in real time.

Q: *How do I know whom to seat where at a business meal?*

A: The seating chart: part logic, part intuition, and just a touch of matchmaking. While there's no one-size-fits-all formula, thoughtful hosting means considering both comfort and chemistry. Here's what to keep in mind:

- Guests of honor deserve the VIP treatment. Traditionally, they sit to the host's right or at the head of the table—but comfort and visibility (to the view, or the room) matter more than strict tradition. Guests of honor may also be seated in the center of a long table.
- Split up couples when possible to encourage mingling—unless they're newlyweds still lost in their own rom-com.
- Consider mobility. Don't seat someone with a cane, stroller, or accessibility need in the most cramped spot in the room.
- Make room for those who need it. Whether it's a left-handed guest who'd appreciate a corner seat or someone needing a little extra elbow room, small accommodations like these show you care.
- Think about chemistry. A vibrant conversationalist next to someone more reserved can spark a great dynamic. Just be mindful to avoid potential ego clashes—this is a meal, not a debate.

In the end, it's not about getting every detail right—it's about creating an environment where people feel comfortable, seen, and able to connect. And if a few elbows bump along the way? That's just part of the charm.

Greeting and Ordering

Meet your guest at the door—it's warm, it's personal, and it sets the tone. Let them order first, and if budget matters, a subtle cue (like mentioning what you're having) helps guide expectations. When possible, handle the check in advance by speaking with the restaurant beforehand and leaving them your credit card—your guest should feel like a priority, not part of the transaction.

Timing the "Business" in Business Meal

Knowing when to dive into work talk can feel tricky. Let the host lead. For multicourse meals, wait about twenty minutes before steering the conversation toward business topics. Remember, the meal is a dance, not a sprint.

The Most Important Ingredient? Consideration

Are you working with a caterer or choosing a set menu for your meal? You don't need a culinary stunt show—just options that are thoughtful, inclusive, and easy to eat. Think: no spaghetti slurping or flying bacon strips. Offer vegetarian, allergy-conscious, and nonalcoholic options without making a fuss. Avoid messy or overly niche dishes and aim for familiar, feel-good flavors.

Final Touches

Leave the restaurant with your guest, not ahead of them. A kind goodbye goes further than you think. And if someone's dietary needs required extra effort, a simple "thank you" to the restaurant staff—paired with a generous tip—shows true appreciation.

Because at the end of the day, hosting isn't about showing off. It's about showing up—with grace, good judgment, and the kind of hospitality people remember long after the dessert menu disappears.

How to Be the Guest Everyone Wants at Their Business Meal

When you're the guest at a business meal, you're not just there for the food—you're there to make a great impression and respect the host's effort. Here's a quick guide to moving through the meal like a pro.

DO YOUR HOMEWORK

Before you even step into the restaurant, check the menu online. Not only does it save time, but it also shows you're thoughtful about the occasion. Bonus: It gives you more time to focus on the conversation, not the menu.

TIMING IS EVERYTHING

Be on time. Not early, not late—on time. If the reservation is at 7 p.m., walk in at 7 p.m. Unlike a casual dinner party where "on time" means slightly after the official start time, business meals are all about punctuality.

> Remember, the meal is a dance, not a sprint.

HOLD OFF ON THAT DRINK ORDER

If alcohol is appropriate (and it's not always), wait for the host to bring it up. Business lunches, especially, are often alcohol-free zones. If you're not sure, stick with water or a soft drink until you get a cue from the host.

ORDERING WELL

Take your cues from the host on how many courses to order. If they're going light, you do the same. Avoid dishes that are hard to eat or make a statement for the wrong reasons—spaghetti, French onion soup, or overly aromatic foods are not your friends here.

HANDLE PROBLEMS GRACEFULLY

When I was in law school, I was involved in the leadership of a student group that hosted lots of guest speakers for speeches, debates, and panel discussions. All the speakers would be invited to lunch after their talks. The timing and restaurant would be the same each time, so the only variables were the speakers. I don't remember much about who knew what to do with their napkin or how to hold a glass with a stem, but I do remember a highly accomplished attorney who was incredibly rude to the restaurant staff—complaining about delays and sending his meal back over what I perceived to be a minor issue. I also remember the speakers who didn't pivot from talking about themselves. They treated lunch as part two of the conversation at the campus event rather than an opportunity to build relationships over a meal. I'm not saying there isn't space to talk business at a business lunch, but balance is key.

All that to say, if you run into a problem with your food, speak kindly and discreetly with the server—with a smile. No one likes drama at the table.

DON'T REACH FOR THE CHECK

As the guest, you're off the hook when it comes to paying the bill. However, keep some cash handy to tip the valet or cloakroom attendant—it's a small but meaningful gesture.

THANK-YOU NOTES AND RECIPROCITY

After the meal, send a thank-you note—either handwritten or via email. Gratitude matters. And if the relationship calls for it, plan to host the next meeting within a few months to keep the goodwill flowing.

Remember, it's not just about the meal; it's about the impression you leave. Thoughtful gestures leave a lasting impact and make you the kind of guest they'll want to invite back.

Was It Something I Typed? Your Guide to Email Etiquette

Email: the lifeline of the modern professional world. It's like the little black dress of communication—versatile, reliable, but all too easy to mess up if you don't accessorize it properly. Whether you're writing to your boss, a client, or the friend who still emails instead of texting, every message says something about you before you even say hello.

So how do we avoid becoming that person—the one who "replies all" unnecessarily, leaves vague subject lines, or accidentally signs their name with "xoxo" when sharing the next staff meeting agenda? Let's dive in.

Subject Lines Are Your First Impression

Think of the subject line as your email's handshake. Would you trust someone who gives you a limp, sweaty handshake? Exactly. A good subject line is clear, specific, and invites action.

- Instead of: "Meeting"
- Try: "Proposal Review Meeting—Thursday at 3 p.m."

It's professional, it's precise, and it's begging for that calendar invite.

Greetings Matter

Skipping a greeting is like walking into a room and launching into your life story without saying hello. Not cool. Always address the recipient by name, and tailor your tone based on your relationship.

- For formal contacts: "Dear Ms. Smith"
- For colleagues or familiar connections: "Hi, Emily"
- For friends you also work with: Avoid the temptation to write "Heyyyy, girl!" Save it for after hours.

Keep It Short and Sweet (but Not Cryptic)

An email should never read like *War and Peace*. Nobody has time for that. Aim to keep your message concise and focused, with one clear ask or purpose. Bullet points are your best friend when you have multiple topics to cover.

Good: "Hi, Sarah, I've attached the report. Let me know if you need edits before Tuesday."

Bad: "Hi, Sarah, I've attached the report, which took a lot of time, but I wasn't sure if you'd want me to add that thing we talked about last month. Thoughts?"

Don't make people decode your message like it's a treasure map.

Reply with Intent

The "Reply All" button is a double-edged sword. Use it sparingly. Ask yourself: *Does everyone on this chain really need to know my response?* If not, spare their inboxes and hit "Reply." And if you're replying late, acknowledge it with grace:

> "Thank you for your patience. I wanted to take the time to give this the attention it deserves."

Sign-Offs That Say "I Mean Business"

Your closing is your final impression—make it count. Avoid overly casual endings like "Cheers" (unless you're actually British) or "xoxo" (unless it's *Gossip Girl*). Keep it professional yet warm:

- "Best regards"
- "Kindly"
- "Looking forward to your thoughts"

Pro tip: Always include a signature block with your name, title, and contact information in the first message you send as part of a conversation. It's the digital equivalent of handing someone a business card.

Spelling, Grammar, and Tone—Oh My!

Emails can't roll their eyes, but poorly written ones feel like they do. Triple-check your spelling and grammar. Use tools like Grammarly or ChatGPT if you need an assist. And before you hit Send, read your email out loud. If it sounds snippy or confusing, rewrite it.

Remember: Tone doesn't always translate in text and often comes across colder without the benefit of body language and tone of voice to supplement that overall impression. If you're upset, draft it, save it, and revisit it later. The Delete key exists for a reason.

Watch Your Words—They Travel

Emails are one of the easiest forms of communication to forward. That witty comment or "just between us" tone could suddenly land in your CEO's inbox—or worse, a client's. Always write with the assumption that your email could be shared.

And remember, depending on your organization's policies, your email account may not be entirely private. Many workplaces retain the right to access messages sent through their systems. Choose your words carefully and stay professional—your inbox could be the modern-day equivalent of an open book.

Attachments: The Bane of Every Email

If you promise an attachment, attach it before you start writing. How many times have you written, "Please find attached," only to realize two seconds after hitting Send that there's nothing attached? We've all been there, but our inboxes deserve better.

Email etiquette isn't rocket science—it's about respecting others' time, being clear in your intentions, and staying polished. Because in a world where your inbox is your digital runway, every message should say, "I know what I'm doing, and I do it well."

The Art of Giving and Receiving Professional Feedback Well

When I started my first job out of college as a TV news reporter, I quickly learned that in that particular newsroom, feedback wasn't optional—it was a sport. The unspoken motto was "Don't trust—triple verify." Every story, even a light segment about a cold snap affecting Vermont's maple syrup supply, was treated with what felt like Watergate-level scrutiny.

One of my earliest stories was met with raised eyebrows from my news director, who asked, "Who reviewed this before it aired?" Then came the line I'll never forget:

"This sounds like it was written by your grandmother . . . if your grandmother were the attorney general."

With all due respect to legal writers, the tone, the structure, the style—it was all too cautious, too stiff, and too disconnected from the audience. That feedback stuck with me. And I remember thinking, *If I ever manage someone who writes like an attorney general in her eighties, I'll find a kinder, clearer way to help her loosen up.*

Because that's the thing about feedback: It's one of the most powerful tools we have for growth. But only if we know how to give it—and receive it—with maturity.

If You're Giving Feedback:

- **Start with what's working.** "Your presentation was compelling and clear. One tweak: Consider trimming it down for time."
- **Be specific, not vague.** No one grows from "Do better." Try: "Adding more context in your emails might reduce the back-and-forth."
- **Focus on the fix.** "This could work even better if you tried . . ." is better than "This isn't working."
- **End with encouragement.** "You've got the skills to make this great. I'm here to help."

If You're Receiving Feedback:

- **Listen first.** Resist the urge to explain—just hear them out.
- **Ask questions.** "Can you give an example? I want to fully understand."

- **Look for the lesson.** Even tough feedback can be useful if you're open to it.
- **Acknowledge and act.** "Thanks for the insight—I'll prioritize that going forward."
- **Don't take it personally.** Feedback is about your work, not your worth.

Business Travel: Maintaining Professionalism on the Go

My first real business trip—the kind that didn't involve a student conference or a job interview—was to Atlanta. I had been an attorney for what felt like five seconds, and suddenly I was boarding a flight with colleagues all old enough to be my parents (and, in some cases, closer in age to my grandparents).

I didn't check a bag, even though I normally would have, because I was afraid I'd seem high-maintenance. I also hadn't yet learned what fabrics hold up on flights or which outfits wrinkle just by looking at them, so I landed in the Peach State looking regrettably disheveled. I was gearing up for days of client meetings, shared meals, a Braves game, and long stretches on the road with people I'd only ever interacted with inside the walls of our DC office. Every little choice—from how I packed to how I ordered at dinner—felt like it carried weight. Because it did.

What I didn't know yet was that business travel is its own form of professional theater. The airport, the hotel, the client dinner—all of it is part of the performance. And your role? A polished, prepared, and pleasant ambassador of your organization (and yourself).

A business trip—even to a vacation hot spot—is still work. From the moment you leave home to the moment you return, how you carry yourself matters. It's not about being perfect. It's about being intentional. Thoughtful. Aware of the impression you're leaving—even when you're standing in a hotel lobby at 7 a.m. looking for the nearest coffee.

Here's how to prepare for a successful business trip and stay polished, professional, and gracious throughout.

- **Understand your objectives and schedule.** Before you set out, make sure you're clear on the purpose of the trip, the schedule, and who you'll be meeting with. Preparation shows that you're serious and ready to make the most of the opportunity.
- **Be organized with your materials.** Ensure all relevant files and documents are saved on your computer or printed as needed. Having hard copies can be a lifesaver if tech issues arise.
- **Pack your tech essentials.** Double-check that you have everything you need, including power cords, adapters, chargers, remote clickers, and any other tech items crucial for your work. Being prepared for any technical situation keeps you looking composed and capable.
- **Confirm your itinerary.** Verify all travel logistics, accommodations, and your daily schedule to avoid last-minute surprises. A smooth itinerary reflects careful planning and respect for everyone's time.
- **Bring extra business cards.** Always pack more business cards than you think you'll need, especially if you're heading to a conference or a large networking event. It's better to have extras than to run out mid-introduction.
- **Dress for success.** Select attire that is professional and appropriate for each event and setting. Align your style with your company's dress code while taking into account the nature of your meetings and cultural expectations.
- **Prepare for international etiquette.** For international travel, learning a few phrases in the local language is a simple yet meaningful way to show respect and cultural awareness. Mastering simple phrases like "hello," "goodbye," "please," "thank you," "nice to meet you," and "where is the restroom?" helps you make a positive impression.
- **Maintain professional conversation.** Keep discussions professional and avoid oversharing about your personal life or prying into the personal matters of others. Gossiping about colleagues is a no-go; it reflects poorly on your professionalism.
- **Understand budget guidelines.** Clarify the budget and which expenses will be approved before your trip, and if you're not sure when and how much to tip for various services on your organization's dime,

ask your supervisor. This ensures you stay within policy and avoid potential misunderstandings.

- **Track your expenses.** Maintain detailed records of your expenses and submit them promptly for reimbursement according to your organization's guidelines. Timely and accurate submissions show attention to detail and responsibility. When in doubt, it's always best to confirm with your organization what is and is not an approved expense.

By following these practices, you'll demonstrate professionalism, preparedness, and respect throughout your business trip, leaving a lasting positive impression and representing your organization with grace.

Q: *How do I politely decline a colleague's invitation to hang out after a day of business travel without seeming rude or antisocial?*

A: Declining doesn't have to feel awkward. Try this: "I'd love to join, but after the day we've had, I need to recharge. Let's definitely catch up tomorrow!"

It's gracious and clear, leaving no room for misunderstanding. Because sometimes the best way to own the room tomorrow is by slipping into pajamas tonight. And honestly, who can blame you for needing a moment to trade the PowerPoint grind for room service and Netflix?

International Travel: Whose Etiquette Rules?

When work takes you across borders—or brings international colleagues to your doorstep—it's natural to wonder: Whose etiquette rules apply? Are the host's customs calling the shots, or should the guest's culture take center stage? It's the kind of question that has launched more than a few awkward toasts and mismatched dress codes. But like most things in the world of grace and good manners, the answer isn't one-size-fits-all.

It's more of a collaborative dance: Sometimes the host leads, sometimes the guest does, and the real magic happens when both are tuned in to each other's rhythm.

If you're the host, think of your role as that of a gracious guide. Your job is to make your guest feel comfortable in your world. Maybe that means serving a vegetarian option when your carnivorous family gathers, or explaining why everyone stands when the king's name is mentioned at a formal British dinner. It's not about losing your traditions but about creating an environment where your guest feels seen, respected, and at ease.

Guests, on the other hand, are like travelers visiting a new city—you wouldn't ignore the local customs just because they're different from what you're used to back home. It's all about blending in, being curious, and showing respect. That means learning to use chopsticks in Japan or leaving your shoes at the door in a Scandinavian home, even if you packed your best stilettos.

The beauty of etiquette lies in the shared effort. Hosts should strive to accommodate reasonable cultural nuances, and guests should make every effort to adapt. The role of the host is to make the guest feel comfortable, while the role of the guest is to make the host feel successful.

For those moments when cultures clash and no one is quite sure who should take the lead, consider this diplomatic middle ground: Create a hybrid experience. Incorporate elements from both cultures—serve sushi alongside lasagna or light a traditional candle to honor your guest's holiday. And if all else fails, lean into universal truths: Politeness, gratitude, and good conversation transcend all cultural divides.

The goal isn't to "win" the etiquette game; it's to play well together. Because when host and guest meet halfway, they create something even better—connection, mutual respect, and a few great stories to tell. And isn't that the real point of entertaining?

Q: *I'm hosting a dinner party for colleagues from different cultures, and I'm terrified of offending someone. Should I stick to my traditions or try to cater to everyone's?*

A: If your dinner party is suddenly feeling less like a celebration and more like a minefield of potential faux pas, take a deep breath and relax—you've got this, and you're not auditioning for the Diplomatic Olympics!

Start by being a gracious host. That doesn't mean abandoning your traditions; it means making your guests feel like they belong in your world. If you're Italian, serve that signature pasta dish your Nonna taught you, but maybe skip the prosciutto platter if your friend from Tel Aviv keeps kosher. It's all about balance: Show off your culture, but leave room for theirs to shine too.

And if you're worried about getting it wrong, remember this golden rule: Curiosity beats perfection. A simple "Is there anything I should know to make you more comfortable?" will earn you more points than obsessing over every detail. So pour the wine, light the candles, and enjoy. Etiquette is about making people feel welcome—and even if you stumble, there's nothing a delicious dessert and heartfelt laughter can't smooth over.

Holiday Parties, Galas, and Other Business Soirées

The social side of business—whether it's a black-tie gala, an office baby shower, or a backyard barbecue—can feel like stepping onto a stage where you're expected to be both professional and personable, all while reading the room in real time. One moment you're clinking glasses at a formal fundraiser, the next you're standing in a conference room celebrating a colleague's wedding you weren't invited to, wondering what to write in the group card that's appropriate but not painfully boring.

And let's not forget the summer pool party where no one's quite sure if "casual" means sundresses or swimsuits. These moments blur the lines between work and play, and they can be as anxiety-inducing as they are well-intentioned.

The stakes? Making an impression that's memorable for the right reasons.

A little timeless wisdom and polished pragmatism will carry you through the sparkle, the snacks, and the social gray areas that come with mixing business and pleasure.

Dress the Part

Consider the dress code your first opportunity to show respect at an event. A cocktail party might call for a sleek dress or tailored suit, while a gala requires full-on glam with floor-length gowns or formal tuxedos. If you're unsure, err on the side of elegance—overdressing is almost always better than being underdressed because it shows respect for the occasion. And whatever you wear, make sure it's comfortable enough to mingle without fidgeting or fussing.

Timing Is Everything

Punctuality matters. For a cocktail party, aim to arrive ten to fifteen minutes after the start time—fashionably late but not rudely so. For seated dinners or galas, be on time. Lateness can throw off the flow of an event and leave a sour first impression.

Mingle Like You Mean It

Holiday parties and galas aren't just about the canapés (though who doesn't love a mini quiche?). They're prime opportunities to network. Approach conversations with genuine interest. Ask open-ended questions like, "What brought you to this organization?" or, "What's been your highlight of the year?"

It's also to your advantage to have a drink (nonalcoholic is fine) in one hand to avoid looking awkward, but don't forget to keep your other hand free for handshakes. And remember, balance is key—drink in moderation and avoid anything too messy on the appetizer tray.

Table Manners 101

If there's a formal meal, this is your time to shine—or at least not stumble. Follow basic etiquette (and read more about table manners in chapter 7 of this book):

- Wait for the host or the majority of the table to begin eating.
- Use utensils from the outside in.
- Keep your napkin in your lap until the meal is over.
- Avoid controversial topics at the table. Stick to light, inclusive conversation that everyone can enjoy.

Show Gratitude Like a Pro

Thank your host before you leave. If the gathering was particularly special, follow up with a handwritten thank-you note. Gratitude never goes out of style, and a thoughtful note leaves a lasting impression.

Holiday-Specific Tips

Holiday parties often blur the lines between personal and professional. While it's fine to let your hair down a little, remember you're still representing yourself—and possibly your company. Avoid overindulging in alcohol or gossiping about coworkers. The mantra here? Celebrate, don't commiserate.

Exit Gracefully

When it's time to leave, do so with warmth and consideration. Thank your host, say goodbye to those you've spoken with, and avoid the Irish goodbye (aka slipping out unnoticed, and a concept with a debated history that my Irish relatives say is more American than Irish). A simple "It was lovely catching up—I hope you enjoy the rest of the evening," will do.

Holiday parties and galas are your chance to shine outside the boardroom, so make the most of them. Bring your charm, your confidence, and your best etiquette game—it's your time to make connections, not just memories.

Q: *What's a subtle way to stand out in a room full of senior professionals at an industry conference without coming across as overly ambitious? I'd like to show I'm capable without overstepping.*

A: There's a fine line between confidence and overkill. The goal is to be memorable without making it seem like you're trying too hard. Think of it as creating a presence that speaks before you even say a word. Start by dressing the part: Choose something that makes you feel like a polished version of yourself but with one small twist—maybe an eye-catching accessory or a bold color that stands out against a sea of neutrals.

Then, focus on listening with intention. People love a good conversationalist, but they're truly captivated by someone who listens and asks thoughtful questions. Instead of trying to impress with everything you know, let your genuine curiosity and interest do the work for you. Remember, when you're in a room with seasoned pros, subtlety is power. Speak clearly and confidently, but make each word count. Leave them with the impression that there's more to you than meets the eye—that's intriguing.

I'll never forget attending a small award luncheon during law school in honor of a former US attorney general. I was one of just a few law students invited and seated among highly accomplished faculty and alumni. I don't say this to impress, but to emphasize what showing up with presence can do. Through a combination of how I carried myself and the advocacy of a trusted professor, that former attorney general later served as a reference—helping me land a coveted clerkship the following semester.

What struck me most, though, was the contrast. One of my fellow students—a sharp, capable classmate who has gone on to do impressive things—sat through the entire lunch in complete silence, looking like he'd accidentally wandered into the wrong event and decided to wait it out. No questions, no conversation, no hint that we were sitting in a room full of influence and insight. Maybe he was just having an off day. But I couldn't help but see the missed opportunity—not just for career growth, but for connection, encouragement, and maybe even a little inspiration. It reminded me that showing up isn't just about being physically present—it's about engaging, noticing, and choosing to participate.

The Takeaway: Polished Isn't Performative—It's Intentional

Whether it's a holiday party, a team dinner, a networking reception, or a regular day at the office, the moments we spend with colleagues matter more than we sometimes give them credit for. They're not just about dressing up or making small talk, or about professional advancement—they're about how you make people feel, how you show up, and how you carry yourself when no one is grading you but everyone is paying attention.

So say yes to the invitation. Write something thoughtful in the group card. Bring your best to that meeting. Send the email with confidence. You don't need to dazzle—but you do need to be present. Because often, it's the quietest moments of grace that leave the most lasting impression.

CHAPTER 5

RELATIONSHIPS IN LOVE AND LIFE

They say that if you want a friend in Washington, you should get a dog. But whoever believes that has never met my friends.

At the height of the COVID-19 pandemic, while most of the world was working from home in athleisure, I was getting dressed in the kind of dry-clean-only clothes you couldn't dry clean and reporting to work each day in the West Wing of the White House. I worked in the small but mighty Office of the Staff Secretary to the President, responsible for managing all the president's documents, including compiling and hand-delivering the president's daily briefing materials—what we called "the book."

We rotated book duty among a handful of us, since it almost always meant staying late—sometimes very late—waiting for the next day's presidential schedule to be finalized. For a number of reasons, I didn't feel safe leaving alone or relying on the Metro, which was operating on a severely limited schedule on my book-duty nights. So I'd text my dear friend Linsey the moment the final schedule came through, and while I printed the documents on the most beautiful gold-embossed stationery I'll probably ever touch and sprinted past the Oval Office, across the colonnade, and to the residence in the East Wing to deliver the book, Linsey would drive from Capitol Hill to pick me up.

She did this for months. Always on call. Always there. Thinking about it still brings tears to my eyes. Her generosity, her loyalty, her quiet consistency—she is one of the great blessings of my life.

I don't share this to make any political statement, but to show you what friendship can look like. Sometimes, one person gives more. One person carries a little more weight. And that's okay. True friendship isn't about everything being perfectly even—it's about love that balances out over time.

For every kindred spirit I've met—those couldn't-live-without-them girlfriends who lift me up—I've also known the pain of friendships that didn't last. I've felt the sting of being left out, replayed conversations, questioned my judgment, and wondered how I ever got into something so imbalanced. If you've been there too, hear this: There is nothing wrong with you. Struggling in friendship doesn't mean you're flawed—it means you're growing. It means you're human.

If you take nothing else from this chapter, let it be this: You deserve excellent relationships in your life—the kind that feel mutual, kind, and safe. And you can learn how to be a source of love and warmth that others are lucky to have.

Friendship, Simplified

Friendships are one of life's greatest gifts. They bring joy, support, and meaning to our lives. Unlike serious romantic relationships, friendships are beautifully complex—you can have many at once, each offering something different. They evolve as we do, sometimes deepening, sometimes drifting. The key is to approach them with kindness, respect, and an open heart.

We may have our friendships for a reason, a season, or a lifetime. Recognizing that truth helps us cherish the ones that lift us up and gently release the ones that no longer fit—without guilt or bitterness.

How to Be an Excellent Friend

Friendship isn't about grand gestures—it's about showing up in small, consistent ways that quietly mean everything. The best friends aren't always the loudest or the most available; they're the ones who make you feel remembered, respected, and safe. Here's how to be that kind of friend with a few simple etiquette habits that speak volumes.

CELEBRATE THEIR WINS

One year, I got a new job that wasn't quite what I'd imagined. It wasn't a bad role—it just felt like a sharp left turn I hadn't seen coming. In Washington, that's not unusual. After my boss lost reelection, I accepted a position that felt like it had been thrust upon me by the universe. Still, I was grateful to have landed on my feet.

The very first day of this new role, a few friends sent me flowers. I felt so seen. About a year later I got promoted—and those same friends took me out to celebrate. We went to a newly opened vegan-friendly restaurant (I'm not vegan, but I have a real appreciation for allergy-friendly menus), and I'm pretty sure I was the only one who truly enjoyed the food. But they didn't care. They were just happy to be there, happy for me. That "drop everything to celebrate you" kind of friendship? It still moves me.

Years later, my sister got a big promotion. Though I couldn't explain her job in any detail, I knew how much the milestone meant to her. As soon as I hung up the phone, I sent flowers her way—just like my friends had done for me. They'd taught me something: When someone you love shares good news, you don't wait. You join them in it.

Personally, I believe in triple-texting good news and calling immediately when someone shares something exciting. If a friend tells me they got engaged, got into their dream school, are expecting, or even finally ended things with someone who was never right for them, I'm picking up the phone. Because deep down, most people want someone to celebrate with. And the quickest way to be that someone is simply to show up with joy.

What to Say When Someone Shares Good News

1. "I'm so proud of you!"

   Why it works: It centers your friend and acknowledges their effort—not just the outcome.

2. "Tell me everything!"

   Why it works: It invites them to relive the moment and signals that you care about the details, not just the headline.
3. "I've always believed in you."

   Why it works: It connects this win to their character and journey, which makes your words feel sincere and meaningful.
4. "This couldn't have happened to a more deserving person."

   Why it works: It reinforces that their success isn't luck—it's earned.
5. "How are we celebrating?"

   Why it works: It shows that you're not just excited *for* them—you're excited *with* them. It turns their news into a shared joy.

What Not to Say—and Why

1. "Must be nice . . ."

   Why to avoid it: Even if meant playfully, it can come across as envious or dismissive.
2. "Wow, I could never do that."

   Why to avoid it: It shifts the focus to you and can make them feel awkward about their success.
3. "I remember when I [insert unrelated story]."

   Why to avoid it: This can sound like one-upping, even if unintentional. Keep the spotlight on them.
4. "Hope you can handle it!" or "You sure that's a good idea?"

   Why to avoid it: Poking holes in someone's happy news—even as a joke—can undercut their moment and cause them to second-guess themselves.
5. "What's next?" or "Now you just need to . . ."

   Why to avoid it: It unintentionally rushes past the current achievement. Let your friend enjoy the moment without already looking ahead to the next milestone.

SHOW UP IN THE HARD TIMES

There's no perfect thing to say when someone is struggling, but your presence is powerful. Whether it's sitting beside them, texting "thinking of you" every few days, or checking in without expecting a response, effort counts.

Etiquette tip: Don't say "Let me know if you need anything." Most people won't. Instead, offer something specific: "Can I drop off dinner Thursday?" "Want to go on a walk this weekend?" Keep it gentle and low-pressure.

We'll do a deeper dive into etiquette during difficult times in chapter 9, exploring how to show up with compassion, sensitivity, and presence when it matters most.

PRACTICE THOUGHTFUL TIMING

You don't need to talk every day, but reliability is key. Follow through on plans, check in regularly, and let your friends know they can count on you. Responding to every text, email, or group chat meme doesn't require urgency—but it does deserve thoughtfulness.

Etiquette tip: Try to respond within twenty-four to forty-eight hours if possible, even if it's just a "More soon, thinking of you!" It's better to reply with kindness than to ghost and assume your friend will understand. And if you're the one waiting? Extend grace—friendship isn't a stopwatch.

KEEP THEIR CONFIDENCE

Are you familiar with the proverb "trust but verify"? To the chagrin of my very protective husband, I've always leaned more toward "trust until given a reason not to." It's who I am—optimistic, maybe a little rose-colored around the edges. Have I gotten burned by it? Absolutely. But I don't see that as a total factory defect. It's part of how I choose to move through the world, though I'm learning to be more discerning as I grow.

There are people I would trust with my life—but what I've come to understand is this: When you're going through something difficult, it matters who you choose to share it with. Confide in people who can not only hold your pain, but also hold a vision of you on the other side of it. The kind of friend who believes in your future, not someone who will keep you tethered to the hardest part of your past or current moment. And of course, be that kind of friend too as you keep their confidence.

Etiquette tip: If someone shares something sensitive with you, don't assume. Ask: "Would you prefer I keep this between us?" That simple question does more than build trust—it shows you're ready to honor their story the way they need it to be held. And that's the mark of a truly respectful friend. And whatever you do, don't gossip. No matter how compelling, it's not a good look.

LET FRIENDSHIPS EVOLVE

Friends become parents. They move. They grow. So do you. What matters most is making space for each other through life's inevitable changes. From experience, I know that clinging to a prior season or becoming territorial about relationships rarely ends well. Friendships aren't meant to stay static—they're meant to stretch, soften, and shift.

Not all friendships will last forever, and that's okay. That doesn't mean the friendship failed—it simply means its role in your life has shifted. The key is to let friendships evolve without resentment and to appreciate them for what they were, even if they don't continue in the same form.

Etiquette tip: Don't take distance personally. Busier schedules, shifting priorities—these things happen. A thoughtful way to stay connected is to say, "I know things are full right now—want to set a time for a quick catch-up call next week?" That little check-in shows you're still invested, even if the rhythm of the friendship has changed.

And if the connection fades? Carry the good with you. A friendship can leave a lasting mark, even if it doesn't last forever.

Ending a Friendship with Kindness

Most friendships don't end with a dramatic conversation—they simply fade with time. I don't have any ill will toward the friend I used to chat with at the laundromat in college, even though we haven't connected in years. Or the colleagues I adored during my first job who slowly drifted out of my life after I moved away. That's the quiet, natural attrition of friendship—something that happens in the background of most adult lives. But every now and then, a friendship ends in a way that feels heavier. It's those unusually painful goodbyes that tend to stick with us, and when they come, we're called to handle them with honesty and compassion.

BE HONEST BUT GENTLE

If a conversation feels necessary, speak from a place of care rather than criticism. Try something like:

"I've really appreciated our friendship, but I feel like we're in different places right now. I'll always value what we shared and truly wish you the best."

LET IT FADE NATURALLY

Not every friendship needs a formal ending. Some naturally drift apart—and that gentle fade can be a peaceful way to move on, especially when there's no hurt or harm involved.

AVOID GOSSIP AND RESIST THE URGE TO REHASH

If the friendship ends, protect what once was by keeping the details private aside from processing with a trusted confidant, counselor, or significant other. Choosing not to gossip is a quiet act of respect—for your former friend and for yourself.

Friendship As a Journey

Whether they're lifelong friends or friends for a season, each one plays an important role in shaping who we are. By showing up with kindness, being intentional, and letting go gracefully when the time comes, you're better able to embrace friendship for what it is—ever-changing, meaningful, and deeply human.

Friendship isn't built on getting everything right; it's a shared rhythm of trust, respect, and understanding. When you invest in your friends, you'll find that the rewards are immeasurable—because a life filled with enriching friendships is a life well-lived.

Q: *My best friend's wedding is the first week of December, but I'm in school and have final exams at the same time. I feel terrible about missing it, but I don't see how I can make it work. What should I do?*

A: First of all, take a deep breath. You're not a bad friend for being in a tough spot, and this doesn't mean you care any less about your friend or their big day. You're juggling a once-in-a-lifetime event for them and a high-stakes moment in your career, and there's no easy answer—but there is a graceful way to handle it.

Here's what I'd do: Call your friend. No texts, no DMs—this deserves an actual conversation. Start by saying how much you love them and how devastated you are to miss their wedding. Be honest about why you can't make it. Something like:

> "I've been dreading telling you this, but my finals fall the same week as your wedding, and I've realized there's just no way I can be there. It's breaking my heart because I've been looking forward to celebrating with you for so long. Please know I'll be thinking of you every second and cheering you on from afar."

They'll feel your sincerity, and that's what matters most. Now, just because you can't physically be there doesn't mean you can't show up in other ways. Maybe send a thoughtful gift with a heartfelt note about how much their love inspires you. Or, record a short video message for them to watch on their wedding day. Something sweet and personal like:

> "I may not be in the room, but you're in my heart, and I'm raising a toast to you both from my study desk. I can't wait to celebrate with you soon!"

And speaking of celebrating, plan something for after finals—dinner, drinks, or even just coffee to hear every detail about their magical day. It shows that even though you couldn't be there on the day, you're still prioritizing their happiness and your friendship.

Finally, let go of the guilt. This doesn't make you a bad friend; it makes you human. Life throws curveballs, and real friendships survive them. If your friend truly loves you—and it sounds like they do—they'll understand and appreciate the effort you're putting in to show how much they mean to you.

You're doing your best, and that's more than enough.

Online Friendships: Finding Your People

I can't be the only one who has ever teared up watching another woman's fertility journey unfold online, or felt oddly invested in a stranger's historic home renovation. Some of the deepest connections happen through screens. Online friendships are real friendships, period. Research from the University of California, Irvine, indicates that many digital interactions among teenagers serve the same purposes and encompass similar qualities as face-to-face relationships. The study found that online communication can provide additional opportunities for friends to spend time together, share thoughts, and display affection, comparable to offline interactions.[1]

Here's the key: Be as present for your online friends as you would for those IRL. Celebrate their wins, check in on bad days, and don't ghost them because life gets busy. Tools like voice notes and video calls add a personal touch that makes your bond stronger.

Q: *I've made an amazing online friend, but I'm worried I might come off as either too clingy some days, or distant others. What's the etiquette for keeping a digital friendship balanced?*

A: Online friendships are like a great conversation—you want to keep the rhythm going without dominating the dialogue. The key is mutual effort, thoughtful gestures, and a touch of patience.

Start by mirroring their energy. If your friend is a once-a-week texter, don't bombard them with daily updates. If they love voice notes or funny memes, lean in to that style of communication—it shows you're tuned into how they like to connect.

But balance is a two-way street. If you feel like you're always initiating, it's okay to pull back slightly and see if they reach out. True friendship, online or otherwise, is about reciprocity.

Want to take things to the next level? Suggest a virtual coffee date or video call to deepen the connection. And when in doubt, just be honest: "I love chatting with you! Let me know if I'm ever overdoing it—I don't want to be 'that' friend."

Online friendships thrive on conscious effort and respect. Show up, be yourself, and trust that the right friendships will feel as effortless as your favorite playlist.

Authenticity vs. Oversharing: The Balancing Act

You want to be real online—research shows that 86 percent of people say authenticity is crucial for brands and influencers[2]—but there is such a thing as too real, and oversharing can feel, well, cringey.

Ask yourself:

- Is this serving a purpose?
- Would I share this with someone I just met?
- Does this align with my boundaries?

It's okay to share parts of your life, but keep some things sacred. Mystery isn't a bad thing.

In an age where a DM can lead to a job interview, a LinkedIn message can spark a mentorship, and a single post can reach millions, your digital presence isn't just a highlight reel. It's an extension of who you are, how you think, and how you make others feel. Online etiquette isn't about playing it safe or curating a "perfect" online image. It's about leading with integrity. It's about choosing thoughtfulness over performance, intention over impulse, and connection over clout. Because in the digital age, good etiquette isn't just nice—it's powerful.

Roommate Etiquette: Respectfully Sharing Space

Sharing a home with someone is a unique relationship—part partnership, part compromise, and sometimes a little chaos. Whether you're moving in with a friend, a stranger, or your partner, roommate etiquette is all about balancing respect, communication, and effort. A well-shared home isn't just about clean counters or who buys the toilet paper—it's about creating a living environment that feels easy, supportive, and peaceful.

Let's start with the basics: respect and responsibility. The living room, kitchen, and bathroom aren't just yours, so treat them as neutral zones. Clean up after yourself, be mindful of your presence, and avoid letting your belongings creep onto every available surface. Dishes don't wash themselves, and laundry doesn't magically migrate from couch to closet. Tidy as you go—it prevents resentment from building and keeps your shared space livable.

While you're sharing space under the same roof, you're not obligated to share every moment. Knock before entering closed doors, give each other breathing room, and honor personal space as much as physical space.

Money can get awkward fast, so fairness is key. Set clear expectations for how you'll split rent, utilities, and household essentials early on. Digital tools like Venmo or Splitwise can help you track expenses without awkward reminders.

And as small as it seems, respect each other's food. That leftover Thai takeout might be someone's reward after a long day—not a free-for-all. When in doubt, label it or ask first. If you borrow something, replace it. No drama necessary.

Communication, unsurprisingly, is the glue that holds it all together. Speak up early and kindly if something bothers you—whether it's noise, dishes, or unexpected guests. Don't let frustrations simmer into a passive-aggressive standoff. And remember: Venting to mutual friends isn't the same as resolving an issue. Talk to your roommate directly.

That said, try not to take everything personally. Everyone has quirks, and part of living well with others is knowing when to seek compromise and when to let things go.

Chores are often where the rubber meets the road. Setting a simple cleaning schedule can work wonders, whether you rotate weeks or divide tasks. From vacuuming to taking out the trash, share responsibilities. Small gestures, like promptly doing your dishes or refilling the toilet paper roll, help build trust and mutual respect.

Social dynamics matter too. You don't have to be best friends with your roommate, but some level of camaraderie makes the day-to-day smoother. Give each other space when needed, and be thoughtful about having guests over. A quick heads-up before inviting friends over—or before a loud FaceTime call—can make all the difference. If you're cooking a big meal, offering your roommate a plate is a lovely gesture that invites connection without pressure.

At the heart of all of this is a simple rule: Treat your roommate the way you'd want to be treated. Whether that's refilling the soap, respecting their downtime, or just asking how their day went, little acts of courtesy make a big impact over time.

Living with someone isn't always effortless—but when approached with consideration and respect, it can be one of life's most rewarding experiences. With communication and a shared sense of care, you can turn your shared living space into more than just a place to sleep—you can make it feel like home.

How to Be a Good Neighbor

Living near others means you're part of an unspoken social contract. While you might not be sharing walls, like with a roommate, you are sharing a sense of community—and the way you show up in that shared space is part of what makes a neighborhood feel like a home. Whether you're waving hello, borrowing a cup of sugar, or negotiating a backyard renovation, treating your neighbors with kindness and respect sets the tone for a harmonious relationship. Here's your guide to neighbor etiquette—centered on simple kindness, respect, and good manners.

Start with the Basics: Greetings and Conversations

SAY HELLO

A smile, wave, or simple "hello" are small gestures that make a meaningful difference. Think of it as the foundation for all future interactions. Even if you're not in the mood for a chat, a quick acknowledgment shows you see and respect them.

MAKE TIME FOR SMALL TALK

Casual conversations over the fence or during a walk are great opportunities to build rapport. That said, be mindful of their time. If your neighbor seems distracted or isn't engaging, take it as a sign to wrap things up. Not every interaction needs to be a deep dive into their weekend plans.

Visiting: Call First, and Don't Overstay

CALL OR TEXT BEFORE DROPPING BY

Spontaneous visits can be charming if you have an established rapport, but most people appreciate a heads-up. A quick text—"Is now a good time to stop by?"—shows thoughtfulness and respects their space and schedule.

KEEP VISITS BRIEF

If you do drop by, be mindful of the time. Look for cues that your neighbor needs to get back to their day. If they're checking their watch or tidying up, it's your signal to leave with a friendly "Thanks for the chat!"

Be a Good Neighbor in Your Space

RESPECT THEIR PRIVACY

Close quarters can make overhearing conversations or noticing personal details unavoidable, but eavesdropping—or repeating what you accidentally overhear—is a no-go. If you find yourself within earshot of a private moment, distract yourself or move away.

MIND THE NOISE

Whether it's mowing the lawn at 7 a.m. or blasting music on a Saturday night, be conscious of how your activities might affect others. If you're planning something particularly loud—like hosting a party—let your neighbors know in advance. A little communication can prevent a lot of annoyance.

TREAT THEIR PROPERTY WITH CARE

Always ask permission before stepping onto their property, borrowing tools, or making use of shared spaces. Their garden isn't a shortcut, and their ladder isn't fair game unless they've offered.

Give and Get Gracefully

DON'T TAKE ADVANTAGE OF THEIR SKILLS

Just because your neighbor is a mechanic, lawyer, or designer doesn't mean they owe you free consultations. If they offer to help, great—just make sure to thank them and avoid turning every encounter into a request.

RETURN THE FAVOR

If a neighbor helps you out, always express your gratitude and be ready to return the favor. Whether it's watering plants while they're on vacation or sharing homemade cookies, small acts of kindness keep the goodwill flowing.

Chores and Common Spaces

BE CONSIDERATE WITH YARD WORK AND MAINTENANCE

Your chores shouldn't become their problem. Choose reasonable hours for mowing, hammering, or other noisy tasks, and let them know if something major—like tree trimming—is happening.

SHARED SPACES REQUIRE SHARED RESPECT

If you have communal areas like hallways, parking lots, or gardens, do your part to keep them clean and functional. Don't leave personal items lying around or create unnecessary clutter.

Neighborhood Living

At the heart of good neighbor etiquette is this: Treat others the way you'd like to be treated. Thoughtful gestures—whether it's a friendly hello, respecting their privacy, or picking up after your dog—help create a community where everyone feels comfortable.

Treat others the way you'd like to be treated.

Because ultimately, being a good neighbor isn't about grand gestures. It's about the small, consistent ways you show up, respect their space, and share your own with grace. You're not just neighbors—you're part of each other's everyday world.

The Etiquette of Family: Showing Kindness Where It Matters Most

Family is where we're most ourselves—where we laugh the loudest, cry the hardest, and sometimes let our guard down a little too much. It's easy to assume that the people who know us best will always understand our intentions, even when we're less than our best. But here's the truth: The ones we love the most deserve just as much kindness, respect, and thoughtfulness as anyone else, if not more.

Family is the foundation of how we give and receive love. When we treat our family members with dignity and care, we create an environment where everyone feels valued and respected. Here's how to bring a little more grace into your family dynamics, even on the messy days.

Speak with Kindness—Even When It's Hard

The way we talk to our family sets the tone for everything. It's easy to snap, interrupt, or say something hurtful in the heat of the moment because we assume they'll forgive us. But words leave marks, even on the people who love us most.

- **Pause before you speak.** Take a breath before responding, especially during arguments. A calm moment can save a relationship from a harsh word.
- **Say the compliments out loud.** Tell your sister she looks radiant, thank your parents for their support, or remind your spouse you appreciate them. Loving thoughts are so much more powerful when expressed.

Respect Their Boundaries

Just because someone is family doesn't mean you're entitled to every corner of their life. Respecting boundaries is a way to show you value their individuality.

- **Ask, don't assume.** Whether it's borrowing a sweater or discussing a sensitive topic, always ask permission first.
- **Give space when needed.** If someone needs alone time or doesn't want to rehash an argument, honor their request.

Share the Load

Family life comes with its share of responsibilities, from chores to childcare to emotional labor. When one person feels like they're carrying too much, resentment builds.

- **Pitch in.** Depending on your season of life, this could look like loading the dishwasher, folding laundry, or running errands. Small acts of effort show you're part of the team. Or it could mean helping aging parents with home maintenance or health issues, planning holiday get-togethers, or other responsibilities of grown siblings.
- **Don't keep score.** It's not about tallying who did what; it's about creating a sense of shared ownership.

Practice Gratitude Daily

It's easy to take family for granted, but expressing appreciation strengthens bonds and fosters connection.

- **Say thank you.** Whether it's for a home-cooked meal or emotional support, gratitude matters.
- **Acknowledge the little things.** Notice and appreciate the everyday ways your family shows up for you.

Thank-You Note Etiquette: Writing Gratitude with Style

Thank-you notes can feel like the broccoli of etiquette—you know they're good for you, but they're easy to put off. I'll be honest: I'm not always perfect about them either. But with a few simple habits, writing notes of gratitude can become something you actually enjoy.

Make It Easy to Follow Through

Keep cards, envelopes, and stamps on hand so your notes don't sit unsent. Block off a regular time—like "Thankful Thursdays"—to make it a rhythm rather than a chore. And invest in stationery you love. When your note feels like an extension of your personal style, writing becomes more fun.

What to Say (and How to Say It)

Skip the standard "Thank you for . . ." opening. Instead, begin with how the gift or gesture made you feel:

"I'm already dreaming of using the olive oil and balsamic vinegar you gave me at my next dinner party."

Then express your appreciation sincerely and specifically. Wrap up with a personal touch—something about the giver's life or when you'll see them next.

When writing on behalf of a couple, avoid signing both names at the bottom. Instead, reference your partner in the body of the note:

"Jason joins me in sending thanks and love to everyone."

For holiday cards, a joint signature—"Jason and Alison"—is perfectly appropriate.

Notes for Monetary Gifts

Thanking someone for money or a gift card can feel tricky, but it's all about intention. You don't need to mention the exact amount—just share how you plan to use it:

"Thank you for your generous gift—I'm excited to put it toward my summer travel plans!"

Letting the giver know their gift will be enjoyed offers a sense of closure and connection.

Handle Conflict

Every family has its share of disagreements—it's how you respond that helps relationships grow or causes them to fracture.

- **Be fair in disagreements.** Focus on the issue, not personal attacks. Avoid bringing up unrelated past grievances.
- **Apologize when necessary.** "I'm sorry" is a powerful phrase that can rebuild trust and repair relationships.

Make Time for Connection

Life is busy, but carving out time for your family strengthens your bond and creates lasting memories.

- **Start small.** Simple rhythms—a regular phone call, a monthly dinner, or a shared hobby—are often what keep relationships thriving.
- **Be present.** Put away your phone and focus on the moment whenever you're with your family.

Don't Forget Yourself

Taking care of your own mental and emotional well-being makes you a better family member.

- **Set healthy boundaries.** It's okay to say no or take time for yourself when you need it.
- **Prioritize self-care.** A well-rested, emotionally balanced you can give more to your family.

Love, but Don't Assume

It's easy to think family relationships will take care of themselves because of shared history and unconditional love. But family bonds, like any relationship, need nurturing. When we treat our loved ones with the same respect and kindness we extend to colleagues, neighbors, and friends, we create a family where everyone feels seen, valued, and loved.

Because if we can't show up for the people who've seen us at our worst, who can we show up for? Family is where grace begins, so why not make it a little more intentional?

Dating Etiquette: Finding Connection with Class

Dating can feel like a high-stakes chess game—strategic moves, unpredictable outcomes, and the hope that someone is playing by the same rules. But here's the thing: Great dating etiquette isn't about playing games. It's about being genuine, respectful, and a little fabulous while showing up well in the sometimes-tricky world of modern romance.

Who Pays? The Dinner-Bill Dilemma

While there's no hard-and-fast rule, etiquette whispers that the person who initiated the date should be prepared to pay. That said, offering to split or cover your share is never a bad idea—it shows consideration and independence. And if your date insists on treating you? Accept graciously, with a heartfelt, "Thank you, that's so kind of you."

As a relationship progresses, it's important to get on the same page about what works best for both of you going forward. Some couples prefer to alternate who pays, while others split costs down the middle or pool their resources. The key is to have an honest, open conversation about your preferences and comfort levels. Talking about finances early on isn't unromantic—it's practical and shows mutual respect.

Whether it's the first date or the fiftieth, the real win is when both people feel appreciated and valued. Honest communication—about money and beyond—lays the foundation for a stronger, more respectful relationship.

The Post-Date Text: Timing Is Everything

Forget the "wait three days" nonsense. If you enjoyed yourself on a first date, there's nothing wrong with a quick, thoughtful follow-up. A simple "I had such a great time tonight—thank you!" leaves a warm impression. And if you didn't feel the spark? A polite "It was lovely meeting you, but I don't think we're a match" is far better than ghosting. Ghosts belong in haunted houses, not in your dating repertoire.

Digital Dating: Swiping with Etiquette

Dating apps can feel like a minefield, but with the right approach, they're just another way to meet great people. A study by Pew Research revealed that nearly 40 percent of couples now meet online.[3]

Tips for dating with class:

- **Craft a thoughtful profile.** Show, don't tell. Instead of "I love to travel," mention your recent trip to Tokyo.
- **Message politely.** Compliment something specific on their profile, not just their looks.
- **Be clear about your intentions.** Whether it's a relationship or casual dating, honesty saves everyone time.

And remember, ghosting is not classy. If you're not feeling it, a short, kind message is always better than disappearing.

Social media is the modern world's cocktail party—fun, dynamic, full of potential, and a place where manners still matter. By staying thoughtful online, you can make genuine connections, build a brand you're proud of, and navigate the digital world with style and grace.

Q: *If someone I'm dating posts a lot about our relationship on social media, how can I ask them to tone it down?*

A: If your partner is all about the posts, but you'd prefer to keep things more low-key, approach it with honesty and a little humor. Try saying something like, "I love that you're excited about our relationship, but I'd like to keep a bit more of 'us' just between us."

Framing it this way lets them know you're not dismissing their excitement—you're just asking for a bit of balance. Reinforce the idea that you value your connection deeply, and it's not about hiding the relationship; it's about savoring it without a running commentary. Most people will understand that sometimes, the best moments are the ones that don't make it to the feed.

Setting Boundaries, Sweetly

Whether it's deciding when to go exclusive or politely saying no to something that doesn't feel right, setting boundaries is a cornerstone of classy dating. The secret? Kind honesty. For example: "I'm really enjoying getting to know you, but I'd like to take things a bit slower." Boundaries are about protecting your space, not shutting people out.

Meeting the Friends: First Impressions Matter

When your date takes you into their social circle, it's a step worth noting. Treat it like an informal interview—be warm, interested, and polite. Compliment the host, engage in group conversation, and avoid monopolizing your date's attention. It's not just about making them like you—it's about showing you can blend seamlessly into their world.

Parting Ways Gracefully

Not feeling it while you're on a date? It's okay. No one is a match for everyone. If you'd rather not continue the date, wait for a natural pause and say, "I've really enjoyed meeting you, but I think we're looking for different things. Thank you for a lovely evening." It's honest, it's kind, and it saves you both time.

Whether it's a relationship or casual dating, honesty saves everyone time.

If you want to politely decline the offer of a second date, be respectful yet straightforward. Say something like, "Thank you so much for meeting up—I really enjoyed getting to know you, but I don't feel the connection I'm looking for. I think it's best if we part ways now, but I truly wish you all the best." Keep it short, sweet, and don't overexplain. You're not obligated to give a detailed reason, but showing gratitude for their time makes the message softer.

Use the same approach if you're several dates into a relationship and don't see a future connection. A gentle message that still honors the connection you shared might include, "I don't feel this is the right fit for something longer-term. I want to be respectful of your time, and honesty felt like the kindest option."

And one more time: Avoid ghosting—it's never classy. Letting someone know where you stand is far more respectful than leaving them wondering.

How you handle these moments shows maturity and care—qualities that matter just as much in dating as chemistry. It may feel awkward, but a kind exit helps preserve dignity on both sides—and leaves the door open for mutual respect, even if romance isn't in the cards.

The Social Media Question

To follow or not to follow after a first date? Consider waiting until you've had a conversation about seeing each other again. Jumping into their Instagram stories or liking their posts from 2017 can feel a little too fast. Let things progress naturally.

Dating with etiquette isn't about getting everything right—it's about showing respect for yourself and the person you're with. And whether it leads to a second date, a lasting relationship, or simply a great story, how you carry yourself matters.

Q: *When is it okay to bring up personal or sensitive topics on a date, and how do you explore deeper topics without it feeling like too soon or too much?*

A: Think of personal or sensitive topics as adding spice to a recipe—you don't want to overdo it too soon. Early dates should focus on getting to know each other's likes, hobbies, and outlook on life. Save heavier topics, like family drama or past heartbreaks, for when you've established a stronger foundation.

If the moment feels right, ease into it. For example, "I'd love to share more about [topic] sometime—have you ever felt the same way?" This keeps the tone light while showing vulnerability. Gauge their reaction, and if they seem engaged, you can go a little deeper.

The golden rule? Share with intention, not just to fill silence. Connection thrives when conversations feel organic and mutual.

Deeper conversations are like swimming—dip a toe in before diving headfirst. Start with open-ended questions that invite thoughtful responses: "What's something you're really passionate about?" or "What's the best advice you've ever received?"

Listen actively and match their energy. If they're enthusiastic and reciprocating, you can explore more meaningful topics. But if they're sticking to lighter answers, follow their lead—it's about creating a space where both people feel comfortable.

And remember, vulnerability is a two-way street. If you're asking personal questions, be prepared to share personal answers too.

Q: *What's a good way to handle it if friends ask intrusive questions about my relationship status? I don't want to brush them off, but I'm also not comfortable sharing too much.*

A: When friends get a little too curious about your love life, it's perfectly okay to set gentle boundaries while still keeping the conversation friendly. Try answering with something light but clear, like, "I'm enjoying where things are right now, but I'll definitely share more when there's something to tell!"

This lets them know that while you're not avoiding the topic, you're also not ready to open the book just yet. If they keep pushing, add a smile and redirect the conversation—"Enough about my love life! How was that new exhibit at the museum? I've been meaning to go!" Humor and gentle redirection can signal that some chapters are meant to stay private—at least for now.

The Takeaway: Lead with Empathy, Speak with Care

Relationships—whether with friends, roommates, neighbors, family, or romantic interests—are at the heart of a well-lived life. And yet, they can be where our best intentions are put to the test. There's no perfect script for every situation, but leading with kindness, showing up with intention, and knowing when to speak up (or hold your tongue) will never steer you wrong.

One of the most meaningful things we can offer the people around us is the benefit of the doubt. That, and a bit of etiquette—not in the stiff, old-fashioned sense, but in the modern, human sense. The kind that says: I respect you. I'm paying attention. I care enough to consider how my actions land.

That's why I'll never ask my dear friend—the whip-smart attorney with the top-tier law degree, who's redefining the future of cryptocurrency by day and belting out Dolly Parton like a country queen by night, who could plan your dream wedding and arrange the florals herself, all while making you laugh until your sides hurt and whipping up a breakfast burrito that belongs in a Michelin Guide—why she's still single. The question might sound harmless, even curious. But it carries an undercurrent that someone's missing a mark, failing to meet an invisible timeline or checklist. And if there's one thing we don't need more of, it's language that makes someone feel like they have to explain away their life.

Every relationship—whether romantic or platonic, brief or lifelong—is nuanced. It's not about getting everything right; it's about building genuine connection. When we communicate thoughtfully, care generously, and move through the world with empathy, we create space for all kinds of relationships to flourish—and for a little bit of magic to find us too.

So the next time you're wondering, *Was it something I said?*, let it be a moment of reflection, not regret. Because when we learn to approach our relationships with emotional intelligence, good manners, and a genuine desire to make others feel seen and valued, the answer will almost always be: No, it was something you did right.

CHAPTER 6

HOSTING AND ATTENDING: WHAT MATTERS MOST

Hosting is my love language. From Galentine's parties to Friendsgivings, bridal and baby showers, birthdays, or even a just-because dinner party, few things bring me more joy than gathering people together. Have I painstakingly put together Pinterest-worthy tablescapes? Absolutely. Have I also served everything on paper plates with paper napkins? You bet.

Hospitality isn't about impressing; it's about making people feel like they belong. Whether you're setting an elaborate table or keeping it casual, the heart of hosting lies in making people feel welcome and appreciated. What follows are some of the lessons I've learned along the way to ensure your gatherings—big or small—are as warm, joyful, and memorable as you desire. Whether you're hosting your first dinner party or attending a friend's birthday, this chapter offers timeless etiquette that brings extra warmth and polish to any occasion—for both hosts and guests.

For Hosts: Timeless Tips for Hosting an Unforgettable Dinner Party

There's something undeniably special about welcoming people into your home—whether it's for a milestone birthday or a casual Sunday dinner. While some people may make hosting look effortless, the most memorable gatherings often reflect a few guiding principles that bring structure, warmth, and ease to the experience.

Skip the fussy traditions, but keep the timeless charm with these thoughtful, personal, and truly modern guiding principles.

Keep It Intimate

The best conversations happen when everyone can actually hear each other. Whether it's six guests or twelve, a smaller group allows for easier connections, better flow, and a more relaxed energy.

Curate, Don't Clone

Mix friends from different areas of your life—just make sure they'll find common ground. A great guest list includes people with shared interests or complementary personalities. Think book club meets brunch crew.

Set the Mood

Lighting, music, scent—ambience matters more than the china. Soft lighting (hello, dimmers or candles), a cozy room temperature, and a curated playlist can make guests feel instantly at ease. Your table doesn't need to be perfect—just clean and inviting. White tablecloths are timeless, but if that's not your style, go with whatever makes you smile.

Your table doesn't need to be perfect—just clean and inviting.

Keep the Menu Simple

You don't need seven courses to impress. Choose a few dishes you love and know how to execute well. Thoughtful, well-prepared food—paired with whatever wine or mocktails fit your budget—sets the tone for a memorable and welcoming affair.

Let the Night Unfold

No need to rush. Serve food at a relaxed pace, build in time for refills and conversation, and don't stress if the timeline shifts a bit. The best dinners feel unhurried, even if you were racing to get the salad plated.

Create Spaces to Linger

If space allows, create little moments beyond the dinner table—whether it's a cozy corner for one-on-one chats or a casual area for games and lounging. People tend to open up more when they're relaxed and free to move around.

Add a Cozy Finale

Dessert doesn't need to be grand—unless you want it to be! End the night with a pot of tea, sliced fruit, ice cream or cookies, and soft lighting. It's a gentle signal that the evening is winding down—and a way to leave everyone with that warm, full-heart feeling.

One of my favorite tips (borrowed from a very clever girlfriend) is to prep store-bought cookie dough in advance—just arrange it on a baking sheet and tuck it in the fridge before guests arrive. Then, while clearing dinner dishes, pop them in the oven. About twelve minutes later, you're casually offering warm, freshly baked cookies like it's no big deal. It's simple, smells amazing, and feels incredibly thoughtful without adding any stress.

Know When to Wrap

A great host knows when the night has peaked. You don't have to kick people out, but subtle cues like clearing plates, offering one last drink, or dimming the lights help signal that the evening is coming to a close. Midnight is a great soft finish—late enough to feel celebratory, early enough to feel considerate.

A great dinner party starts with intention—not perfection. It's about creating a space where people feel seen, comfortable, and cared for. Whether you're working with a shoebox apartment or a spacious dining room, these guiding principles will help you host with heart—and pull off a gathering that feels easy, elegant, and completely your own.

Now let's walk through a get-together from start to finish and explore how thoughtful etiquette—whether you're the host or a guest—can elevate any evening.

For Hosts and Guests: Making, Canceling, and Postponing Plans

In the world of entertaining, plans can feel as fragile as a champagne flute—beautiful but prone to shattering if not handled carefully. Whether you're hosting or attending, the way you handle your commitments says a lot about your respect for others' time and effort. Here's how to handle making, canceling, and postponing plans tactfully.

Making Plans: Setting the Tone for Success

As a host making plans, clarity and communication are key.

- **Be specific.** Suggest a date, time, and location when proposing plans. "You should come over for dinner soon" is nice, but "How about dinner at our place at 7 p.m. next Thursday?" gets the ball rolling.
- **Confirm early.** Once plans are agreed upon, send a follow-up confirmation closer to the date. A simple "Still good for tomorrow?" ensures everyone's on the same page.
- **Know your audience.** Be mindful of your invitees. If it's a casual group hang, flexibility is fine. For formal events, provide clear expectations—like dress code or timing—to help guests prepare.

Canceling Plans: When Life Gets in the Way

Sometimes, things come up, and canceling is unavoidable. If you're a guest who has to send last-minute regrets, the trick is to handle it with kindness and accountability.

- **Give notice.** Cancel as soon as you know you can't make it. Ideally, aim for at least twenty-four hours' notice. The earlier, the better—it gives others time to adjust.
- **Apologize, don't overexplain.** A sincere apology goes further than a laundry list of excuses. Try, "I'm so sorry, but I need to cancel our plans for tonight. Something unexpected has come up." Use your discretion regarding if it's best to provide a reason. If it's your college roommate's wedding, this level of vagueness may not fly, but more often than not, erring on the side of less-is-more while still being polite and warm suffices.
- **Offer to reschedule.** Show you value the relationship by suggesting a new time: "Can we find another date soon? I'd love to catch up."

Postponing Plans: Managing Expectations

If you need to postpone, the same rules apply as canceling—timeliness and thoughtfulness are key.

- **Acknowledge the inconvenience.** "I know you've carved out time for this, and I really appreciate your understanding."
- **Be specific about rescheduling.** Avoid vague promises like "Let's do it another time." Instead, suggest a clear alternative: "Can we move it to Friday at the same time?"
- **Follow through.** Make the new plan happen. Consistently postponing without follow-up can come across as flaky.

Bonus Tips for Etiquette Ease

- **Don't ghost.** Ignoring plans or failing to confirm leaves everyone in limbo. Respond promptly, even if it's a no.
- **Be honest about your capacity.** If your schedule is tight, it's better to decline up front than to overcommit and cancel later.
- **Respect group dynamics.** For group events, communicate directly with the host, and depending on the relationships, you might avoid canceling in a group chat unless absolutely necessary because it can feel impersonal.

The Takeaway: Rescheduling Can Still Reflect Respect

Plans are more than dates and times—they're a reflection of your respect for others' time and effort. By approaching changes with grace, clarity, and accountability, you ensure your relationships remain strong, even when the plans themselves don't. Because at the end of the day, good manners make any change of plans feel seamless.

For Guests: "Just Bring Yourself" and What That Really Means

When a host invites you to a gathering and tells you to "just bring yourself," it's usually meant to ease your stress—not to suggest you arrive empty-handed. This phrase is their way of saying you don't need to bring food or drinks for the actual meal, so there's no need to show up with a casserole or a bottle of wine and expect it to be served.

Why Hosts Might Not Use What You Bring

While it may seem thoughtful to bring something for the event, asking the host to serve it can disrupt their carefully planned menu or decor. A bottle of wine might not pair well with the dishes they've chosen, and adding an unplanned dessert could throw off their timing. When in doubt, think of your contribution as a gift for the host, not something for immediate use.

The Risks of Alcohol

Alcohol can be tricky—it's a common host gift, but it's not always appropriate. Some hosts don't drink or prefer to curate the beverages themselves. If you choose to bring alcohol, stick to something versatile like a quality bottle of wine, but don't expect it to be opened that night.

Considerations for Flowers

Flowers can be a lovely gesture, but they come with their own etiquette challenges. Avoid bringing fresh flowers that require the host to stop what they're doing to trim, arrange, and find a vase. And if the event already has a floral theme, your bouquet might clash or feel redundant. A better option? Send a pre-arranged bouquet ahead of time or a potted plant that can be displayed later.

Gifting After the Party

If you didn't bring something to the event, sending a thoughtful gift afterward is always a graceful option. A handwritten thank-you note paired with something small, like specialty chocolates, a candle, or a bottle of olive oil, lets your host know how much you appreciated their effort.

The bottom line? "Just bring yourself" means you don't need to worry about contributing to the event itself, but it's never a bad idea to show your gratitude with a thoughtful gesture—before, during, or after the party.

For Guests: Signature Host Gifts Add a Personal Touch

If you're on the guest list for a party, having a go-to host gift you love to give makes host-gifting easier and potentially a little more special. One of my personal favorite gifts for hosts is chocolates from the Harbor Candy Shop in Ogunquit, Maine—their vegan truffles are absolutely divine. Guests always light up when they see that little box, and it gives me a chance to share about my family in Maine, shout out the small business I admire, and debunk the myth that dark chocolate sans milk can't be delicious.

Go-To Host Gift Ideas

Not sure what to bring? Here's a list of thoughtful options that work for nearly any occasion:

FOR THE ENTERTAINER

- Vases
- Serving utensils
- Platters
- Cheese knives
- Cutting boards
- Little display bowls
- Coasters

FOR FOODIES

- Perishable gifts like pastries or bread
- Specialty food products (like infused olive oil or honey)
- Homemade compotes or jams along with appropriate accoutrements
- Specialty salts
- Caviar
- Nice olive oil or balsamic vinegar
- Wine—if you are confident this sort of gift would be appreciated, and never pressure a host to serve the gift you gave them at an event you are attending
- Cookbook
- A subscription to a culinary magazine and/or website

FOR HOME LOVERS

- Luxurious hand soap and lotions
- Candles or tea lights
- Home fragrances
- Coffee-table book on a topic of the host's personal interest—options abound!

FLORAL AND FUN TOUCHES

- Flowers—so long as it is a casual event where flowers are not already taken care of, or you are sending flowers after a party as a thank-you
- Subscription for floral deliveries on a continuing basis
- Tea towels

FOR SOMETHING DIFFERENT

- A unique board game
- Puzzle

A host gift doesn't have to be extravagant—thoughtful is the goal. Whether it's a beautifully wrapped jar of compote or a pair of simple tea towels, the gesture expresses gratitude and sets the tone for a warm, memorable evening.

For Hosts: Receiving a Gift

Receiving a Host Gift

If your kind guests have brought you a gift, here are some guidelines for receiving it graciously:

DON'T WORRY ABOUT OPENING IT IN PERSON

If you're hosting, you're juggling food, drinks, and conversation—unwrapping gifts in front of everyone can throw off the flow. Plus, it might make anyone who didn't bring something feel awkward. Hosts can save the unwrapping for later, guilt-free.

NO THANK-YOU NOTE NECESSARY

There's no obligation to send a thank-you note for a host gift—but a quick follow-up text or message of appreciation is always a gracious touch. A host gift is a thank-you in itself, so there's no need for the host to send a thank-you note afterward. As a guest, your presence at their gathering—and your thoughtful gift—are more than enough.

For Guests: What to Wear?

Whether you're attending a party, a wedding, or any event with an attire recommendation, understanding dress codes allows you to show respect and step into the moment feeling confident. Let's break down common dress codes so you can strike the right tone—without second-guessing your outfit at the door.

Business Casual

Business casual—or smart casual—has a way of being as elusive as a text back from your crush. It's more like a vague suggestion that leaves room for interpretation—and missteps.

For men, a blazer or sports jacket is always a safe bet. Pair it with trousers like chinos, corduroys, or even a nice pair of jeans. No need for a tie. Polo shirts are fair game as long as you keep it classy.

For women, dresses, long skirts, trousers, shirts, and blouses are all good options. A word of caution: Strapless looks should stay home unless it's a beach wedding. Flats and practical heels like wedges strike the perfect balance between chic and comfortable. And then there are leggings—a perennial wild card. If styled right, with ankle boots, a glam oversized sweater, and a long coat, they can work. Just don't try to pass off your workout leggings as office-ready.

Business casual is all about finding that sweet spot where comfort meets polished style. When in doubt, err on the side of being a little overdressed—it's easier to tone it down than to elevate an outfit that started too casual.

Business Attire

Business attire is the structured sibling of business casual. It's what you wear when the stakes are higher, the dress code is clearer, and first impressions really count.

For men, this usually means a suit or blazer with matching trousers, a collared shirt, and dress shoes (yes, polished). A tie is typically expected unless you're told otherwise—and even then, it never hurts to bring one along, just in case. Think tailored, not tight. Crisp, not flashy.

For women, tailored dresses, suits, blouses with trousers or pencil skirts, and closed-toe heels or flats all fall safely in the business attire zone. Patterns and color are welcome, as long as they're not distracting. Sleeveless tops are fine with a blazer, and yes, you can absolutely look professional without wearing heels that pinch. The goal is structured and polished, not costume-y or stiff.

This is not the moment for linen that wrinkles on contact, denim anything, or sandals. And while trends shift, business attire tends to reward timeless choices over fashion risks. Keep it elegant, well-fitted, and clean. You want your work to speak for itself—but a sharp outfit never hurts your case.

When in doubt? Ask. Every industry and office has its own version of "business formal," and it's far better to clarify than to guess. Think of business attire as your visual résumé—what story do you want it to tell?

Cocktail Attire

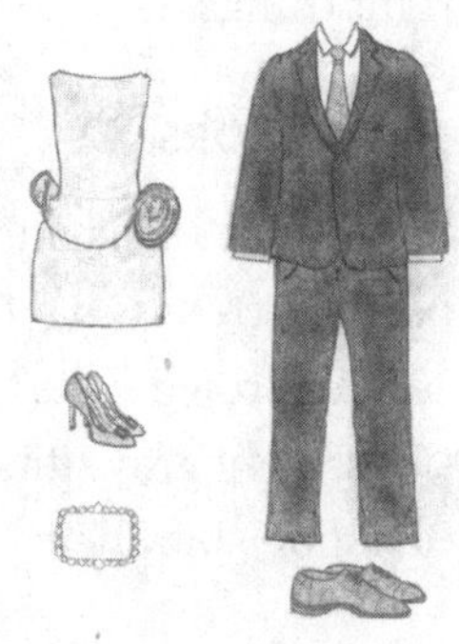

Cocktail attire is where elegance meets ease—it's that perfect balance of formal and fun. For women, it typically means a cocktail dress: something festive, slightly above the knee, and perfect for a night out (think sequins, beads, celebratory flair—polished but not overly fussy). Feeling adventurous? A chic jumpsuit or a tailored pantsuit in a luxe fabric works too. Whether it's a swanky hotel wedding or a casual beachside soirée, let the venue and invitation clues guide your style.

THE COCKTAIL BAG: YOUR SMALL BUT MIGHTY ACCESSORY

When it comes to cocktail attire, the bag you choose isn't just an afterthought—it's the punctuation mark on your entire look. The right bag is small, elegant, and effortlessly chic. Think of it as your stylish sidekick, holding only the essentials while complementing your outfit like a perfectly chosen piece of jewelry.

A sleek clutch is the gold standard for cocktail events. It's compact, polished, and sends a clear message: "I'm here to mingle, not to lug around my life." If the idea of juggling a clutch all night stresses you out (how will you manage a cocktail and a canapé?), opt for one with a discreet chain strap. It's a functional upgrade that doesn't sacrifice style.

As for materials, this is your time to shine—literally. Satin, velvet, metallics, and embellished details all scream "evening chic." Leave the casual options, like straw or canvas, at home where they belong. Your bag should feel as dressed up as you are.

When coordinating your look, aim for balance. A jewel-toned clutch adds just the right pop of drama to a little black dress, while a metallic mini bag perfectly complements bolder colors or patterns. Remember: This isn't the time to overpack. A cocktail bag is about the essentials—a phone, a lipstick, a credit card, ID, and maybe a breath mint. That's it.

Menswear Tips

Let's talk about the rules of menswear. You're not simply wearing an outfit; you're making a statement. Here's how to ensure yours says all the right things.

SUIT COLORS

For formal occasions, stick to classic dark gray or navy. While black has become trendy, it's traditionally reserved for funerals—it can feel a bit severe. Brown suits? Leave those for the countryside or more casual settings. Light gray suits, often seen in warmer climates, can be tricky. When in doubt, skip them.

STRIPES, CHECKS, OR PLAIN?

The pattern is a personal choice. Stripes, like pinstripes or chalk stripes, add character. Pinstripes are subtle and close together, while chalk stripes are bolder. Stripes suit taller men but can overwhelm shorter frames, so tread carefully.

JACKET LENGTH

A well-tailored jacket should hit just past the seat. To check, let your arms hang naturally by your sides; the hem should rest in the cupped palms of your hands.

JACKET BUTTONS

- **Sleeve Buttons:** Functional sleeve buttons (also called surgeon's cuffs) are a hallmark of a quality suit. Always ask for them when tailoring.
- **Front Buttons:** For single-breasted suits, stick to two- or three-button styles. On a two-button suit, fasten only the top button when standing. For three-button jackets, fasten the middle button

only. Always unfasten buttons when seated to avoid strain. Double-breasted jackets? Fasten all buttons when standing.

SHIRTS

- **Collars:** A turndown collar is essential. Button-down collars may be beloved by baby boomers, but they're too casual for formal wear, especially with a tie.
- **Colors:** Plain white is always the sharpest choice, but light blue, pale pink, or soft yellow can work if done subtly.
- **Cuffs:** Double cuffs (French cuffs) add a touch of formality and require cuff links, while button cuffs are perfectly acceptable for less dressy occasions.

TIES

- **Design:** Ties give you an opportunity to inject a little personality into your look, but, as always, context is key. For somber occasions like funerals or serious business meetings, a darker tie is the way to go. Black is a modern staple for funerals, but dark blue or maroon can also work. Avoid wearing a tie with a design tied to private clubs, schools, or military regiments unless you're part of that world. Do a little homework before you don something with hidden meaning.
- **Style:** A bulky knot can throw off the entire look. Windsor or half Windsor knots are solid go-tos, but ultimately, the choice comes down to personal preference. Just make sure it complements the width of your jacket's lapel.
- **Length:** Your tie should end just above your belt, where your trousers begin. Too short or too long, and it throws off the balance of your entire outfit.

OTHER ITEMS

- **Belts:** Match the belt color to the shoe color.
- **Trousers:** Trousers should break just over the first few laces of your shoe. Too long, and you're drowning in fabric; too short, and you're channeling a high-water vibe.
- **Socks:** Socks are like ties—they're where personality gets to shine.

Bold stripes, playful checks, and vibrant solids are all fair game when the occasion allows.
- **Shoes:** Shoes say a lot about your attention to detail and personal care. Keep them polished, replace fraying laces, and stay on top of maintenance. Brown shoes may be fashionable in certain circles (hello, Italy!), but they're still considered a country look or more casual choice.
- **Hats:** Hats are strictly an outdoor accessory. This applies not only to bowler hats and fedoras, but also beanies and baseball caps.
- **Top-Pocket Handkerchiefs:** The pocket square is a stylish accessory for any gentleman, adding a personal touch to your outfit. Whether silk, wool, or cotton, it's all about complementing or contrasting with your tie—never matching it exactly. If you're unsure, a classic white pocket square is always a reliable choice. Keep the edges neatly tucked in for a polished look.

Evening Dress: The Art of Black Tie

Black tie, the pinnacle of most formal wardrobes, is the dress code most will encounter for galas, weddings, or formal dinners. Here's how to master the black-tie look with poise and sophistication.

A Gentleman's Guide to Black Tie

- **Shirt:** Start with a white dress shirt with a turndown collar. The shirt front might feature marcella fabric or subtle frills for texture. A hidden placket (where the buttons are concealed) is ideal, and cuff links are a must, as double cuffs (French cuffs) are the standard.
- **Bow Tie:** Opt for a hand-tied silk bow tie (not a black necktie). Avoid pre-tied versions, as they are tricky to disguise and take away from the bespoke elegance of your ensemble.
- **Jacket:** Dinner jackets are typically black or midnight blue—though a cream-colored one works in a tropical climate. They can feature shawl or peaked lapels, have covered buttons for a

sleek finish, and lack vents. Single-breasted styles remain unfastened if paired with a waistcoat or cummerbund. Double-breasted jackets are always buttoned.

- **Trousers:** Match the jacket fabric and color. Black-tie trousers usually feature a single silk braid down the side seam. Use suspenders (not belts), preferably in black, to keep them in place.
- **Accessories:**
  - **Pocket Squares:** If you choose to wear one, it should be white. Pocket squares are traditionally styled as a plume, with no visible corners.
  - **Socks and Shoes:** While black silk socks are technically correct, black wool or cotton socks are more practical and widely accepted. Shoes should be polished black leather; patent leather is a classic choice but not essential. Velvet slippers are still acceptable for non-state occasions.
  - **Decorations:** If the invitation specifies, miniature medals or decorations may be worn, usually at formal military events or special ceremonies. Wear medals on the left—unless they're borrowed from a family member, in which case, wear them on the right.

Black tie's appeal lies in its simplicity: an understated palette, impeccable tailoring, and an attention to detail that speaks volumes. Whether you're donning your tuxedo for a lavish gala or a sophisticated evening event, remember: It's not just about dressing to impress—it's about embodying timeless elegance with every step.

A Lady's Guide to Black Tie

When it comes to black-tie events, ladies have the delightful opportunity to combine their personal style with formal allure and a touch of glamour.

THE DRESS

- **Length Matters:** A gown that falls between just below the ankle and floor-length is perfectly suited for the grandeur of black-tie occasions.
- **Color Palette:** Whether you opt for a classic black dress or a vibrant hue, the simplicity of men's tuxedos is designed, in part, to allow women's attire to shine even brighter.
- **Design Details:** Consider the "pick one" rule for dramatic elements. If your dress features a low-cut neckline, an open back, or a high slit, let that be the standout feature. Showcasing one striking detail keeps your look elegant and avoids overwhelming the ensemble.
- **Practical Elegance:** While it's tempting to select the most dazzling gown, practicality should not be overlooked. Ensure you can sit comfortably if the event includes a long dinner, and consider ease of movement for dancing or navigating crowded spaces. Feeling comfortable will help you shine without distraction.

HAIR AND ACCESSORIES

- **Hairstyles:** If dancing is on the agenda, an updo or styled-back hair can keep you looking polished all night. For events without dancing, wearing your hair down is perfectly acceptable.
- **Handbags:** Use a sleek clutch, one that's understated enough not to detract from your overall look.
- **Shoes:** Closed-toe shoes are the standard for black-tie events, but tasteful open-toe shoes are acceptable in warmer climates. Remember, comfort is key, especially if you'll be on your feet mingling or dancing.

STOCKINGS AND TIGHTS

- **Personal Preference:** Once considered mandatory, wearing stockings or tights is now a matter of personal choice. If you wear them, avoid pairing them with open-toe shoes.

FINAL TOUCHES

- **Shoulders:** Traditionally, black tie has called for shoulders to be covered. While this tradition isn't as strictly observed today, consider bringing a wrap or shawl to conservative venues or cooler environments.

Celebrate both tradition and personal expression through black tie. Select attire that balances elegance with practicality, and you'll not only look stunning but also feel at ease throughout the event.

Q: *I just got invited to a party where the dress code is black tie, but it's not a formal dinner—I'm not even sure there will be chairs. Is this weird? And what do I do?*

A: You're right that black tie usually signals an elevated level of formality, typically reserved for events like galas, weddings, and sit-down dinners with exquisite hospitality. The dress code sets expectations for dinner or at least seating, so a setting without those can feel mismatched.

If the invitation says black tie, however, take it as a cue to respect the host's vision. Dress codes are about more than attire—they set the stage for the vibe the host wants to create. Even if the level of hospitality doesn't seem to match, wearing black tie shows that you value the effort they've put into planning. And here's the thing: It's poor etiquette to correct a host's etiquette. Even if the host isn't following traditional norms, it's considerate (and classy) to go with the flow.

Think of it as an opportunity to embrace a bit of glamour. You might feel slightly overdressed if the setting is casual, but trust me, being overdressed always leaves a better impression than the alternative. Plus, adhering to the dress code reflects your thoughtfulness and adaptability. As a guest, your role isn't to question the choice—it's to show up with grace and maybe a little sparkle. Let the host's party shine for what it is, quirks and all.

For Hosts: Creating a Thoughtful Welcome

The doorbell has rung, warm greetings have been exchanged, and perhaps you've accepted a lovely gift your guests have brought with them. Now it's time to make them feel at home. When guests walk through your door, your welcome sets the tone for the whole evening. It doesn't have to be dramatic—just warm, sincere, and grounded in the little things that show you care.

One of the most understated, elegant gestures? Helping someone with their coat. It sounds simple, and it is, but it carries that old-school charm that makes people feel truly looked after.

I'll never forget one winter dinner party when my friend Rachel arrived balancing her purse, a bottle of wine, and a massive faux fur coat. I gently took everything from her arms and helped her get settled. She let out a little breath and said, "Oh wow, I already feel taken care of." That stuck with me—hosting doesn't mean everything's perfect. It just means your guests don't need to think too hard.

If you're helping someone with their coat, take it at the shoulders and mind the hem—nothing says "oops" like dragging someone's favorite wool across the floor. Hang it neatly (a hanger is ideal, but a hook works in a pinch) and offer a clear spot for bags or scarves.

And at the end of the night, the reverse is just as thoughtful: Help them slip their arms back into their coat, check for tucked-away gloves, scarves, or hats in the sleeves, and send them off with that same warmth you welcomed them with.

Drinks Before Dinner: Hospitality Begins with a Glass in Hand

Imagine arriving at someone's home and being ushered straight to the dining table before you've even taken off your coat. A little disorienting, right? On the flip side, waiting too long to be offered a drink can feel a touch awkward. That's why a welcoming drink—offered early and with a smile—is one of the most graceful ways to say, "We're so glad you're here!"

After coats are taken and bags are set down, hand your guest something light and lovely: a chilled sparkling water with a citrus slice, a sprig of mint in a coupe glass, or whatever signature sip fits your mood. It doesn't have to be fancy—just intentional.

Offering drinks before dinner isn't about playing bartender all night. It's about setting a rhythm. It buys time for late arrivals, gives you a few more minutes to finish up in the kitchen, and most importantly, gives guests a moment to ease into the evening.

A few unexpected benefits:

- It sparks conversation naturally.
- It gives your home a sense of flow—people mingling, chatting, laughing.
- It allows you to skip a plated appetizer, if you like, by offering hearty hors d'oeuvres with their drinks instead.

No chairs? No problem. Pre-dinner drinks are often best served standing, napkin in hand, letting guests float from one conversation to the next.

For Hosts Who Want to Keep It Simple

Light Fare, Full Heart

If the thought of preparing a full meal makes you break into a stress sweat—don't. Hosting can be as simple as pre-dinner drinks with a few thoughtful snacks.

A beautiful cheese board, a signature cocktail (or mocktail), and a well-set coffee table can create just as much connection as a five-course meal. What matters is that people feel seen, appreciated, and at ease.

I've hosted my fair share of seated dinners with meticulously set tablescapes, but the party my friends still talk about the most? A Halloween gathering in our small row home, where we were shoulder to shoulder, costumes askew, and I turned our only table into a grazing board by rolling out butcher paper and covering it with snacks. It was casual, a little chaotic, and most of us stood the entire night—but we laughed, we mingled, and it worked.

Some of my favorite nights have been these kinds of gatherings:

low-lift, high-impact, filled with easy conversation and genuine connection. And not a single person missed the main course.

For Guests: Things That Might Seem Polite, but Actually Aren't

I share this next section lovingly, knowing that many of these things happen with the very best of intentions. We've all been there—trying to be helpful, thoughtful, or polite, only to realize later that our efforts may have added stress instead of easing it.

Think of these not as strict don'ts, but gentle reminders that sometimes the most gracious thing you can do is simply show up, follow your host's lead, and enjoy yourself.

Arriving Early

Being too late is rude, yes. But showing up too early? Surprisingly, that's just as disruptive. Your host is likely still in prep mode—fluffing pillows, lighting candles, hiding clutter in closets, and possibly scrambling to finish cooking. An early arrival means they now have to shift into host mode before they're ready.

The sweet spot? Aim to arrive right on time—or fashionably five to ten minutes late.

Insisting on Helping

Offering to help your host is lovely. Insisting on helping after they've politely declined? Not so much. The "too many cooks in the kitchen" cliché exists for a reason. If they say they've got it, believe them—and give yourself permission to just enjoy being a guest. If they need a hand later, they'll ask, and they'll appreciate that you're game.

Showing Up with a Dish They Didn't Ask For

You baked your famous brownies, and you're sure everyone will love them. But if your host didn't ask you to bring food, it's best to resist the urge. Adding a new dish can throw off their menu or table setup, and it may come across (unintentionally!) as a vote of no faith in what they've planned. Instead, bring a thoughtful host gift they can enjoy later—like nice olive oil or wrapped chocolates—and leave the menu to them.

Waiting to Go Through the Buffet Line

At a buffet-style dinner, it can feel awkward to be the first person to grab a plate—but once your host invites guests to begin, hanging back can actually create more hesitation. If you're standing closest, take the plunge. You're not being greedy—you're helping set the pace.

Cleaning Up Without Asking

If you spill something, it's tempting to spring into action—but don't go rifling through drawers for paper towels. Ask first: "Can I grab a cloth to help clean this up?" That quick check-in respects your host's space and boundaries.

Same goes for post-dinner tidying. Some hosts love help in the kitchen. Others have a very specific way of loading the dishwasher and would rather take care of it themselves. When in doubt, ask: "Would you like help clearing or should I just relax?" Either way, they'll feel supported.

A thoughtful arrangement can take a gathering from good to gracious.

For Hosts: Seating Arrangements That Create Comfort and Connection

Once guests are refreshed and comfortable, perhaps glasses have been raised and warm words have been said; it's time to take a seat. But where?

Every year, as I start sketching out the seating arrangement for Friendsgiving (a pre-Thanksgiving tradition in the Cheperdak household that my husband and I love!), a full-on internal monologue kicks in. Who needs a little more space because they'll have a baby on their lap? Who's new to the group and might appreciate sitting next to someone friendly and easygoing? Who do I think would really hit it off and end up talking for hours over pie? Who's almost definitely going to bring up politics? And then there's that pair who dated years ago—they're cordial now, but let's be honest, it's probably best to keep them on opposite sides of the table.

These are just a few of the things swirling through my head as I put together the seating chart. And while it might sound like overthinking, I genuinely believe that a thoughtful arrangement can take a gathering from good to gracious—creating an atmosphere where everyone feels seen, included, and maybe even a little delighted.

Depending on the formality of the event, this might mean individual place cards at each setting or a seating chart near the entrance—like at a wedding—so guests know where they're headed. Either way, the goal is the same: to make people feel considered before they even sit down.

A well-planned seating arrangement can remove the guesswork and set the tone for any gathering, whether it's a formal dinner, a casual brunch, or a business luncheon.

Formal vs. Informal Settings

FORMAL EVENTS

In formal settings, place cards are a must. This prevents confusion and ensures everyone knows where to sit without hesitation. Use neatly written or printed cards to guide guests to their spots.

CASUAL GATHERINGS

For less formal meals, place cards are always a nice touch, but letting guests choose their own seats is also perfectly fine. However, if you're hosting a dinner where introductions are key—such as a networking event—and you don't have place cards, consider lightly directing seating to ensure everyone connects.

General Rules of Seating Etiquette

THE HOST AND HOSTESS POSITIONS

Traditionally, the host and hostess (or two cohosts) are seated at opposite ends of the table. This ensures they can manage the flow of conversation and tend to guests easily.

HONORED GUESTS

The most honored guests sit to the right of the host and hostess, with the next most distinguished guests to their left. This rule applies to formal events where rank, seniority, or guest-of-honor status matters.

CREATING A BALANCED TABLE

In more traditional etiquette guides, hosts were often encouraged to alternate seating between men and women to create visual balance and encourage conversation across perspectives. While that may have been the norm in decades past, today's gatherings call for a more thoughtful and inclusive approach.

Instead of following a gender-based formula, focus on mixing personalities, energy levels, and interests. Consider pairing a chatty guest with a quieter one, or seating newcomers next to great conversationalists. The goal remains the same: to spark meaningful connections and help everyone feel comfortable, seen, and engaged—no matter who they are or where they're seated.

AVOID EMPTY CHAIRS

If someone cancels last minute, adjust the arrangement to avoid awkward gaps. A well-balanced table keeps the energy of the gathering intact.

Additional Tips for Specific Scenarios

- **Rectangular Tables:** Longer tables are ideal for larger gatherings, but they can create conversational divides. To combat this, consider serving family-style meals or organizing activities that keep everyone engaged.
- **Round Tables:** Round tables are excellent for creating an inclusive atmosphere, as everyone can see and hear each other. These are perfect for smaller gatherings or intimate settings.

Whether you're hosting a formal dinner or a casual get-together, a little planning helps create a welcoming, inclusive, and memorable experience.

Q: *What's the best way to handle it if a guest arrives late to a sit-down dinner? Should I wait for them to start, or is it okay to begin without them?*

A: When it comes to a sit-down dinner, timing is everything—but so is keeping things comfortable and relaxed for everyone. If a guest is running a bit late, it's perfectly fine to start the meal with the guests who've arrived on time. You can wait a few extra minutes if you think they're just around the corner, but after that, your on-time guests will appreciate not waiting too long.

When the latecomer arrives, greet them warmly and make them feel welcome without drawing too much attention to their arrival. You can even keep their first course ready, so they can join in seamlessly. This way, everyone can enjoy the evening without feeling held up, and your late-arriving guest can settle in without feeling like they've derailed the event.

Q: *I'm hosting my first dinner party, and I'm stressed because my apartment isn't perfectly decorated, and I can't cook like Ina Garten. How do I still make it special?*

A: The best gatherings aren't flawless—they're full of warmth and intention. Picture this: Your friends walk into your cozy apartment, greeted by a playlist that sets the vibe (think jazzy classics or upbeat indie hits), you looking relaxed (even if you're not), a glass of wine in hand.

If you're short on space, get creative. No dining table? No problem! Lay out cushions on the floor and create a casual, bohemian-style dinner setup. Add a throw blanket or two and some candles, and voilà—it's charming and intimate.

Worried about the menu? Keep it simple. A deli roast chicken or a store-bought quiche can pair beautifully with a big salad and crusty bread. Or, make it a potluck! Guests often love contributing a dish, and it takes some of the pressure off you. Bonus: It gives everyone something to talk about and taste.

As for décor, it doesn't take much—a clean space and a few personal touches like a vase of fresh flowers, a string of fairy lights, or even just neatly folded napkins create an atmosphere that feels both warm and intentional. The real magic, though, isn't in the setting or the food; it's in how you make people feel. Compliment their outfit, ask about their week, and share a story that gets everyone laughing.

At the end of the night, guests won't be wishing the meal had been served on the finest bone china. They'll remember how you made them feel—and that's the secret to hosting that Ina herself would applaud.

For Everyone: Polite Portions and Other Considerations

Dining with others is about more than just the food—it's about creating a warm and enjoyable experience for everyone at the table. Whether you're hosting or attending as a guest, knowing how much to serve and to eat is part of that experience and reflects both your manners and your cultural awareness. Here's how to navigate the delicate balance, whether the dinner is buffet style, family style with dishes passed around the table, or individually plated in the kitchen.

As a Guest: Respect the Host's Effort

TRY A LITTLE OF EVERYTHING

When attending a meal, it's polite to sample a bit of everything your host has prepared, especially if it's a seated dinner with limited options. Even if something isn't your favorite, taking a small portion (if you're serving yourself) or tasting a small bite (if your food is already plated) shows appreciation for the effort and thought the host put into the menu. A simple "This looks wonderful" as you take a serving can make your host feel genuinely appreciated.

THE "NO THANK YOU" PORTION

If there's something you'd rather not eat and you're serving yourself, consider taking a very small amount. This allows you to graciously participate in the meal without declining outright. Politely leaving the portion mostly uneaten is acceptable in many cultures and avoids offending a well-meaning host.

BE AWARE OF CULTURAL SENSITIVITIES

To that point, in some cultures refusing food outright can be seen as a serious affront. For instance:

- Middle Eastern and Indian cultures often view a guest's refusal as disrespectful to the host's hospitality.
- In Chinese culture, not trying at least a small portion of each dish can be interpreted as a lack of gratitude.
- Mexico is another place where turning down food can be considered impolite, as it may be seen as rejecting the host's kindness and effort.

If you're traveling or dining with friends from different cultural backgrounds, it's worth brushing up on local customs to ensure you're respectful.

As a Host: Create a Comfortable Atmosphere

SERVE APPROPRIATELY SIZED PORTIONS

If you're plating your guests' food, aim for portions that are generous enough to satisfy, but not so large that they feel overwhelming. For buffet-style meals, arrange the flow so it's intuitive and well-labeled, allowing guests to help themselves comfortably without bottlenecks. With family-style service, set out serving utensils for each dish and encourage guests to pass thoughtfully, ensuring everyone gets a fair and timely chance to enjoy the meal.

No matter the format, offering a variety of dishes—especially when it comes to dietary preferences—helps guests feel considered and cared for.

PAY ATTENTION TO GUESTS' NEEDS

Not every guest will feel comfortable eating everything you've prepared—whether due to dietary restrictions, allergies, or personal preferences. Encourage guests to serve themselves when possible, or politely ask how much they'd like if plating dishes individually.

AVOID PRESSURING GUESTS

While it's tempting to urge someone to try your special dish, avoid making guests feel obligated. Gentle encouragement is fine, but respect their decision if they politely decline.

Striking the Right Balance

As a guest, your goal is to show appreciation without overindulging or drawing unnecessary attention to your choices. As a host, your role is to create an environment where guests feel comfortable enjoying the meal at their own pace.

By understanding and respecting these dynamics—along with cultural sensitivities—you can elevate the dining experience for everyone. The best meals are about connection, not just the food on the plate.

For Hosts: After-Dinner Details

When the final course has been enjoyed and as conversation continues, what comes next helps gently usher the evening to a close. Traditionally, there's a thoughtful order to this part of the meal—and while it's helpful to know the classic structure, there are many gracious ways to adapt it to suit your guests and setting.

In the most formal settings, the sequence goes like this:

- Dessert is served and enjoyed on its own.
- Digestifs—small, often spirit-based drinks meant to aid digestion—are offered.
- Coffee or tea follows, typically as the final gesture of the evening.

This pacing allows each element to shine on its own while also preserving the natural rhythm of the meal.

That said, in more casual or modern settings—especially in American homes—it's perfectly acceptable to serve coffee and dessert together. Many hosts find that this approach keeps the evening flowing naturally, particularly if guests are eager for coffee or the meal is more relaxed in tone. If you go this route, just remember: While it's perfectly fine to pair coffee with sweet desserts, it's best not to serve it with a cheese course, which is often considered a savory final note on its own.

If you're choosing to serve coffee after dessert, consider offering it at the table with a small sweet—like a piece of dark chocolate, a mint, or a petit four—or moving to a cozy sitting area to encourage guests to linger. This simple shift in location can subtly signal the winding down of the evening while still making everyone feel welcome.

Now, about those digestifs—if you don't serve one with dessert, you can offer it right after. Think of them as the elegant bookend to the meal. Classic choices include:

- Cognac or Armagnac
- Amaro, grappa, or limoncello
- Fortified wines like port, Madeira, or Sauternes

They're typically sipped slowly and served in small pours, offering guests a chance to relax and savor the final notes of the evening.

For guests who don't drink alcohol, consider offering an herbal tea (like peppermint or chamomile), a caffeine-free coffee option, sparkling water with lemon, lime, or even a sprig of thyme, or a spiced cider in cooler months. The goal is the same: to offer something warm or special that brings the meal to a thoughtful close.

Whether you follow the traditional order or craft your own variation, what matters most is the feeling you create—one of care, comfort, and graceful hospitality.

Q: *I'm not a big coffee or tea drinker, but I want to have options for guests with different preferences. What should I keep in stock?*

A: Even if your daily beverage lineup doesn't go beyond water and the occasional juice, having a well-rounded drink selection for guests shows thoughtfulness and hospitality. Here's a simple guide to stocking your cupboard like a pro host:

For the Coffee Crowd

- **Ground Coffee or Pods:** A medium roast is a safe bet for most tastes. If you have a single-serve machine, keep a few pod options handy, including decaf.
- **French Press or Drip Coffee Maker:** If you don't have a fancy setup, a French press is compact, affordable, and easy to use.
- **Creamer and Milk Options:** Regular milk and a nondairy option (like almond or oat milk) cover most bases.
- **Sugar and Sweeteners:** Keep sugar, stevia, and honey on hand for guests who like their coffee sweet.

For the Tea Enthusiasts

- **Tea Bags or Loose-Leaf Tea:** Go for a variety with black, green, herbal, and decaf options.
- **Lemon and Honey:** Essential for tea drinkers, especially in cooler months.
- **Hot Water Kettle:** A basic electric kettle will quickly become your best friend.

Bonus Beverages for Non-Coffee/Tea Drinkers

- **Hot Chocolate Mix:** A crowd-pleaser for kids and anyone looking for a cozy treat.
- **Sparkling Water:** Keep a few cans in fun flavors for a refreshing alternative.
- **Juice or Kombucha:** These add variety and can double as mixers for casual entertaining.

Presentation Tips

If you have overnight guests or will be hosting a larger gathering, designate a small tray or corner of your kitchen as the beverage station. Arrange everything neatly—coffee, tea, sweeteners, mugs, and spoons—so guests can serve themselves with ease. A small gesture like this makes even a simple drink feel special, and a thoughtful beverage setup ensures every guest feels considered—even if you're not partaking yourself.

For Guests: Departing with Kindness and Care

Goodbyes at a party can be as tricky as finding the perfect party outfit—there's a balance to strike between a proper farewell and knowing when to slip out quietly. While styles of departure vary, your approach should depend on the event and the company. Let's decode the etiquette of saying goodbye like the gracious guest you are.

Thank the Host (Without Disrupting the Flow)

While it may be tempting to sneak out when your hosts are swarmed by guests, resist the urge. A proper goodbye and a sincere thank-you are essential. If your host is deep in conversation, don't hover like a helicopter waiting to swoop in. Instead, observe from a polite distance, and seize a natural pause to express your gratitude and farewell. Keep it short—this is not the moment to recap your favorite party highlights.

The one exception? Weddings. Interrupting the couple mid-dance or as they're savoring their cake is more disruptive than polite. As long as you've greeted the families or thanked the couple earlier in the evening, you can quietly slip away without causing a stir. They'll appreciate your thoughtfulness in letting them enjoy their celebration.

Know When to Leave and How Long to Stay

Every event has its rhythm, and your departure should respect it. If the invitation specifies a start and end time, plan to stay for the full duration. For shorter drop-in-style gatherings, thirty to forty-five minutes is perfectly acceptable—just long enough to connect with your host and celebrate the occasion.

For more formal events, like weddings or milestone parties, leaving too early can feel dismissive of the effort your hosts have put into the evening. If you can't stay until the couple's send-off, plan to leave after the main highlights—dinner, toasts, dances, and cake cutting. Departing immediately after the meal signals more of a snub than a polite exit.

The Irish Exit vs. the Midwestern Goodbye

There are two schools of thought when it comes to farewells: the quick getaway or the lingering goodbye. The Irish exit—leaving a party without saying a word—serves as one extreme. But as my family in Ireland would tell you, it's not common there, its history is debated, and it might be more of an American concept. Still, we'll use it here as a symbol of the quick, no-fuss departure.

On the other hand, the Midwestern goodbye represents the opposite extreme: a long and winding series of farewells to every person in the room, often followed by conversations at the door, the driveway, and possibly even by text on your way home.

Your best bet? Aim for a happy medium. Express your thanks to your host, say goodbye to those closest to you, and exit gracefully without overstaying your welcome or disappearing without a trace.

Saying goodbye is a small moment, but one that leaves a lasting impression. The key is to honor the host, respect the tone of the event, and depart with warmth and gratitude. The most gracious guests are remembered long after the party ends—for all the right reasons.

Q: *I love hosting, but one friend always stays long after everyone else has left. She's even said that that's her favorite part of parties at my apartment. How can I signal it's time to wrap up without being rude?*

A: The classic party lingerer! While it's flattering that she loves hanging out after everyone else has gone, there comes a point when even the best host wants her apartment back. Try signaling the wrap-up with small cues: start tidying up a bit, brighten the lights, or even change into comfier clothes if you're feeling bold. You could also gently say something like, "It's been so great catching up—I'm winding down, but let's grab coffee soon so we can keep chatting!"

This way, you're showing her you appreciate the extra time together while hinting that the evening's officially over. And it'll hopefully help her realize when it's time to take her exit cue next time too.

Q: *Our friends' kids are wonderful, but I'm hoping to host an adults-only event so everyone can relax and enjoy themselves. What's a polite way to let people know it's a no-kids gathering without offending anyone?*

A: Hosting an adults-only event can be tricky, but charm and humor can help set the right tone. When sending out the invitation, you could add something like, "This one's a night off for the grown-ups—think cocktails, fabulous music, and zero interruptions!" Or try a lighthearted line like, "Let's make this one a grown-ups' night—just us, a little sparkle, and some uninterrupted fun!"

This way, you're setting the vibe without making it about excluding anyone's little ones. Many parents will appreciate the excuse to have a night to themselves! And for those who need a gentle reminder, a quick follow-up closer to the date never hurts. Everyone will get the message, and you'll have the adults-only evening you're dreaming of. From a practical perspective, it's considerate to choose a time that works well with parents' schedules and to send invitations far enough in advance to give everyone time to find a sitter or other arrangements for their kids.

The Takeaway: Good Manners Set the Table—Warmth Makes the Meal

Before you send or accept those invitations, remember: Entertaining isn't about having the fanciest setup or getting every detail just right—it's about presence. Some of my favorite gatherings in DC weren't formal dinners at all—they were book club brunches eaten off paper plates while sitting cross-legged on the floor. No place cards, no polished silver—just laughter, good conversation, and a genuine sense of connection.

Whether you're hosting a seated dinner or showing up with a smile and a thoughtful gift, the goal is the same: to create a moment when people feel welcome. With a little intention, a touch of planning, and a whole lot of heart, every gathering becomes a chance to make someone feel seen, appreciated, and at home.

CHAPTER 7

AT THE TABLE

When I was a junior attorney, a friend who was just a few years ahead of me told me something I've never forgotten: "BigLaw is a lot easier if you grew up chatting with adults at cocktail parties." At the time, I hadn't really thought about it, but looking back, I see her point.

BigLaw—a nickname for the country's largest and most prestigious corporate law firms—isn't just about legal acumen. It's also about client dinners, partner lunches, and polished interactions in polished settings. Most of my interviews and more casual recruitment moments with large corporate law firms had some sort of dining component: coffee and donuts in a law school career center, finger foods at a mixer, or a series of lunches with partners quietly considering whether they'd like to work alongside me. And while no one handed me a pop quiz on utensil placement, how I carried myself at the table absolutely mattered.

That's why I care so much about helping people feel confident in these settings—not so they can memorize the history of the teacup or perfect a pinky pose (spoiler alert: we don't do that), but so they don't have to think about their table manners at all. When you know the basics, they become second nature—and that frees you up to focus on what truly matters: connection, conversation, and showing up as your best self.

So what do you actually do with your napkin when you step away from the table? Which way should you pass the bread basket? And how are you supposed to use that oddly shaped fork? This chapter will walk you through all of it—from how to set a beautiful table to how to hold your cutlery with confidence—so you feel prepared, not performative, wherever you're dining.

Elements of a Flawless Table

Have you ever seen a picture-perfect tablescape in a magazine or on social media and thought, *How in the Martha Stewart does anyone even begin to create something that beautiful?* If so, same.

It all starts with knowing the basics—where things go, what each piece is for—and then layering in your own artistic flair. Let's start from the foundation up and examine every element of a well-set, welcoming table.

Chairs

Place the chairs first, aligning them where diners will sit. This ensures even spacing and avoids having to reset the table if something is off.

Tablecloths or Placemats

Choose between a crisp tablecloth or felt-backed placemats (often called table mats)—never both. While tablecloths are traditional, many prefer to showcase polished wood and opt for placemats instead. If using placemats, ensure they sit an inch away from the table's edge and are perfectly parallel, with the design facing the diner.

Now, tablecloths do have their perks. They add a touch of glamour to any meal and even soften the acoustics in the room—perfect for when Aunt Linda gets a little too enthusiastic about family gossip. Whatever color you choose, remember, like a good outfit, your tablecloth should coordinate with the rest of the setting.

When it comes to sizing, think proportions. Measure your table and allow for a stylish overhang (the extra fabric that drapes over the edge). There's no hard rule, but longer tables look more elegant with deeper overhangs. For very formal events, like state dinners, the drop is deeper and more dramatic. For a buffet or round table, the cloth should sweep all the way to the floor. Beneath it all? A "silence cloth" or table protector—layered insulation that not only shields against heat but also keeps the clatter of dinnerware from interrupting the conversation.

For those who prefer placemats, you've got options: wood, bamboo, leather, mirrored tiles—you name it. Size matters here too. Standard mats are usually around 9 by 12 inches and should align neatly, depending on the table's edge. Straight-edged tables? Leave about an inch of space. Beveled edges? Go flush with the bevel. And for round tables, circular mats are your best friend. Keep in mind that unless your placemats are supersized, they're meant for plates only—utensils find their place directly on the table.

Centerpieces

Candles and flowers are a timeless table pairing. The key to selecting the right flowers is striking a balance between beauty and subtlety—they should enhance, not overpower. Fragrances should be kept light so as not to compete with the culinary experience, and it's wise to choose blooms that are gentle on the senses for guests who may be sensitive to pollen or prone to allergies.

Keep floral arrangements either low or high enough to allow eye contact and conversation to flow freely across the table.

Candles are the hallmark of an evening affair; they are best reserved for after dark. While opinions differ, many etiquette experts suggest using fresh, new candles for each gathering as a gesture of extra effort and thoughtful hospitality. If you love the look of romantic, dripping candles, know that there are dripless varieties that offer ambiance without the cleanup.

And remember: For a graceful end to the evening, extinguish your candles with a candle snuffer. This simple tool ensures the wax stays put and prevents any messy mishaps.

You don't need to stick to flowers and candles, however. You might also consider incorporating:

- fresh fruit and vegetables;
- paper flowers;
- books;
- terrariums;
- natural elements like branches, pine cones, seashells, sea glass, or driftwood;

- a bud vase with fresh herbs or small potted herbs that are mild enough so as not to overpower the meal; or
- a collection of potted plants, such as succulents.

Plates

Main plates (dinner or luncheon) should be centered in the setting and placed about an inch from the table's edge. A service plate (or charger) may be set flush with the table's edge for visual alignment, but it should always be removed before the main course is served—typically after the appetizer or soup course. Chargers are decorative and not meant to be eaten from directly.

- **Bread Plates:** In American settings, they're placed above the largest fork, to the top left.
- **Salad or Appetizer Plates:** They are larger than a bread plate and smaller than a dinner plate. They may be placed on top of the charger, if one is used, and are cleared before the main course arrives, at which point the charger is also removed. If no charger is used, these courses are served directly on their own plates.

Cutlery

Align the bottom edges of the cutlery with the lower edge of the main plate, leaving about an inch between the plate and the table's edge. Even if you're removing the plate later, use it as a guide to arrange the settings.

- **Handling Cutlery:** Hold utensils by their handles as you are setting the table, so you don't touch the part that will touch diners' mouths.
- **Placement Rules:** Arrange cutlery in the order of use, working from the outside inward. We'll explore cutlery in much more detail next (with pictures), but basically, knives and spoons go on the right, forks on the left, reflecting historical norms from when swords were held in the right hand. Left-handed diners can quietly adjust as needed without altering the table's symmetry.
- **Knife Blades:** Always face blades to the left (meaning toward

ourselves, not our fellow diners), a tradition dating back to medieval times that shows we come in peace.

- **Bread Knives and Butter Spreaders:** Bread knives are either placed alongside the other knives or horizontally on the bread plate. Butter spreaders are always placed horizontally on the bread plate.
- **Forks:** Prongs face upward in British and American settings but downward in French settings—a nod to historical frilly cuffs that could snag on upward-facing tines.
- **Oyster Forks:** These are the only forks set on the right side, parallel to other utensils, never angled or resting against a neighboring spoon.
- **Dessert Cutlery:** Traditionally placed at the top of the plate in American place settings, the spoon is set above the fork with the handle facing right and the fork handle facing left.

Finishing Touches

For a polished finish, consider wearing cotton gloves or using a dry tea towel when setting cutlery to avoid fingerprints.

Napkins

Napkins can be placed either on the dinner plate, where the dinner plate will go, or to the left of it. Skip the paper options for a formal dinner and opt for timeless plain linen or linen damask. While elaborately folded napkins can feel overdone, simple folds like the Bishop's Mitre or Prince of Wales plume add a touch of elegance without overwhelming the table. Modern etiquette often leaves napkins flat on the side plate. And let's be clear: Napkins never belong in glasses.

Salt, Pepper, and Condiments

Condiments should be spaced evenly along the table for easy access. At the grandest of dinners, each place setting may even have its own set. For formal occasions, salt and pepper pots are used (save the mills for casual meals). Place salt and pepper side by side, with mustard pots positioned in front. If there's no mustard, the salt goes in front of the pepper. Ideally, salt and pepper and other condiments should be set about every four people or so.

Pro Tip: Relish and chutneys should always be served in a sauceboat or a small bowl with a spoon, depending on the consistency—never straight from the bottle.

If you're serving finger food that could get messy, set a finger bowl slightly to the left, above the forks, for guests to dip and rinse their fingers. While floating lemon slices may add flair to finger bowls in restaurants, they're unnecessary at home. The water in the bowl should be cold to prevent food smells from lingering on the hands. Finger bowls may be served after a dessert course or after messy seafood courses, especially crab, lobster, or shrimp served in the shell. Finger bowls are removed once they have been used and before the next course, if applicable.

Glassware

Glasses go on the table last to avoid smudges or accidental spills. Arrange them to the right of the place setting, just above the dinner knife, in the order they'll be used, moving front to back.

- The water glass sits slightly behind and to the left of the wine glasses. While perfectly matched sets are no longer a strict requirement, keep the basics in mind: White wine glasses are narrower, red wine glasses are rounder, and champagne is best served in flutes (although coupes are making a nostalgic comeback).
- Skip the coasters for formal dinners, no matter how valuable the table. When placing glasses, hold them by the stem to avoid fingerprints on the bowl.

Cups and Saucers

Cups and saucers are placed about an inch beyond the outermost piece of flatware, with the saucer's top edge aligned with the plate or bowl. Handles should point to three o'clock for easy grabbing. However, cups and saucers shouldn't be part of the initial lunch or dinner table setup—they're brought out only when it's time for coffee or tea.

By paying attention to these small but meaningful details, your table will reflect the perfect balance of tradition, elegance, and modern practicality, ensuring your guests feel both impressed and comfortable.

Poise at the Plate: Dining Posture Dos and Don'ts

Perhaps it's all those years of classical ballet training and figure skating, but how to stand (and sit) up straight is ingrained in my psyche. I still think of Miss Jessica, my childhood ballet teacher, reminding me to imagine a string pulling upward from the top of my head like a puppet. Whether I'm speaking on live television or maintaining good form at the gym, that mental image still sticks.

That same posture matters at the table. It projects self-assurance, respect, and enthusiasm, not to mention that it minimizes potential spills on your clothes.

Let's start with the chair. Don't lean back like it's movie night, and skip the armrests—they're posture saboteurs. Instead, imagine a delicate egg between your back and the chair. You wouldn't want to crush it, would you?

Then, sit about one-and-a-half hands' width from the table. Too close, and it looks like you're ready to pounce on your plate. Too far, and you'll be leaning in like you're trying to hear a secret. Aim for that sweet spot: upright, balanced, and not touching the table.

As for the classic elbow debate—just don't. Not at the dinner table, not during a client lunch, and not at your anniversary dinner. Yes, leaning in conveys attention and rapport, but there are more elegant ways to show you're engaged.

Hand placement? In the US and UK, hands rest politely in your lap when you're not eating. In much of Europe (but not Italy or the UK), wrists may rest lightly on the edge of the table. Being mindful of cultural differences shows attentiveness and respect.

And yes—your legs matter too. Avoid crossing at the knee, which can throw off your posture. Instead, keep both feet on the floor or cross at the ankles for a poised, polished look.

These dos and don'ts aren't about being rigid or performative. They're about sitting tall, showing presence, and letting your posture reflect the confidence and composure you bring to the table.

Serving Etiquette: Passing Food and Drink at the Table

The first Thanksgiving I spent without my family was during my first year of law school, when we were welcomed to the home of friends in Virginia. The table was stunning—honestly, the nicest I'd ever seen outside of a wedding. There were place cards, flickering candles, beautifully folded napkins . . . it all felt very grown-up.

Back home, Thanksgiving was loud and lovable. There were kids everywhere, dogs underfoot, and someone was always reaching across the table to grab the rolls. But this dinner felt quieter and more composed. At one point, someone asked for the gravy. It was sitting right in front of me, and I hesitated. Is it my job to pass it? Should I offer it to them first? Just hand it over?

It reminded me that even the simplest gestures—like passing a dish—carry meaning at the table. When done thoughtfully, they help create a sense of ease, flow, and connection.

In casual or semiformal settings, passing food around the table is part of the rhythm of the meal. Typically, dishes are passed to the right in the US and most Western cultures—ensuring a smooth, counterclockwise flow. In the UK, however, tradition flips, and food is passed to the left. If you're unsure, follow the host's lead or take a cue from the guest of honor.

If a serving dish is already in front of you, offer it to the person on your left first, then serve yourself, and continue passing to your right. It might feel counterintuitive, but it keeps the dish moving in one direction without skipping anyone.

Avoid reaching across others or stretching over the table. It's not just about formality—it's about making others feel seen, included, and comfortable. Small gestures like offering before serving yourself and passing with intention help set a gracious tone.

In some family-style meals, the host may choose to serve each guest rather than pass dishes. When in doubt, observe what others are doing. Good etiquette always begins with thoughtful attention to the moment you're in.

Eating at the Table: How to Use a Place Setting

Now that we've covered how to set the table from the host's perspective, let's shift gears. Once you sit down at a formal place setting, how do you use it all? This is all about handling your meal with grace and awareness—so you can enjoy the moment without distraction. Let's break it down, piece by piece.

Using a Napkin

Once you sit down at a perfectly set table, what do you do first? You pick up your napkin. At a restaurant, your napkin should go directly in your lap as soon as you sit down. But if you're dining at someone's home, etiquette calls for waiting until the host places their napkin on their lap—this simple gesture signals that the meal has officially begun. We also want to wait to begin eating until the host does as well, unless they encourage everyone to begin sooner.

When placing your napkin on your lap, first fold it horizontally and then place it so that the crease is closest to your hips, and the opening of the fold is closest to your knees. If you get any food or drink on your face during the meal, slightly open the napkin fold and gently dab (not wipe) in the necessary areas until the food or drink has been removed. Then refold your napkin and place it back on your lap, unless it becomes very dirty, in which case it's fine to ask for a new napkin. And what if you drop it? If you're dining in someone's home (*Downton Abbey*–style estates excluded), simply retrieve your own napkin as discreetly as you can and carry on. If you're at a restaurant, it's okay to ask for a new one.

Again, when using your napkin, dab lightly at your lips—don't wipe.

Think of it as a gentle touch, meant to refresh rather than scrub. This subtle dabbing helps keep things tidy without drawing attention.

The Many Types of Napkins

Napkins—so simple, yet so full of subtle signals. First, let's talk sizes. Dinner napkins are larger and meant to be folded in half and placed on your lap. Lunch and tea napkins? They can stay unfolded on your lap, and cocktail napkins are strictly for fingers—don't even think about putting one on your lap. In the world of dining, even the smallest details—like napkin size—help set the stage for the perfect experience.

Napkin Type	Size	Purpose
Dinner Napkin	22 to 26 inches squared	The largest of the bunch, perfect for formal meals and special occasions.
Luncheon Napkin	18 to 20 inches squared	A versatile size ideal for casual lunches and midday gatherings.
Tea Napkin	Approximately 12 inches squared	Petite and charming, just right for elegant tea service or light snacks.
Cocktail Napkin	6 to 9 inches squared	Small but essential, designed for holding drinks, appetizers, and keeping fingers clean.

Using Forks

The humble fork hasn't always had a seat at the table. Once considered vain and even ungodly, it took centuries to evolve from a kitchen tool into a proper dining utensil. Today, its placement to the left of the plate signals its role in most courses, and different sizes—salad, fish, entrée, dessert—may appear throughout a formal meal. Your modern fork simply asks that you use it gracefully: no spearing, no shoveling, and no waving mid-story. Here are a few kinds of forks you might encounter.

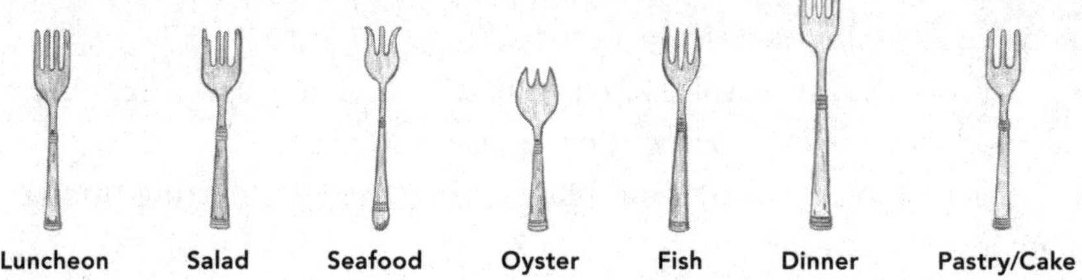

Luncheon Fork *(Slightly smaller than a dinner fork, measuring about 6.75 inches)*
Paired with the luncheon knife or pudding/dessert spoon.

Salad Fork *(About 6 inches)*
Features an extra-wide, sometimes grooved, left tine for cutting greens. Rarely seen today; a luncheon fork often substitutes.

Seafood Fork *(Typically 4.5 to 5.5 inches)*
Also known as the cocktail fork, this three-pronged fork has short tines and a long handle for spearing shellfish and seafood appetizers like shrimp cocktail. Uniquely placed to the right of the plate.

Oyster Fork *(About 4 inches)*
Small with short, wide, and curved tines for eating oysters. Held upturned in the dominant hand, used in informal settings.

Fish Fork *(Typically 7 inches)*
Introduced around 1870 alongside fish knives, often decorative and "pinched" in the middle. Held like a standard fork. In the UK, aristocratic homes and the Royal Family use two forks for fish.

Dinner Fork *(Typically around 7.5 inches in length.)*
The primary fork used with the dinner knife, also known as the table fork.

Pastry/Cake Fork *(Smaller—around 5 inches)*
A Victorian invention still used today, mainly in hospitality, with a thicker left tine for cutting pastries and small cakes. Held upturned in the dominant hand.

Using Knives

Knives have been a staple of dining for centuries, though they weren't always used the way we imagine. You may have noticed some rather warlike references to knives (and even swords) throughout this book—and it's true: Their origins were more battlefield than breakfast table.

But that fascinating history helps explain many of the unspoken rules and etiquette we still observe today.

Over time, knives evolved from utilitarian tools into specialized utensils, each designed with a specific purpose in mind:

Serrated blades, like steak knives, are perfect for cutting through tougher cuts of meat.

Dull edges, such as dinner, luncheon, and fruit knives, are suited for softer or cooked foods.

Pointed tips are helpful for carving meat, peeling fruit, or separating fish from the bone.

Blunt ends, like butter knives and spreaders, are ideal for—no surprise—spreading soft foods with ease.

From practical tools to refined utensils, knives have evolved with the needs and trends of each era. Today, they remain an essential part of any dining experience.

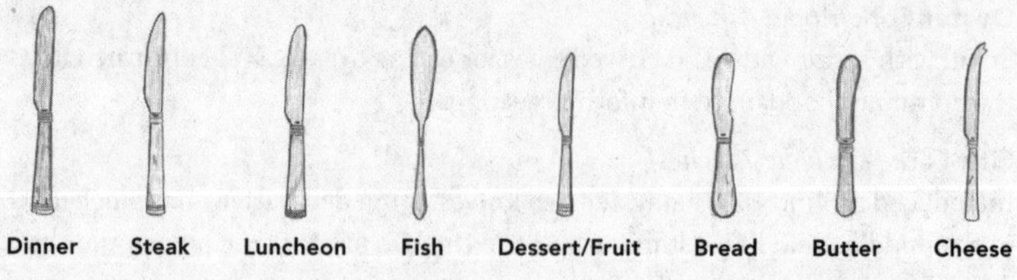

Dinner Knife *(Approximately 9 inches)*
The largest knife, used for cutting and pushing food during main courses. Also called a table knife.

Steak Knife *(8.25 to 9 inches)*
A specialized knife for cutting thick meats like steak or chops. Not used in very formal dining.

Luncheon Knife *(8 to 8.75 inches)*
Smaller than a dinner knife, often used for lighter meals, first courses, cheese, or smaller dishes.

Fish Knife *(8.75 inches)*
Designed in Victorian England to flake fish off bones, often decorative. Rarely used today if fish is served boneless.

Dessert/Fruit Knife *(7.5 to 8 inches)*
Sharp, often with a serrated blade and pointed tip, used to cut or pare fruit.

Bread Knife *(Smaller than a luncheon knife)*
Common in British settings, used to butter bread or cut cheese. Also called a tea knife.

Butter Spreader *(5 to 6 inches)*
Designed to spread soft foods like butter, with no sharp edges.

Cheese Knife *(6 to 8 inches)*
Features a short, often serrated blade with tines at the tip for slicing and lifting firm cheeses.

Using Spoons

Now on to the first utensil most of us learn to use as children. From soup and cereal to dessert and tea, spoons come in a variety of shapes and sizes designed for specific purposes.

While you don't need to memorize every variation, it's helpful to know the basics:

Teaspoons: Ideal for stirring beverages or enjoying smaller portions like yogurt or pudding.

Tablespoons: Larger and more utilitarian, often used for serving or eating hearty soups and stews.

Dessert Spoons: Slightly smaller than a tablespoon and designed specifically for enjoying sweets with just the right touch of elegance.

Soup Spoons: Recognizable by their rounder, deeper bowls, perfect for holding more liquid and minimizing spills.

Good etiquette always begins with thoughtful attention to the moment you're in.

Iced Tea Spoon *(7 to 10 inches)*
Long handle and small bowl, typically used for iced tea or tall drinks.

Oval Soup Spoon *(Up to 8.25 inches)*
Similar to a tablespoon, ideal for soups with chunks of meat or vegetables.

Dessert Spoon *(7 to 7.25 inches)*
Designed for desserts, with a slightly rounded bowl.

Cream Soup Spoon *(Approximately 6 inches)*
Slightly deeper oval bowl, used for most types of soup.

Teaspoon *(5.5 to 6.25 inches)*
Commonly used to stir tea or transfer condiments.

Demitasse Spoon *(3.75 to 4.5 inches)*
Smaller spoon used for after-dinner coffee or espresso.

Citrus Spoon *(5.5 to 6.5 inches)*
Pointed tip, sometimes serrated, used for citrus fruits like grapefruits.

Salt Spoon *(2.5 inches or smaller)*
Small spoon with a gilded bowl, used to serve salt.

Caviar Spoon *(3 to 4 inches)*
Made of natural materials to avoid reactions with fish roe.

How to Hold Utensils with Style and Grace

Now that you're well acquainted with your cutlery, it's time to pick it up and put it to good use. Holding your utensils properly can help you feel at ease and avoid those awkward fumbles that can distract from an otherwise lovely meal.

Let's start with the basics:

Hold utensils with a relaxed but secure grip. Think of the handle as an extension of your hand. Your index finger should gently guide the top, never gripping too tightly.

When using just a fork, hold it in your dominant hand with the tines facing up—ideal for pasta, salads, and similar dishes.

When using both fork and knife, hold the fork in your left hand (tines down) and the knife in your right. Then you have two options: Continental or American style (more on that in a moment). But the shortest way to get each bite into your mouth? Continental style: Cut one bite at a time, then bring the food to your mouth without switching hands.

Avoid stabbing at your food or holding your utensils like a pen. Think controlled, graceful movements that match the ambiance of the meal.

Once your utensils are in hand, keep them off the table. If you pause, rest them on the edge of your plate (fork tines down, knife blade inward). Placing them on the tablecloth mid-meal is a no-go.

Two Styles: American and Continental

So what's the right way to use your fork and knife? The answer depends on where you are—and what feels natural to you. Living in the US, I didn't grow up dining Continental style. In fact, I didn't even learn it until adulthood, when I began to study etiquette more seriously. At first, it felt awkward—like I was trying to rewrite muscle memory. But during the 2020 lockdown, while others were baking sourdough, redecorating their apartments, or enjoying newfound TikTok stardom, I read *Emily Post's Etiquette* cover to cover . . . and practiced my Continental dining technique until it felt natural. Spoiler: It eventually did.

In American style, the fork starts in the left hand while you cut, but once you've sliced a few bites, you place the knife down (blade facing inward) and switch the fork to your right hand to eat, tines facing up. This switching-hand method is uniquely American and stems from nineteenth-century dining habits. It's thoughtful, deliberate, and completely correct in US settings.

Just avoid two common missteps:

- Don't cut all your food at once (that's reserved for toddlers).

- Don't cut one piece at a time with constant switching—that gets fussy fast. Try to find your pace by cutting enough for three or four bites, then switch.

In Continental (or European) style, the fork stays in your left hand and the knife in your right throughout the meal. There's no switching—the knife cuts, the fork (tines down) lifts the food, and you maintain a steady rhythm as you go. It's sleek, efficient, and widely used across Europe. I personally use Continental in the US and abroad, and I recommend it in more formal and business settings. But whichever style you choose, consistency is key. Pick one and stick with it throughout the meal.

Q: *When I'm traveling abroad, should I adapt to Continental dining etiquette, or stick with what I know?*

A: If you're dining in Europe, adapting to Continental style is a lovely gesture of cultural awareness. It shows you've done your homework—and it looks polished too. But if you're not quite comfortable with it yet, don't worry. Most hosts will appreciate the effort more than flawless technique. Just observe, follow the lead of those around you, and, most importantly—enjoy the meal.

The real goal of dining etiquette isn't flawless execution—it's helping everyone, including yourself, feel at ease.

TYPES OF GLASSES AND HOW TO HOLD THEM

Champagne Flute

More commonly used than the champagne saucer or coupe. Its tall, narrow shape keeps champagne cooler and preserves bubbles longer, maintaining the fizz. Hold by the stem and fill two-thirds of the way.

Champagne Saucer/Coupe

Less popular today but still favored in France. The wide, shallow bowl causes bubbles to dissipate quickly, resulting in flat champagne. Hold by the stem and fill two-thirds of the way.

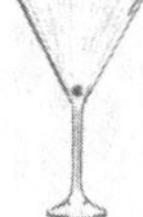

Cocktail/Martini Glass

Features a long stem and a wide, angular bowl. Often frozen to keep drinks chilled. Traditionally used for martinis but can serve other cocktails. Hold by the stem and fill as appropriate for the cocktail.

Highball Tumbler/Collins Glass

Used for carbonated soft drinks or mixed drinks with ice, often for low-strength alcoholic beverages. Its height retains fizz and minimizes ice melt. Not typically seen at formal dining tables.

Lowball Tumbler/Old-Fashioned Glass

Common for whiskey or single-spirit drinks like gin and tonic. The wide bowl allows the aroma to develop, and the heavy base prevents the drink from warming. Hold by the lower half or base.

Port Glass

Small size suited for the high sugar and alcohol content of port wine. Fill just over halfway and hold by the stem.

Red Wine Glass

The larger bowl allows tannins in red wine to breathe and develop flavor. Fill just below halfway, where the glass tapers. Hold by the stem to maintain the wine's temperature.

Water Goblet

Distinct from a stemmed beer glass, this is filled two-thirds of the way. Hold by the lower portion of the bowl.

White Wine Glass

Designed with a smaller bowl and narrower shape to keep chilled wine cool while enhancing its delicate aroma. Fill just below halfway and hold by the stem.

American Place Settings: A Guide to Elegant Dining

A helpful way to remember your place setting is the acronym BMW: bread on the left, meal in the center, and water on the right. As for the napkin, it may be placed in one of three locations: to the left of the forks, beneath the forks, or centered on the main plate. Regardless of where it appears, it should always be neatly folded.

Everyday Place Setting

The essential pieces needed for a simple, unfussy meal.

a - Bread plate; **b** - Butter knife; **c** - Place card; **d** - Water goblet; **e** - Napkin; **f** - Main dining fork; **g** - Main dining plate; **h** - Main dining knife

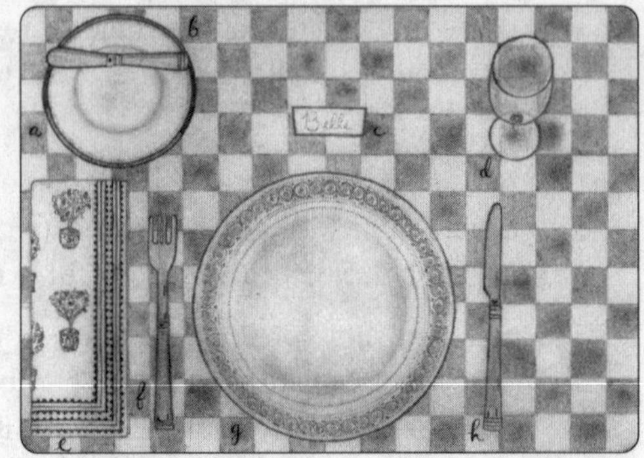

Casual Place Setting

An expanded setting that introduces additional elements often used when more than one course is served.

a - Bread plate; **b** - Butter knife; **c** - Salt and pepper shakers; **d** - Place card; **e** - Water goblet; **f** - Napkin; **g** - Main dining fork; **h** - Main dining plate; **i** - Soup bowl; **j** - Main dining knife; **k** - Soup spoon

Semi-Formal Place Setting

A structured setting that shows how flatware and glassware expand as additional courses are added.

a - Bread plate; **b** - Butter knife; **c** - Place card; **d** - Dessert spoon; **e** - Dessert fork; **f** - Wine glass; **g** - Water goblet; **h** - Tea cup; **i** - Saucer; **j** - Teaspoon; **k** - Main dining fork; **l** - Charger or service plate; **m** - Napkin; **n** - Main dining knife; **o** - Soup spoon

Formal Place Setting in the American Style

A complete place setting with full flatware and glassware placed in advance for a traditional multicourse meal.

a - Bread plate; **b** - Butter knife;
c - Salt and pepper shakers; **d** - Dessert spoon;
e - Dessert fork; **f** - Place card; **g** - Water goblet;
h - White wine glass; **i** - Red wine glass;
j - Champagne flute; **k** - Salad fork;
l - Dinner fork; **m** - Charger or service plate;
n - Napkin; **o** - Dinner knife; **p** - Fish knife (if served); **q** - Soup spoon

Q: *What should I do if I accidentally use the wrong utensil at a fancy dinner?*

A: First, don't draw attention to it. Quietly place the utensil on your plate (not the table, because the utensil has already been used) and smoothly pick up the correct one. No need for an apology or a dramatic confession—most people won't even notice, and those who do will appreciate your composure.

If you're mid-bite, finish confidently. Set the utensil down afterward and move on like nothing happened. The real goal of dining etiquette isn't flawless execution—it's helping everyone, including yourself, feel at ease.

And remember, even the fanciest host knows the real star of the meal isn't the fork—it's the conversation. So relax and carry on. A small slip-up never stood between anyone and dessert.

Knowing the Parts of Your Plate: Dining with Intention and Ease

Now that you've mastered utensils and settings, let's talk about how to manage the food on your plate. Imagine your plate as a clock, with twelve o'clock at the top. This approach not only keeps your plate looking tidy but also makes it practical for dining and courteous for those around you. Any items you won't be eating—such as garnishes, bones, or lemon rinds—should be set aside at the eleven o'clock position. This keeps them out of the way without cluttering the areas of your plate meant for actual bites.

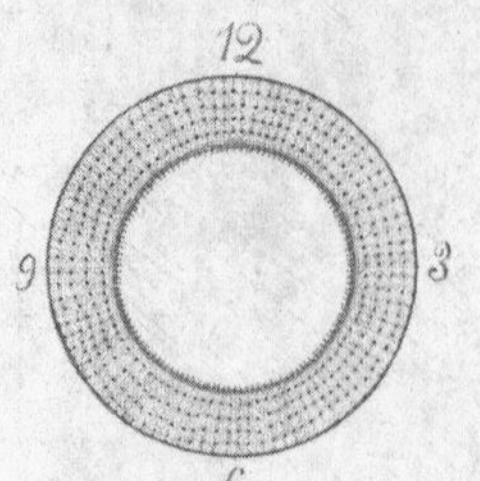

For sauces, butters, or other condiments, place them at around five o'clock. This positioning puts the elements you're actively eating closer to you, creating a more organized dining experience. It also keeps your main food within easy reach, allowing for a smooth, natural flow while eating.

Finally, keep the rim of your plate clean. Not only does this make your plate more visually appealing, but it's also respectful to the servers or your hosts, who will be handling it. A clean rim ensures they can handle your plate without any mess, allowing them to function with ease and you to enjoy your meal with polished etiquette.

Decoding the Modern Dinner Set: A Blend of Tradition and Personal Taste

So what about all the other dishware you might encounter? It depends on what's in your host's dinner set. The notion of a dinner set, all neatly matching, is actually a pretty recent concept from the 1950s, born from clever marketing. Before that—and even now—most collections are curated from individual pieces, carefully chosen to fit the host's taste. This makes it tricky to pin down exactly what each service includes. It's more useful to know about the individual items that might be part of a service. While dimensions are provided as a rough guide, each maker has their own measurements, and older or antique plates tend to be larger than their modern versions. Sizes generally refer to the widest part.

Name	Size	Description
Charger, Service Plate, or Lay Plate	12 to 13 inches	Also known as a charger, this plate is used as an underplate for the first course, adding elegance to the table setting. It's never eaten from and is removed before the main course.

Name	Size	Description
Dinner Plate	10 to 12 inches	The largest plate in a traditional setting, meant for the main course. Its size reflects the importance of the main dish.
Fish Plate	8 to 10 inches	A smaller plate used specifically for fish courses, making the serving more attractive. It can also be used as a luncheon plate or for cheese courses.
Side Plate	6 to 7.5 inches	Often used for bread and butter, this plate sits to the left of the forks. Historically, bread was placed directly on the tablecloth.
Soup Plate	9 to 10 inches	A wide and shallow dish, traditionally used for serving soup in formal settings. Its design allows for cooling and easy spooning. In casual dining, soup plates might be slightly larger, but for formal settings, they stay within this size range to complement the overall table layout.
Soup Bowl	6 to 8 inches	A deeper alternative to the soup plate, typically used for casual dining or serving thicker soups, stews, or chowders.
Meat Dishes (Platters)	Varies; large	Oval or rectangular serving pieces, designed for presenting and serving larger cuts of meat or roasts at the table.
Soup Cup	6 to 8 ounces	Similar to the bouillon cup but larger and without a saucer, it is used for serving soup in less formal dining.
Crescent Salad Plate	Crescent-shaped	A uniquely shaped plate designed to sit alongside a dinner plate for serving salads, especially in formal multicourse meals.
Teapot	16 to 32 ounces	A vessel with a spout, handle, and lid, used for brewing and serving tea. A key element of tea service. This is not to be confused with a kettle, which is used for boiling water.
Hot Water Jug	12 to 24 ounces	A jug or pitcher designed for holding hot water, typically used to dilute tea or for serving alongside tea in formal settings.

Name	Size	Description
Teacups	Sizes vary, but generally 4 to 8 ounces	Small cups with handles, used for serving tea. Typically paired with a saucer in formal or casual settings. Round and deep teacups maintain the temperature better. Wide and shallow teacups cause the tea to cool more quickly. In the UK, tea is served piping hot.
Tea Plate	6 to 7 inches	A small plate, slightly larger than a saucer, used for serving tea sandwiches, cookies, or scones. Even though tea plates are small, once you begin using utensils, place them neatly on the tea plate, not the tablecloth.
Cake/ Bread and Butter Plate	7 to 10 inches	A versatile, small plate used for serving slices of cake or bread and a pat of butter in both formal and casual dining. Use the bread plate on your left and break bread into small pieces rather than cutting it.
Covered Sugar Bowl	Sizes vary, but a 6-to-8-ounce capacity is common	A lidded bowl designed to store and serve sugar in tea or coffee service, helping keep it fresh and clean. Use the provided spoon or tongs to serve sugar, never your hands or personal utensils.
Sugar Bowl	Varies	An open bowl for serving sugar, often part of a tea or coffee set. Place the sugar bowl to the right of the teapot or coffee pot for easy access with a sugar spoon, which is very similar to a teaspoon, but deeper.
Coffee Pot	Varies	A tall, slender pot with a spout, handle, and lid, used for brewing and serving coffee. When serving coffee, fill cups halfway unless guests request more.
Coffee Cup	Sizes vary, but 6 to 8 ounces is common	A medium-sized cup, typically with a saucer, used for serving coffee. Place the saucer on the table, not in your lap, and avoid clinking the spoon against the cup.
Jug/ Creamer	Sizes vary, but 8 to 12 ounces is common	A small pitcher for serving cream or milk alongside coffee or tea. Always pour cream or milk after the coffee or tea, allowing guests to specify their preference.

Name	Size	Description
Demitasse Cup	2-to-3-ounce capacity and 2 inches high	A petite cup, usually accompanied by a saucer, used for serving espresso or strong coffee. Sip espresso slowly and enjoy it without sugar to appreciate the flavor.
Mug	Typically 8 to 16 ounces	A larger, handle-equipped cup used for informal tea, coffee, or hot chocolate. Avoid overfilling the mug to prevent spills, especially when sharing drinks in a casual setting.
Soup Tureen and Stand	Varies	A large covered dish with a stand, used for serving soup in a formal setting. Use the provided ladle to serve soup, and avoid tilting the tureen to scoop the last portion.
Vegetable Dishes (Open or Covered)	Sizes vary, but 8 to 12 inches is common	Serving dishes designed to present and serve vegetables, either open for ease or covered to retain warmth. Serve vegetables with the provided serving utensil, not personal cutlery.
Sauceboat or Gravy Boat	Sizes vary, but an 8-to-12-ounce capacity is common	A vessel with a spout for pouring gravy or sauces, often accompanied by an underplate to catch drips. Pass the gravy boat with the handle toward the next person, and pour carefully to avoid splashes.
Dessert Services	Varies	
Cream Tureen and Stand	12 to 16 ounces	A covered serving dish with a stand, used for serving whipped cream or custards in formal settings. Always serve cream with a clean dessert spoon, and avoid double-dipping or touching the lid with fingers.
Fruit Stands	6 to 18 inches tall	Tiered or pedestal serving dishes for displaying and serving fruits, often used in elegant presentations. Arrange fruits attractively, and provide small forks or picks for easy serving.

When You Are Finished: The Silent Service Code

Say you need to briefly leave the table. Where do you place your utensils and napkin? You can use the silent service code to discreetly and clearly signal whether you are finished or taking a break during a meal. Remember: As a general matter with cutlery, once we pick up a utensil, it doesn't go back on the table, and that includes resting the handles of cutlery on the table. The reason for this is trying to keep the table and linens, if applicable, as clean as possible during a meal. You may notice that a recurring theme in dining etiquette is making things easier and more pleasant for anyone who will be cleaning up. Here's your guide to finished or resting positions, as well as using your napkin as a signal:

Finished Eating Position *(US)*

Place the tines of the fork up and the knife with the blade in. Imagine that if your plate were a clock and the cutlery were the hands of the clock, the cutlery would be at about the 4:20 position.

This same position is used in France and some other parts of Europe, with the only difference being that the tines of the fork would face down.

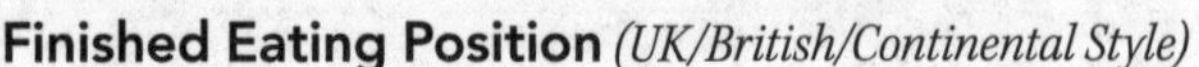

Finished Eating Position *(UK/British/Continental Style)*

The fork faces up, the blade of the knife faces in, and the cutlery are placed so that they would be at a 6:30 position.

If you have a fork and spoon, the same position applies but the spoon replaces the knife, and the bowl of the spoon faces up.

Finished Eating Position *(parts of Europe)*

Utensils are placed in a 3:15 position in parts of Europe, such as the Netherlands. Here the tines of the fork face up and the blade of the knife also faces in. And it's worth noting that in some parts of Europe, if you place your utensils apart on either side of your plate, it means you didn't like your food, so be extra careful how you place them.

Resting Position *(US)*

The fork tines face up and the fork is placed in the center of the plate with the handle at the 4 o'clock position. The fork and knife should be parallel to each other with the knife placed across the upper rim of the plate.

Resting Position *(British/European/Continental Style)*

Create an "X" with the fork and the knife, with the fork tines facing down and the fork crossed over the knife. The blade of the knife remains facing inward. Historically, this was to show that the knife was not going to be used as a weapon.

Resting with Dessert Cutlery *(British/European/ Continental Style)*

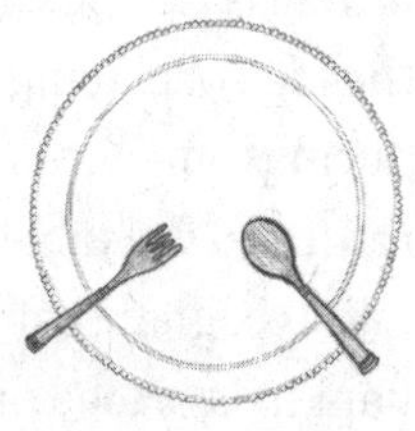

When pausing during dessert, your cutlery should be placed in a clear resting position to signal you're not finished. Unlike the main course, where a knife might cross over a fork in the European style, dessert utensils are handled a bit more simply.

If you're using both a fork and a spoon, rest them at an angle on your plate—handles at approximately 4 o'clock, and the tines of the fork and the bowl of the spoon pointing toward 10 o'clock. The fork tines should face down, while the spoon faces up. They do not need to be crossed; in traditional etiquette, the spoon was never considered a weapon, so the crossing convention doesn't apply.

If you're using only a spoon or fork, rest it similarly—placed diagonally across the plate with the handle at 4 o'clock and with tines or bowl at 10 o'clock. This angled placement lets servers know you're still enjoying your dessert.

Finished Position with Dessert Cutlery *(British/European/Continental Style)*

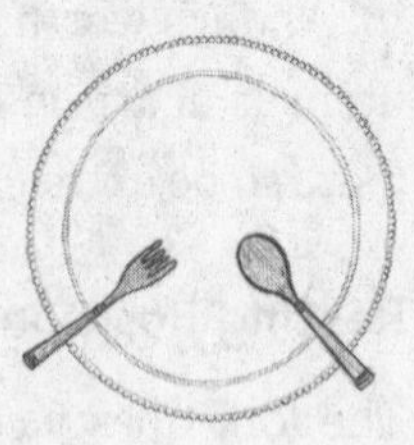

To indicate that you've finished your dessert, place your utensils parallel to each other on your plate. The traditional position is with the handles at 4 o'clock and the tips pointing to 10 o'clock.

If using both a fork and a spoon, place them side by side, not overlapping. The fork tines should face down, and the spoon bowl should face up.

If using only a fork or spoon, position it the same way—placed neatly at an angle from 4 to 10 o'clock. And yes, this is one of those situations where the resting and finished positions are quite confusingly the same.

Avoid laying your utensils haphazardly or leaving them in a resting position, as this may confuse servers or hosts.

Napkins

If a napkin is placed on a chair, it means the diner will return. If possible, putting the napkin on an arm of a chair is best for hygiene purposes, but if that is not possible, the seat of the chair works too. If you do not like the idea of placing your napkin on your seat when you get up temporarily during a meal, you can politely ask a server for a fresh napkin when you return to the table, if at a restaurant or professional venue.

To signal that you are leaving the table for good and not returning, a napkin is placed on the table in a neat but not perfectly folded way, to the left of the place setting.

Elegant Etiquette for Life's Trickiest Dishes

Some foods require a little extra finesse, but with the right approach, you can enjoy even the most challenging bites with ease and elegance. Certain delicious delicacies are challenging—looking at you, lobster!—but a little awareness and practice certainly help.

Here's your guide to eating confidently and elegantly, no matter what's on the plate.

- **Apples:** For a polished approach, slice them before eating. If you're biting into one, do so discreetly and avoid loud crunching, and save eating apples whole for very informal scenarios.
- **Artichokes:** Pull off leaves with your fingers, dip in sauce, and then use your teeth to pull off the "meat." The heart can be eaten with a fork and knife.
- **Asparagus:** If it's tender, use a fork. For firmer stalks, using your fingers is perfectly fine. If served as a first course instead of an accompaniment vegetable with a main course, eat with the left hand and dip in Hollandaise or similar sauce.
- **Bacon:** Enjoy it with your fingers if crispy, but use a fork and knife if it's softer.
- **Bananas:** If served as a dessert, cut both ends off with dessert cutlery and then slice down the skin to unwrap. Cut into slices and enjoy with a fork and knife.
- **Bread:** Bread is not cut, nor is an entire piece buttered all at once. Instead, tear off bite-sized pieces and butter each piece individually.
- **Burgers:** While burgers were made for hands, today's towering creations often demand a knife and fork. Simply remove the top bun, cut the burger into manageable pieces, and enjoy. That extra bun? Slice it up and savor it throughout the meal.
- **Cheese:** Keep the wedge intact. When cutting a piece off a triangle-shaped cheese that is being passed around the table, avoid slicing off the point. Instead, cut to maintain its original shape, leaving it neat and presentable for the next person.
- **Crème Brûlée:** Gently crack the caramelized top with your spoon, scoop small bites with both the crunchy topping and creamy custard, and avoid scraping the dish loudly as you finish.
- **Crêpes:** Fold and eat with a fork and knife, especially if they have a filling.
- **Grapes:** If scissors are available, snip a small branch to take just what you need. No scissors? Snap off a portion of the bunch with your hands. Either way, avoid leaving the stem looking picked over.

- **Kebabs:** Remove the pieces from the skewer onto your plate by holding the stick in one hand and using your fork to slide the pieces onto your plate one by one. Once the food is on the plate, use utensils as you normally would.
- **Condiments:** When using condiments like ketchup, place a small portion on the side of your plate for dipping. Avoid spreading it across your food, especially in a formal setting.
- **Mussels:** Use a fork to gently loosen the mollusk and enjoy it directly from the shell. Empty shells should be placed on a designated plate or bowl—keep your dining space tidy.
- **Oysters:** Loosen the oyster with a fork before eating. You can either spear it with the fork or tip it directly into your mouth from the shell. Either approach is elegant as long as it's done smoothly.
- **Pasta:** Twirl long pasta with a fork. Avoid cutting it. (See spaghetti.)
- **Peas:** Avoid scooping peas with an upward-facing fork. Instead, spear a few at a time or use mashed potatoes (or another similar side) to help them stay put on your fork as you convey the bite to your mouth.
- **Pizza:** In Italy, casual pizza is often eaten with hands, but when things get messy—or the setting is more formal—use a knife and fork to cut small, manageable pieces.
- **Salad:** Cutting lettuce was once considered an affront to the host (thanks to historical poison paranoia!), but in today's world it's perfectly fine to use your knife and fork for oversized or awkwardly shaped pieces that cannot be easily folded.
- **Salt and Pepper:** Pepper is sprinkled on food, whereas salt etiquette depends on how it's presented.
    - If using loose salt: Place a small pile on the side of your plate and dip your food into it, rather than scattering it all over.
    - If using a salt mill: Gently sprinkle it onto your food, as a mill is designed for precision.
    - Asking for salt and pepper when they're not already on the table can signal that the dish isn't to your liking, so it's best to avoid if possible.
- **Soufflés:** Savory soufflés are eaten with a fork, and sweet ones (usually served in ramekins or small bowls) call for a spoon.

- **Spaghetti:** Spaghetti should be twirled with a fork alone—no cutting, and definitely no spoon. If you're not confident in your skills, skip it when you're at an important event. Since spaghetti is one of the trickier of the tricky foods to master, it's not recommended to include on a menu for a formal occasion or to order for a date or business meal.
- **Steak:** Rather than drenching your steak in sauce, pour a small amount onto the side of your plate. Cut one piece at a time and dip it into the sauce for a polished dining experience.
- **Sushi:** Chopsticks are standard, though clean fingers are acceptable in informal settings if others are doing the same. Always dip sushi fish-side down to avoid breaking the rice.

Dining with elegance is less about following rules than about showing respect for the meal, your host, and yourself. Done well, even the simplest meal can feel like an occasion.

The Takeaway: It's Less About the Fork and More About the People

Over the years, I have often had friends visit with me in Maine, where my family has a long-standing tradition of treating guests, especially out-of-towners, to lobster. For many of our guests, it's their very first time tackling a whole lobster—and let's just say, it can be a humbling experience. There are crackers and picks involved, butter dripping, shells flying . . . It's the opposite of dainty, and yet, it's one of the most joyful meals we share. What makes it work isn't flawless technique—it's the willingness to dive in with curiosity, a bit of guidance, and a spirit of warmth and good humor. I think the same spirit applies to even the most formal of table settings.

You've now learned the basics of place settings, the proper use of cutlery, and the secrets behind those tableware pieces we might not see every day. With this foundation, you can approach any meal—formal or casual—feeling prepared, relaxed, and able to focus on what truly matters: the people at the table.

Because ultimately, etiquette isn't about rigid rules or impressing others. It's about making everyone at the table feel comfortable, seen, and welcomed—whether you're lifting a delicate dessert spoon or cracking open your very first lobster.

CHAPTER 8

DINING OUT WITH DECORUM

Have you ever been at a nicer-than-usual restaurant and suddenly felt like everyone knows what to do except you?

I felt that way the night my husband, Jason, and I got engaged. We were at the fanciest restaurant either of us had ever been to. It was the kind of place where someone gently reminded you to "watch your step" as you left the dining room, and replaced your napkin the second you left the table, even if you had gotten up many, many times because of what I like to call "about to pop the question" nerves. Jason was so nervous—he kept whispering, "I feel like someone is watching me eat." And honestly, I did too.

Most of us don't grow up dining in settings like that. But once you feel comfortable at a formal table, something shifts. You start to notice the rhythm of it all—the unspoken cues, the pacing, the little details that make everything feel smooth. And the best part? Once you know how to dine formally, it's easy to tone it down for any setting. But trying to level up in the moment, when you're already feeling unsure? That's much harder.

This chapter will walk you through what to do in both formal and informal settings so you don't have to overthink it. The focus isn't flawlessness; it's about being present, thoughtful, and self-assured—no matter where you're seated.

Valet Parking

First, let's start with what happens before you even enter the restaurant. If you've driven to your destination and valet parking is on offer, taking advantage of it can make your evening go smoothly. And of course, you want to use this service with kindness and class. Valets are the unsung heroes of our modern hustle, dashing through rain, snow, blistering heat, and wind to ensure your evening starts and ends without a hitch. Handing over your car—one of your most cherished possessions—to a stranger might feel like a leap of faith, but it's one that deserves a proper thank-you. And what's the chicest way to say thanks? A thoughtful tip, of course. It's more than just a kind gesture; it's a nod to their hard work and attention to detail.

Most valets earn an hourly wage, but those tips you slip them add a little sparkle to their take-home pay. A generous tip, especially when service exceeds expectations, is like giving them the VIP treatment they've just extended to you.

Here are a few valet tips to keep your drop-off and pickup experience seamless and oh-so-sophisticated:

1. **Have your tip ready.** Don't let an awkward cash scramble ruin the vibe. Prep your tip in advance (before you get out of the car), so you can hand it over seamlessly.
2. **Tip both on arrival and departure.** Offering a tip when you hand over your keys sets a courteous tone and may encourage extra care in return.
3. **Tip thoughtfully.** For most valet services, a tip of $3 to $5 is standard, but if the service is exceptional or the weather is dreadful, consider tipping $10 or more as you hand over your car keys. It's a small price for peace of mind and stellar service.
4. **Hand tips discreetly.** Slide your tip like a pro—with the smallest bill on the outside and all of them folded in half. It's classy, considerate, and ensures the exchange feels polished.
5. **Be clear about special instructions.** Does your car have a secret quirk, or do you prefer a shaded parking spot? Communicate your preferences clearly to avoid any misunderstandings.

6. **Don't leave valuables in the car.** Think of your car as your castle. Would you leave your crown jewels lying around? Remove wallets, laptops, or anything precious before handing over the keys.
7. **Be polite and patient.** Valets work under immense pressure, especially during peak hours. A smile and a little patience make their job a whole lot brighter—and your experience smoother.
8. **Check the hours of service.** Before you sashay away, confirm the valet's operating hours. Nobody wants to be Cinderella at midnight without her ride.
9. **Inspect your vehicle.** When your car is returned, give it a quick once-over. If something feels off, address it promptly and politely. You're aiming for resolution, not drama.
10. **Know when not to use valet.** If the thought of someone else driving your car gives you hives, or if your vehicle is a bit . . . temperamental, self-parking might be your best bet.

Valet etiquette will help you not only leave a great impression but also spread a little kindness to the hardworking individuals behind the service.

Coat Check Charm: Etiquette for Effortless Exchanges

You've made it inside, and now it's time to take off your coat and stay a while. Coat check services are a little slice of sophistication that keep your hands free and your outfit sleek while you dine. But just like any moment of elegance, there are a few rules to follow to keep things smooth and stylish.

Tipping

In the US, a tip of $1 to $5 per item is customary when you retrieve your coat. Larger or more complicated situations—like a coat with multiple accessories—may call for a more generous tip. If you've ever felt unsure about tipping at coat check, here's the golden rule: If someone's helping you, a small thank-you in the form of a tip is always appreciated. Whether it's spare change from your wallet or a crisp dollar bill, it's a simple way to show gratitude for the service. (For more on tipping, see 253.)

Writing Your Initials and Phone Number on Your Ticket

Ever wonder what to do with that coat check ticket besides keeping it safe in your purse or pocket? Write your initials and phone number on the back. This tiny detail can save the day if your ticket is misplaced or if there's any mix-up. Think of it as your stylish safety net.

Additional Tips for a Seamless Experience

1. **Be polite and patient.** The coat check staff are there to make your evening easier, so a warm smile and kind words are appropriate. Even during busy times, a little patience keeps the vibe friendly.
2. **Check before you go.** Before you hand over your coat, make sure to empty the pockets of any valuables like keys, wallets, or lipstick. It's better to keep these essentials with you than risk losing them.
3. **Keep your ticket secure.** Store it somewhere safe but accessible, like a designated pocket or wallet compartment.
4. **Avoid last-minute rushes.** If you're at a large event, consider retrieving your coat a few minutes before the crowd rushes the coat check. It saves time and makes the process smoother for everyone.
5. **Know what's expected.** Some venues charge a coat check fee, which may or may not include gratuity. If the fee doesn't cover a tip, be prepared to show your appreciation with a little extra.

By following these simple yet thoughtful guidelines, you'll elevate your coat check experience from a routine transaction to a graceful part of your evening.

Dining with Finesse: Ordering and Wine Etiquette

So you've seen to your car, stowed your coat, and are seated comfortably at your table. When the server approaches, you have another chance to use good etiquette to make the evening smoother, kinder, and more genteel for everyone involved, especially the waitstaff. Ordering at a restaurant is more than just picking something that sounds delicious—it's an artful dance of timing, consideration, and strategy. From the first sip of a pre-dinner cocktail to the final swirl of wine, every choice contributes to the experience, not just for you, but for everyone at your table (and even your server's other tables).

Separate Checks? Speak Up Early

We'll talk more about handling the check later, but it's best to know from the start: If you are dining in a group and you plan to split the bill, mention it right away—before the first drink is even ordered. Asking for separate checks at the end of the meal can slow service for everyone, as your server has to divide everything retroactively. If you're unsure whether the restaurant allows separate checks, call ahead or ask as you're seated.

Drinks: Cheers to Good Timing

Feel free to order your preferred drinks as soon as the server asks, even if everyone in your party hasn't arrived. You might consider waiting to order wine if there may be interest in getting a bottle of wine for the table. Latecomers can catch up when the server returns. If you're hosting, take charge and help your guests decide by suggesting options or asking their preferences.

THE BASICS OF ORDERING

After drinks are served, your focus turns to the menu. Being ready when your server arrives to take your order shows respect for both their time and the dining experience. If you're still deciding, let them know you need more time—it's far kinder than holding them hostage while you change your mind. Remember, they have other tables to tend to, food to deliver, and customers waiting. The universal signal that you're ready? A closed menu.

When the server approaches, skip the casual and demanding "I'll have" and opt for something more polished and polite, like "May I please have the salmon?" or "The tenderloin, please." Avoid pointing at the menu or waving it around—it's a dining room, not an auction. While it's perfectly fine to request modifications, and it is more acceptable at a restaurant than in a private home, keep them purposeful. Focus on dietary restrictions or major dislikes, not a laundry list of tweaks for minor preferences. The goal? To balance your needs with respect for the chef's craft and the flow of service. A thoughtful approach transforms dining out from a routine meal into a gracious experience.

The Food Order: What to Keep in Mind

Number of Courses: It's not mandatory to match your companions course-for-course. If you're the only one ordering an appetizer, enjoy it while they sip their drinks or chat. Just avoid slowing the meal down for others.

Sharing Is Caring: Splitting an appetizer, dessert, or even a main course is perfectly fine. Just let your server know in advance, and consider tipping a bit extra to account for the shared service.

Ask for Recommendations: Narrowed down your choices but still unsure? Ask your server for their opinion. If specials catch your eye, don't hesitate to ask about the price—they're often a splurge. If you're a guest, leave cost-related questions to your host.

Choosing Foods to Match Your Plans: If the evening calls for leisurely conversation, avoid dishes that demand too much attention, like shellfish in the shell or anything notoriously messy. Stick to meals that allow you to stay engaged and elegant.

Unfamiliar Dishes: Dining adventures are exciting, but if you're not sure how to eat an artichoke or tackle a crab claw, it's better to stick with something familiar to avoid stress.

Pairing Your Meal with Wine

Before you place a wine order, there are a few things to consider: how much you want to spend, what will pair well with your meal, and how to handle the wine when it arrives at the table. Here's what to keep in mind as you move through the process with confidence and composure:

Wine Lists and Prices: Not all wine lists are created equal. Some offer detailed descriptions that help guide your choice, while others are more basic. The best lists include a variety of familiar and unique options at prices that align with the entrées.

To subtly communicate your price range to your server—or sommelier, if the restaurant has a wine expert on staff—point to a wine on the list at your preferred price and ask their opinion. Place your finger on the price, not the name, to keep things discreet. A good rule of thumb for ordering bottles is half a bottle per person, or, for larger groups, a mix of red and white to accommodate diverse tastes.

Selecting the Wine: If memorizing wine regions and varietals isn't your style, opt for reliable crowd-pleasers. A Pinot Noir (red) or a dry Riesling (white) pairs well with most dishes. For more adventurous diners, reviewing the wine list online before your visit gives you a chance to familiarize yourself with options and even practice pronouncing them.

The Sommelier: If the restaurant has a sommelier, or wine expert, don't hesitate to ask for their help. Be ready to share your preferences, what you're eating, and whether you're open to trying something new. When it comes to budget, there's no need for a big announcement—simply point discreetly to a price on the menu (perhaps a bottle in your preferred range) and say something like, "We're looking for something around here—what would you recommend?" A good sommelier will take the hint and make recommendations accordingly.

Wine by the Glass: Ordering by the glass is a fantastic way to sample different wines. But be mindful that wine from a previously opened bottle might not be as fresh. Ask your server when the bottle was opened, and if it's been a day or more, consider another choice.

Etiquette for Inspecting the Wine

So you've ordered wine for the table. When the wine arrives, the server will present the unopened bottle to confirm your order. Once it's uncorked, they'll pour a small taste. Swirl, sniff, and sip to check for flaws—if it smells or tastes off. If it's acceptable, a simple "It's fine" lets the server know to proceed. If something is amiss, politely let them know.

From there, the server will pour for the guests first, with the host or person ordering served last. If you're skipping wine, simply say, "No, thank you." Glasses are traditionally filled three-quarters full for white wine and halfway for red to allow the aromas to shine.

A well-executed restaurant order isn't just about the food—it's about creating an experience that's smooth, enjoyable, and considerate of everyone involved. With a little thought and a dash of charm, you'll make dining out feel effortless and oh-so-stylish.

When to Start Eating

Timing your first bite is a subtle yet significant part of dining etiquette. From the hosting chapter, you may recall that in someone's home, you wait for the host to begin, unless otherwise directed. In a restaurant, it's polite to wait until everyone at the table has been served before starting your meal. That said, in larger groups where service may be staggered, it's common for those still waiting to encourage others to begin, ensuring no one's meal goes cold. As a guest, if your food hasn't arrived yet, a kind word like, "Please start," signals to others that you're comfortable with them eating first.

For Small Groups

At intimate dinners with just a few people, it's best to wait until everyone is served to start eating. This approach fosters a sense of togetherness and ensures no one feels left out.

Large Events

At large-scale events like weddings or galas, the dynamics shift. Plates may arrive at different times, often with significant delays between tables or even among guests at the same table. In such cases, a delicate balance is key. Guests who haven't been served yet can politely encourage those who have to begin, creating a shared understanding that accommodates both warmth and practicality.

Knowing when to start eating is a subtle art that blends mindfulness with social awareness. By observing these guidelines, you'll show respect for your host, fellow diners, and the meal itself—making every dining experience feel effortlessly elegant.

When Things Go Wrong at a Restaurant: Grace Under Pressure

Dining out is supposed to feel like a mini vacation—good food, great company, and no dishes to wash. But every so often, things don't go as planned. A dropped fork, an undercooked steak, or even an unexpected spill can threaten to derail your evening. The secret to staying chic in the face of chaos? Handle it all with the finesse of a rom-com heroine who always manages to land on her feet.

Dropping Something: Let It Go

So you've dropped your fork. Or your knife. Or—heaven forbid—your napkin. Resist the urge to dive under the table like you're rescuing lost treasure. Anything that hits the floor belongs to the restaurant now, not your plate. Simply catch the server's attention with a discreet, "I seem to have dropped my fork. Could I trouble you for a fresh one?" Trust me, no one will bat an eye, and you'll avoid the embarrassment of placing a dirty utensil back on the pristine white tablecloth.

Food That Misses the Mark: Be Smooth

Not every dish is a hit. Maybe your steak is rare enough to audition for *The Walking Dead* or your soup is more salt than broth. Whatever the issue, don't panic—and definitely don't broadcast it to the whole dining room. Instead, channel your inner diplomat with your server.

"I'm so sorry to mention this, but my chicken seems a bit undercooked. Would it be possible to have it replaced?"

"It looks like there's something in my salad that shouldn't be there—could I have a fresh one, please?"

Polite, confident, and effective. Remember, the goal is to give the restaurant a chance to make it right, not to ruin everyone's appetite with a tirade.

Facing Unfamiliar Food: Stay Cool

You ordered something adventurous, and now you're face-to-face with a dish that looks more like modern art than dinner. Approach it with curiosity and grace. Try a bite, savor the experience, and if it's truly not for you, focus on the other courses without making a fuss. No need to turn your table into a Yelp review in real time.

Spills Happen: Own It with Style

Knocked over your wine? Spilled your water? It's not the end of the world—or your outfit. Take a breath and wave down the server with an apologetic, "I'm so sorry—I seem to have made a mess. Would you mind helping with this?" Let them handle it with their professional tools while you handle it with your professional poise. If the spill is on your clothing, excuse yourself to the restroom where you can more easily have the privacy to mitigate the matter and have the benefit of a mirror.

Service Issues: Be Constructive, Not Catty

Slow service or a forgotten order can feel frustrating, but remember: This isn't your moment to become the main character. Instead, summon your inner problem-solver.

"I wanted to check on my order—it seems like it's taking a little longer than expected."

And if things still feel off, a quiet word with the manager—emphasis on quiet—is far more effective than a public display of exasperation. But whatever you do, do not be rude. Being unkind to restaurant staff is not a good look!

Incorrect Check: Keep It Drama-Free

Few things kill the post-dinner glow faster than confusion over the bill. If there's an error, point it out kindly. "I think there might have been a mix-up here—could we take another look?" No snapping fingers or eye rolls required.

Above All, Stay Composed

Here's the thing about restaurant mishaps: They're rarely about the food or service and always about how you handle the moment. Stay calm, stay gracious, and stay focused on what really matters—the company and the experience. Because even when things go wrong, a little charm and a lot of grace can turn it all around.

Q: *What do I do if I spill something, like a drink or sauce?*

A: Accidents happen to everyone. Signal your server and say, "I'm so sorry—I've spilled my drink. Could you help clean it up?" This is easier said than done, but unless you need to stop a large spill from getting worse immediately, avoid trying to clean it yourself with your napkin, as it's best to let the staff handle it with proper cleaning tools. If the spill affects another guest, offer a sincere apology and to have their clothing professionally cleaned, or replaced if irreparable.

Q: *Should I tip if something went wrong on the restaurant's end?*

A: If the issue was minor and resolved well, tip as you normally would. If the service or resolution was unsatisfactory, tipping slightly less is acceptable—but avoid skipping the tip altogether unless the experience was truly egregious. If the problem was with the food and not the service, don't penalize the server, as they likely had minimal control over it.

Grace and composure in these moments show that you can handle challenges with poise. The true mark of etiquette isn't avoiding problems—it's how you handle them when they arise.

Splitting the Check: Etiquette for Handling the Restaurant Bill

When the bill arrives at the end of a fabulous meal with a group, it can feel like the ultimate mood-dampener—but it doesn't have to. With a little planning and the right etiquette, you can keep the evening's glow intact while settling up like a pro.

Set the Plan Before the Meal

As I mentioned earlier, it's best to set your intentions beforehand. Before the first sip of wine or bite of bread, decide how the bill will be handled. Will it be split evenly? Divided based on individual orders? Or does one person plan to treat the group? A quick discussion up front saves confusion (and awkwardness) later.

Designate a Bill Collector

Every group needs a leader, and when it comes to the bill, having a designated collector is key. This person can manage payment logistics, whether it's splitting the total, collecting cash, or swiping a card and being reimbursed. They're the hero who ensures the process stays smooth and organized.

Consider Other Diners

Splitting the bill evenly might seem like the easiest solution, but it's not always the fairest. If some diners enjoyed multiple courses or indulged in cocktails while others stuck to simpler fare, adjusting for individual expenses shows thoughtfulness. That said, tax and gratuity should always be shared among the group—the server worked equally hard for everyone.

The Guest of Honor

If there's a guest of honor—whether it's a birthday, promotion celebration, or another special occasion—there's an unspoken rule: They shouldn't pay for their meal. The cost is typically divided among the rest of the group as a gesture of celebration and generosity.

Alcohol: The Wild Card

Alcoholic drinks can add up quickly, and not everyone may partake. When splitting the bill, consider handling drinks separately to avoid confusion or uneven contributions. This approach ensures fairness while letting those who indulged enjoy their cocktails guilt-free.

Keep It Classy

Whatever the arrangement, handle the bill with discretion. There's no need for loud math debates or a detailed breakdown at the table—keep the process smooth and seamless. If issues arise, address them quietly or step aside to sort things out.

The way you handle the bill says as much about your etiquette as the way you hold a fork. With a little foresight and grace, you'll leave the restaurant not just well-fed but admired for your effortless efficiency.

Brewing Good Vibes: Coffee Shop Etiquette

Coffee shops are the cozy living rooms of modern life—part caffeine haven, part work sanctuary, part social hub. Whether you're dashing in for a latte or setting up shop for an afternoon of productivity, small acts of courtesy make the coffee shop experience better for everyone.

Tip Your Barista

Your barista isn't just handing you coffee; they're handing you life's little liquid miracle. Show your gratitude with a tip, even for the simplest order. If you're a regular, tipping generously is a great way to build goodwill and brighten someone's day.

Minimize Phone Calls (and Use Headphones Wisely)

Loud phone conversations are the ultimate mood disruptors in a coffee shop. If you need to take a call, step outside. Listening to music or watching videos? Use headphones or earbuds, and keep the volume low enough that only you can hear it.

Share the Space

Community tables are just that—for the community. Don't spread out your belongings like you're moving in. Stick to one seat and leave room for others. Be kind to those around you, especially if they're working or reading. And remember, coffee shops aren't libraries—don't expect silence. It's about creating an atmosphere that works for everyone, not just you.

Be Aware of Others

From holding the door for someone juggling their espresso and pastry to clearing your dishes when you're done, small acts of consideration make a big difference. If the shop is busy, avoid overstaying your welcome. A good rule of thumb? Make a purchase about every hour and a half if you're lingering.

Respect the Rules

Each coffee shop has its own vibe and guidelines. Whether it's a no-laptops policy during peak hours or a minimum purchase requirement for seating, respect the house rules. Being a good guest ensures you'll always be welcome.

Be Warm and Kind

Coffee shops thrive on community, and your kindness contributes to that. Smile at the staff, greet familiar faces, and treat everyone with warmth. If you're a regular, get to know the people who make your coffee magic happen—it turns a simple transaction into a human connection.

Coffee shop etiquette is about balancing your needs with those of the people around you. With just a little effort, you can sip your cappuccino, answer emails, and soak in the ambiance without stepping on anyone's toes. After all, good manners pair perfectly with a good cup of coffee.

Afternoon Tea

Going out for a meal may be festive, but there are few things as charming and sophisticated as going out for an elegant afternoon tea. Steeped in tradition, this special occasion stands in for a light meal in the midafternoon, just when you're starting to need a pick-me-up. It features both savory and sweet options, with treats that are as delightful to the eyes as they are to the palate—think dainty brownies, airy macarons, slivers of carrot cake, or tiny fruit-filled tarts. This is where the pastry chef's flair shines, showcasing their creativity in a small yet impactful showcase.

In the refined world of afternoon tea, even the humble fork gets a touch of elegance. Enter the pastry fork: a delicate tool often seen in the finest hotels. What sets this fork apart? Its three slender tines, unlike the usual four, and a subtly thicker left side designed to cut through cake with ease. And yes, there's even a left-handed version with the thicker edge on the right, making sure no one is left out of the cake-cutting finesse. For those occasions where the cake is served in heartier slices, it's perfectly acceptable to enjoy it with your hands—no raised eyebrows necessary.

Table Settings for Tea

When it comes to the table for afternoon tea, there's no universal standard; each venue—whether a private home, restaurant, or hotel—adds its unique flair to the arrangement. This flexibility harkens back to English drawing rooms, where tea was enjoyed informally, with guests balancing plates on their laps. But if you're using a table, here's what you'll find.

Cutlery: Traditionally, a cake or pastry fork is placed on the right alongside the knives, owing to its smaller size, while luncheon forks are positioned on the left. Fork tines typically face upward, adhering to English custom. Knives are included but are not intended for cutting bread or cake; they're for spreading butter, creams, and jams. Teaspoons are set exclusively for stirring tea; any additional spoons required for food items are provided with the respective course.

Plates: A small plate, often referred to as a tea or bread-and-butter plate, is centered in the setting. In some establishments, this plate is replaced with a clean one after a savory course, while others may provide an additional bread plate on the left for sweet items or discards.

Glasses: Including a water goblet has become common, especially in hospitality settings, to offer guests a refreshing option alongside the sweet tea offerings.

Accoutrements: Milk, sugar, and other accompaniments are arranged just before the tea service to ensure freshness. Tea strainers are placed near the teacup—often one per guest—to maintain the distinct flavors of different teas.

Napkins: Napkins are either placed in the center of the setting, to the left of the fork(s), or underneath the fork(s), typically without elaborate folds, maintaining a simple elegance.

Variations by Venue

Private Homes: Tea is often served in a more relaxed setting, possibly in the drawing room, with guests serving themselves and perhaps balancing plates on their laps. The use of a tablecloth is optional and depends on personal preference.

Restaurants or Tea Rooms: Tea may be served at dining tables or low coffee tables, with settings adhering to standard dining etiquette but allowing for the establishment's unique interpretation. A tablecloth might be used to enhance the dining experience.

Hotels: Often, hotels have their own signature tea services, with specific table settings reflecting their brand's style. A tablecloth is commonly used to add a touch of formality. Tea strainers are usually provided per guest to accommodate different tea selections.

Private Home versus Hotel Tea Experiences

Afternoon tea may have started in the cozy parlors of English homes, but these days it's more the domain of chic hotels and quaint teashops, where tradition meets indulgence. The difference? Homes are about intimate charm, while hotels and teashops are commercial hubs where the sky's the limit—especially if you're footing the bill. Let's spill the tea on how the service and menu stack up between these two quintessential venues.

Aspect	Private Home	Hotel
What It's Called	Simply "tea"—no frills, just the essentials.	"Afternoon tea," complete with elegance and a bit of pomp.
Who's Pouring?	The host or a guest takes charge—tea-pouring is part of the charm.	It's all about being served—staff handles the pouring.
The Spread	Minimalist: think buttered bread slices and a couple of cakes.	Abundant: three or four courses brimming with variety.
How It's Served	Plates casually set on a side table—no fuss, no tiers.	Tiered cake stands steal the show, with flat plates making a supporting appearance.
Sandwich Style	Delicate, thinly sliced squares of bread.	More robust rectangles with thicker, fluffier bread.
Cake	Big cakes sliced down to size—Victoria sponge in summer, fruitcake in winter.	French patisserie perfection—petite, pretty, and Instagram-worthy.

Teatime	The clock strikes 5 p.m., and it's teatime for about an hour.	Offered from as early as 11:30 a.m. to 6 p.m.; most popular time is 4 p.m. Sittings last about two hours.
Coffee	Rarely served; tea remains the focus.	Coffee is readily available upon request.

Regardless of the venue, the arrangement of afternoon tea strikes a balance between honoring tradition and ensuring practicality. Whether enjoyed in the cozy intimacy of a private home or the opulent setting of a luxury hotel, afternoon tea remains an elegant and timeless experience.

TEA ACCESSORIES

Item	Size	Description
Tea Caddy	Varies	An elegant container for tea, once a status symbol. Early ones were silver and small, often locking. Over time, they became larger and more decorative, made from exotic materials like ivory or tortoiseshell. By the nineteenth century, wood caddies, especially mahogany, were common. The tea bag eventually ended their use.
Caddy Spoon	Approx. 1.5 to 2.5 inches	Used to measure loose-leaf tea, following the "one per person and one for the pot" tradition in the UK. Mostly silver, highly decorative, and once essential. Now they're perfect for serving small snacks. The size has reflected tea's value—earlier spoons were small with short handles, later ones resembled teaspoons but with smaller, molded bowls.
Hot Milk Jug	Varies	Once a staple for tea, served piping hot for health benefits. When European porcelain was delicate, hot milk was used to protect it before adding boiling tea. This trend showed off your expensive china and lasted until sturdier porcelain came along.

Hot Water Jug	Varies	Silver-plated and arriving in the late nineteenth century, hot water jugs became essential in large hotels for topping up teapots. Today, they're a rarity in private homes.
Strainer	Varies	A must-have from the late nineteenth century, mainly in silver or silver plate in the UK and Netherlands, with porcelain versions popular in Germany and France. Perfect for catching those pesky tea leaves.
Sugar Bowl	Varies	A status symbol, sugar bowls started small and covered, often in silver or gold. As sugar became more affordable, bowls grew larger but stayed covered until the 1840s. These covered bowls, called sucriers, were often porcelain. By the mid-nineteenth century, open bowls appeared, becoming smaller with granulated sugar in the twentieth century. Silver bowls with twin handles are often part of a tea set.
Sugar Tongs	3 to 5 inches	Essential for serving tea with a touch of elegance. Originally, sugar was expensive and came in solid cones that needed to be chipped. Hostesses used silver sugar tongs to serve these lumps. Early tongs resembled fire tongs, but by the late eighteenth century, they were crafted from a single U-shaped piece of silver. With granulated sugar, smaller tongs were introduced. Though less common today, they add a refined touch to tea service, often seen in hotels.

TEA ACCOMPANIMENTS

The following are traditional and commonly served at private homes.

Lemon	A traditional companion, served in elegant half slices or wedges, seeds delicately removed.
Milk	The classic, always cold, and never cream—a staple in traditional tea service.
Sugar	A must-have, with sugar cubes being more formal than loose sugar. Tongs are essential for cubes, while a spoon is used for loose sugar.

Tea Sandwiches: A Slice of History and Etiquette

Teatime elevates sandwiches to a whole different level. Think dainty, crustless, and impeccably refined. Traditional fillings include smoked salmon, egg mayonnaise, coronation chicken, ham, and of course, cucumber. Why cucumbers? They were a Victorian status symbol. Back then, growing them required expert gardeners, so offering cucumber sandwiches was a subtle flex about your household staff. A bit snobby, yes, but very on-brand for the era.

Tea sandwiches must be small, elegant, and easy to manage. The royal household in Britain serves them square, while others go for rectangles or triangles. Whichever shape you choose, they shouldn't be overfilled—nobody wants a bite to turn into a messy explosion of fillings.

When it comes to serving, tea sandwiches are meant to be picked up from the platter with your fingers, not tongs. While some hotels in Asia or the Middle East may provide tongs for hygiene reasons, it's strictly fingers-only in Britain. Sandwiches are presented on a platter at your table, and guests help themselves to the closest ones, taking one or two at a time. Piling your plate high? That's a no-go. It's perfectly fine to have seconds—just remember to offer your neighbor another before you snag the last one for yourself.

In a well-run hotel or private house, your sandwich platter will be replenished promptly, so there's no need to rush or hoard. The elegance of tea sandwiches isn't just in their size or fillings—it's in the etiquette surrounding them. And that, my friends, is the ultimate bite of sophistication.

The Savory Side of Tea: A Tasty Twist on Tradition

Savories are the wild card of afternoon tea—a little unexpected, a little indulgent, and oh-so-delightful. Some luxury hotels opt to serve a savory treat alongside, or even instead of, traditional finger sandwiches. Whether you're reaching with your fingers or a petite knife and fork depends entirely on the dish—there's no hard-and-fast rule here.

These pre-tea bites are often served cold, though occasionally they arrive warm, adding a touch of cozy surprise. Think along the lines of delicate smoked salmon blini topped with crème fraîche or a perfectly crafted mini quiche Lorraine. At the most exclusive tea experiences, you might find truffle-infused gougères or a petite tartlet filled with caramelized onions and goat cheese.

Scones: An Afternoon Tea Essential

Scones may be synonymous with afternoon tea, but their origins are as rugged and fascinating as the Scottish Highlands. Back in the day, they were triangular, made from oats, and cooked on a griddle[1]—a far cry from the round, flour-based, oven-baked versions we know today.

Traditionally, scones were plain and unassuming, but modern takes often include fruit like currants, sultanas, or raisins. Whether to add them is entirely up to the baker or the eater. As for accompaniments, strawberry, raspberry, or damson jam are the usual suspects. The cream of choice? Clotted cream, rich and heavenly, but often hard to come by outside the UK due to its short shelf life. In a pinch, butter or whipped cream can fill the void—though, let's be honest, it's just not the same.

Interestingly, scones weren't originally part of the traditional afternoon tea spread. English muffins (or tea cakes) held that honor. But somewhere along the way, scones became the star of the show. These days, an afternoon tea without them feels incomplete.

Cheese scones, on the other hand, are in a category of their own. Warm, buttery, and savory, they're more of a stand-alone treat, perfect for a midmorning or afternoon pick-me-up. They don't typically make an appearance at tea service, but they share the same comforting warmth as their sweet counterparts.

So whether you're team plain, fruit, or cheese, there's no denying scones are more than just a teatime treat—they're a delicious slice of history.

ELEGANTLY ENJOYING SCONES

When offered a scone, always choose the one nearest to you—this etiquette applies to any food at the table. In hotels, you might find a tempting mix of plain and fruit scones, while at a friend's place, you might have just one choice.

Freshly baked scones should be broken open with your hands, following their natural seam—no knives needed, unless they're store-bought and need a little extra help.

When it comes to jam and cream (or butter), use separate utensils to keep things neat. Never apply them directly from the pot unless you're dining solo; put a small dollop on your plate.

Whether you prefer cream or jam first is up to you—just layer in small, bite-sized portions. Use your plate as a base, keeping the scone grounded—precision is key, not slathering.

The Takeaway: When You Know What to Do, You Can Focus on Who You're With

Whether you're celebrating a milestone, having a delicious break during your afternoon, or simply enjoying a night off from cooking, dining out is about more than just food and drink—it's about the experience. The time, care, and investment that go into a special outing deserve to be met with equal attention and respect.

Good manners aren't about being fancy or fussy. They're about making everyone—your fellow diners, your hosts, your servers—feel at ease. They help ensure that a shared experience, whether simple or grand, goes as smoothly and enjoyably as possible.

Now many years beyond our first experience at an impossibly elegant restaurant where my husband and I got engaged, we've put in a little more practice to overcome the nerves and newness of all those subtle details.

I've come to appreciate that once you learn the rhythm of fine dining, you don't need to think about every little detail—it becomes second nature. And that's the real gift of etiquette: It lets you relax, be present, and fully enjoy the moment.

Because dining well isn't about showing off—it's about showing up, with grace and appreciation, for an experience meant to be savored.

CHAPTER 9

ETIQUETTE FOR CHALLENGING TIMES

Several years ago, my husband and I had the great privilege of visiting the Holy Land as part of a church group trip. We retraced Jesus' steps through Jerusalem, Bethlehem, Nazareth, and along the shores of the Sea of Galilee. As my husband will cheekily tell anyone who asks, it was not a vacation. It was one of the most spiritually rich and worthwhile experiences of our lives, but it was also intense: long days, a demanding schedule, stretches between meals, an element of vigilance in certain areas, and—how do I say this kindly?—not exactly five-star accommodations.

By the time we returned home, I was spent. I'm an introvert by nature, and after ten days of nonstop travel and togetherness, I was craving solitude in the deepest way. I had just slipped into comfy clothes and was moments away from an early bedtime when a dear friend reached out. She said she needed to talk—and needed to do it in person.

My first thought was, *Can't this wait until tomorrow?* But what she had to say was far more important than my exhaustion.

What she shared was some of the hardest news I've ever had to hear: Her husband—whom she had married just two months earlier in a stunning black-tie wedding at a historic property on the water—had left without warning or explanation. This was the same friend who had just picked out delicate crystal and registered for linens embroidered with their new monogram. The same friend who had poured her heart into creating a home and a future. And now, all of that had shattered—silently and suddenly.

So I did what any good friend should do. I listened. I didn't try to solve it or minimize it. I sat with her in it.

The next morning, she had a brunch scheduled that she'd planned weeks before. She wanted to follow through, to show up as if everything were normal, and I respected that. I picked up paper towels and biscuits and came over early to help her set up. I helped her host by doing little things like setting up the buffet and making sure the bathroom had toilet paper, knowing full well she was holding herself together by a thread.

For a while, I was one of the only people who knew. When she was ready to let others in, I offered to share the news with our mutual friends so she wouldn't have to explain it over and over again. She said yes. Not because she was ashamed, but because repeating the story meant reliving the pain. It meant absorbing the weight of other people's sadness while she was still learning how to carry her own.

Years later, I'm thrilled to say that my friend is now happily remarried to the most wonderful man. He's steady, kind, and adores her—as well he should!

I often think back to that moment—and how important it is to show up for the ones we care about when the stakes are high. It reminded me that etiquette in hard times isn't about having the perfect response, having consistently selfless thoughts, or being endlessly composed. It's about caring enough to inconvenience yourself. It's about stepping into someone else's pain with quiet compassion.

It's not about getting everything "right." Being a kind, caring human will suffice.

Difficulty and disappointment are, regrettably, part of life. And while we can't always prevent the pain, we can choose how we respond to it—both in our own lives and in the lives of those we care about. The pages that follow offer gentle guidance for moving through life's hardest moments with empathy, respect, and quiet strength—because especially in times of heartbreak, thoughtful gestures and steady presence truly matter.

Sharing and Receiving Difficult News

Sharing or receiving difficult news—whether it's about health, family, relationships, or another serious issue—requires a level of care that can sometimes feel overwhelming. But at the heart of these conversations is the goal of communicating with empathy, respect, and, above all, a willingness to listen. Here's how to handle these moments gracefully, whether you're the one sharing difficult news or the one receiving it.

Sharing Difficult News

When you're the one delivering hard news, clarity and compassion are key. Choose a quiet, private setting, giving both of you the time and space to have an uninterrupted conversation. Start with a gentle lead-in like, "I have something difficult to share, and I wanted to tell you in person." This prepares them emotionally, allowing the news to be less of a shock.

Be straightforward but considerate, avoiding excessive details unless they're truly necessary. Offer the information with pauses so the person can process, and give them time to respond in their own way. Some people may react with questions, while others might need silence. Let them set the pace for how the conversation unfolds.

If you sense that they need space to take it in, acknowledge that: "I know this is a lot to absorb. Take whatever time you need." Remember, sharing difficult news isn't just about delivering the message; it's about creating a safe space for whatever response comes next.

Receiving Difficult News

Hearing hard news from someone you care about can be just as challenging, and it's easy to feel at a loss for what to say. In these moments, being present is more powerful than trying to find the right words. Start by simply acknowledging their courage: "Thank you for telling me this—I'm here for you." This shows that you're ready to support them however they need, without judgment or pressure.

Avoid jumping in with solutions, platitudes, or comparisons. Phrases like "Everything will be okay" or "I know how you feel" may come across as dismissive, even if well-intentioned. Instead, keep the focus on their experience. "I can't imagine how you're feeling, but I'm here to listen" or "How can I support you right now?" allows them to steer the conversation based on what they need most.

Give Space for Emotions

When sharing or receiving difficult news, emotions can run high. Letting tears, anger, or silence be part of the conversation is natural and healthy. If you're the one sharing, be prepared for a range of reactions, and give the person time to process their emotions. If you're receiving the news, avoid rushing to smooth things over; sometimes, just sitting with someone in silence is the greatest show of support.

Follow Up Thoughtfully

After a difficult conversation, a thoughtful follow-up can be incredibly meaningful. If you've shared the news, send a message the next day saying, "Thank you for listening—it means a lot to me." If you've received the news, a simple "I've been thinking of you. Here if you need anything" can be comforting, showing that your care continues beyond the initial conversation.

Respect Boundaries

Difficult news often takes time to process, and everyone has a different approach to coping. Some may need time alone, while others may reach out for more frequent support. Respecting their boundaries without prying or pushing ensures that your support is felt without being overbearing.

In these difficult moments, it's not about having the perfect response; it's about being present, respectful, and compassionate. The goal is to make the other person feel heard, respected, and supported, creating a foundation of trust and empathy even in the most challenging of times.

Visiting Hospitals, the Ill, and Bereaved: A Guide to Being Present with Compassion

When someone we care about is going through illness or loss, knowing how to show support can feel daunting. Visits to hospitals, homes, or funeral gatherings call for a gentle balance between offering comfort and respecting boundaries. Here's how to approach these sensitive situations thoughtfully and with compassion.

Visiting Someone in the Hospital

Hospital visits can be a great way to show support, but it's essential to check in first. Reach out to see if they're ready for visitors, and respect any visiting hours or limitations. Keep your visit brief unless they specifically ask you to stay longer—hospital environments can be tiring and even overwhelming. When you're there, focus on positivity. Bring small, thoughtful gestures like a card, flowers (if allowed), or a book to lift their spirits.

Keep the conversation light and avoid excessive questions about their condition unless they bring it up. Sometimes a simple "I'm here if you want to talk about anything" is all they need to feel supported.

Visiting Someone Who Is Ill at Home

When visiting someone who is ill at home, ask ahead of time if they're up for a visit or if there's anything specific they need. Bringing a meal or small gift can be a lovely gesture, but ensure it's something they actually need and can use. As with a hospital visit, keep it short unless they ask you to stay longer.

It's important to focus on being a comforting presence rather than a distraction. Avoid discussing anything overly negative, and allow them to set the tone. Sometimes all they need is your quiet company, and respecting that can mean the world.

Visiting the Bereaved

When visiting someone who is grieving, the simplest gestures are often the most meaningful. Begin by offering your condolences with sincerity and kindness, avoiding clichés like "They're in a better place" or "Everything happens for a reason," which can almost always feel empty or dismissive. Instead, try "I'm so sorry for your loss. I'm here for you."

Offer specific support if you can—"Can I bring you a meal?" or "Let me know if you need a hand with any errands." Don't expect the bereaved to guide the conversation; instead, be prepared to listen if they want to share memories or talk through their feelings, or simply sit in silence if that's what they need.

Respect Boundaries and Know When to Leave

Whether you're visiting someone who is ill or grieving, pay close attention to nonverbal cues. If they seem tired, distracted, or if the conversation starts to lose energy, take it as your sign to gracefully wrap things up. You might say something like, "Thank you for letting me stop by—I'll let you get some rest, but I'm so glad I got to see you."

They may be too polite—or too emotionally exhausted—to ask you to leave, even when they need space. The goal of your visit should always be to comfort, not to burden. Respecting their need for rest or privacy is one of the kindest things you can do.

And if you're ever the one being visited, and you find yourself unsure how to bring the visit to a close, it's perfectly acceptable to set a gentle boundary. A simple "I'm so grateful you came—it means the world. I think I need to rest now, but I really appreciate you for being here" communicates both warmth and honesty.

Illness and grief are tender, unpredictable places. Sometimes, the most gracious thing we can do is give someone permission to take a break—whether that's leaving quietly or kindly asking for a little space.

Thoughtful Follow-Up

After your visit, a simple message like "I'm thinking of you" or "I'm here for you" can mean so much. This lets them know your support continues beyond the initial visit and reminds them they're not alone. Sometimes, offering to stay in touch or checking in on significant dates (like anniversaries or birthdays) can be comforting reminders that you're there, even when others may have moved on.

Stay Mindful of Your Role

Remember, when visiting the ill or bereaved, your presence should be a source of comfort rather than a distraction. Avoid focusing on your own feelings, and let the person take the lead on what they need from you.

Simply being there, listening, and offering practical support may speak louder than well-meaning words.

Death and Funerals: Offering Support with Sensitivity

When someone experiences the loss of a loved one, knowing what to say—or do—can feel overwhelming. Grief is deeply personal, and honoring the customs and etiquette around death and funerals requires empathy, patience, and thoughtful restraint. But even the smallest kindness can offer comfort in a time of profound sorrow.

I grew up in a family where funerals weren't just attended—they were honored. My dad was an altar boy for countless Irish Catholic funeral masses as a child, and later, one of his most trusted mentors was a beloved local funeral director. In our community, paying respects was more than a gesture—it was a way of life. To this day, I watch my dad take time off from work to attend funerals—not because he's playing hooky (as a small business owner, he's never short on responsibilities), but because he believes deeply in the importance of showing up to mark the end of a life and to support those left behind. That sense of reverence, of presence, has stayed with me.

I have the utmost respect for the people who dedicate their lives to honoring the end of life—hospice nurses, doctors, grief counselors, funeral home staff, and the quiet heroes who handle the details behind the scenes. Their work is more than a job; it's a ministry of presence, dignity, and care. They often step into moments when others feel lost or overwhelmed, and they do so with steadiness and grace.

Across different cultures and faith traditions, there's a kind of rhythm to how we honor those we've lost. Whether it's the murmurs of a rosary, the gathering of neighbors around casseroles and stories, a Shiva call with quiet hugs and covered mirrors, or a traditional tea ceremony held in memory—what these moments have in common is presence. They give structure to sorrow and remind the bereaved that they are not alone. This section is written with deep respect for those varied traditions, and with the hope that you'll find comfort and clarity here, no matter what rituals or customs are familiar to you.

So much of etiquette during times of grief is about showing up—quietly, respectfully, and without expectation. This isn't the time for clever words or grand gestures. It's a time to be of service, whether that means writing a heartfelt note, dropping off food without fanfare, or simply sitting beside someone in silence.

The following pages offer gentle guidance on how to support others during some of life's hardest moments. There's no one right way to grieve, but there are ways to walk alongside someone with compassion and care.

- **Expressing Condolences:** A heartfelt condolence doesn't need to be long or elaborate. Sometimes, a simple "I'm so sorry for your loss" or "I'm thinking of you" is enough. If you were close to the deceased, sharing a brief memory can also be comforting: "I'll always remember how they made everyone laugh at gatherings." Avoid clichés like "They're in a better place," as they can feel empty to someone grieving. Remember, your words should show understanding, not attempt to explain the loss.
- **Attending the Funeral:** If you're attending a funeral, arrive a few minutes early to allow yourself time to find a seat quietly. Dress in conservative, respectful clothing, usually in dark colors, unless the family has specifically requested otherwise. During the service, keep conversations to a minimum; your presence alone is often enough. When interacting with the family, offer a simple greeting, express your sympathy, and avoid overwhelming them with questions or lengthy conversations.
- **Offering Practical Support:** In times of grief, people often appreciate gestures that require minimal effort on their part. Offering specific help—such as providing meals, assisting with errands, or helping to organize post-funeral arrangements—can be a true comfort. Instead of saying, "Let me know if you need anything," try something more concrete, like, "I'd love to drop off a meal this week. Would that be helpful?" Thoughtful support lets the bereaved focus on their grieving without the added stress of managing daily tasks.
- **Sending Flowers or Donations:** Sending flowers is a traditional and

thoughtful way to show support, but if the family has requested donations in lieu of flowers, respect their wishes. This might mean donating to a charity that was important to the deceased, which shows you're honoring their legacy in a meaningful way. If you do send flowers, include a brief, warm note, such as, "With deepest sympathy" or "In loving memory of [Name]."

- **Respecting Cultural or Religious Customs:** Different cultures and religions have unique traditions when it comes to funerals and mourning, so take the time to understand any specific customs. If you're unfamiliar with the family's practices, it's perfectly acceptable to ask beforehand or look it up. Showing respect for their customs, whether by observing a moment of silence, participating in a prayer, or refraining from certain behaviors, demonstrates your sensitivity and respect.
- **Following Up After the Funeral:** Grieving doesn't end with the funeral, and many people feel an increased sense of loneliness in the weeks that follow. A thoughtful follow-up, like a text, card, or call a few weeks after the service, can mean a lot. You might say, "Just checking in—I'm here if you need to talk or meet up," which shows continued support without putting pressure on them to respond. On significant dates like birthdays or anniversaries, a quick message to let them know you're thinking of them can also be a quiet yet powerful gesture of solidarity.
- **Respecting Boundaries and Privacy:** Grief is deeply personal, and everyone mourns in their own way. Avoid pressing for details about the death or asking intrusive questions about the family's feelings or plans. Give them space to share as much—or as little—as they feel comfortable with, and respect their need for privacy. Your role is to offer comfort, not answers.

Approaching death and funerals with respect, humility, and gentleness allows you to be a supportive presence in someone's life during a difficult time. Remember, it's often the quiet, thoughtful gestures—the ones that require little effort from the grieving—that mean the most.

Pregnancy Loss

Pregnancy loss is a deeply personal and often painful experience, one that can leave even the most well-meaning friends and family unsure of what to say or how to help. At its heart, etiquette around pregnancy loss is about offering support in a way that respects the grieving person's emotions and their unique way of processing loss.

- **Acknowledge the loss thoughtfully.** Sometimes people hesitate to bring up a loss, thinking it might add to the person's pain, but often the opposite is true. A simple, heartfelt acknowledgment can mean the world. You could say, "I'm so sorry for your loss. I'm here for you if you want to talk or just need someone to sit with." By acknowledging their grief, you're showing them that they're not alone and that their experience matters.
- **Avoid clichés or unsolicited advice.** When comforting someone, there's a natural impulse to say things like, "Everything happens for a reason" or "You can always try again." While these phrases are well-intentioned, they often feel dismissive. Instead, focus on their feelings in the moment. "I can't imagine how hard this must be for you" or "Please know that I'm here for whatever you need" can be much more comforting than any attempt to make sense of the situation.
- **Offer specific help.** After a loss, many people are too overwhelmed to reach out, even if they need support. Rather than saying, "Let me know if there's anything I can do," offer specific forms of help: "Would it be okay if I dropped off a meal this week?" or "I'd love to go on a walk with you if you ever want to get outside."

  Being specific shows that you're not just offering empty words; you're genuinely prepared to be there in ways that might ease their burden.

And it's worth noting: Depending on the circumstances, especially in cases of miscarriage, stillbirth, or infant loss, your friend may also be physically recovering in ways that are intense and often invisible.

A midwife once shared with me that the physical demands on a woman's body in these situations can be just as significant as those following a live birth, often requiring ongoing medical care and rest. People don't always realize this, so your awareness can be a quiet, powerful kindness.

Whether it's practical support or simply lightening the load, your thoughtful offer could be the thing that helps someone get through the day.

- **Respect their privacy.** Everyone processes loss differently, so respect their pace and privacy. Some may want to share their feelings openly, while others may need space. Avoid pressing for details or updates, and let them take the lead on what they're comfortable discussing. Simply let them know that you're available whenever they feel ready to talk.
- **Be mindful of anniversaries.** A thoughtful message on a significant date—like the due date or the anniversary of the loss—can be incredibly meaningful. A gentle "I'm thinking of you today" can remind them that their experience isn't forgotten, even as time moves on. It's a small but powerful way of letting them know they have your continued support.
- **Keep the door open.** Grief can ebb and flow, and the need for support may come and go too. Sometimes the hardest days come weeks or months after the initial loss, when others might have moved on. Let them know you're there in the long term: "I'm always here if you need anything, no matter when."

By approaching the topic of pregnancy loss with care, sensitivity, and a focus on the other person's needs, you create space for them to feel supported and seen without feeling overwhelmed. It's a small but meaningful way of letting someone know they're not alone, honoring their journey without trying to dictate or diminish it.

How to Acknowledge Someone's Loss When You Didn't Know the Person

It can feel tricky to know how to support someone when you didn't know the person they've lost. But here's the thing: Acknowledging their loss is less about your relationship with the person who passed and more about showing you care about the person grieving.

Start simple. A heartfelt, "I'm so sorry for your loss" can offer real comfort. If you knew something about the person who passed, mentioning something specific can make your gesture even more meaningful:

- "I heard your dad was an incredible storyteller. I'm sure he'll be deeply missed."
- "I didn't know your friend, but I can tell they meant so much to you. I'm so sorry for your loss."

Sometimes, just letting them know you're there is enough. A text, a card, or even just being present can speak volumes. Remember, this isn't about having the perfect words—it's about showing up with compassion and letting them know they're not alone.

Best Practices for Acknowledging Condolences

When the loss is yours, it can be overwhelming to receive the outpouring of support. People mean well, but let's be honest—it's a lot. Acknowledging condolences doesn't have to be elaborate or immediate, but it is a kind gesture that lets people know their support meant something to you.

It used to be expected that every single person who sent flowers, a meal, or a card would receive a handwritten thank-you note in return. And while that tradition was rooted in thoughtfulness, we also have to acknowledge the reality: Grief is exhausting. I believe we now can offer one another a bit more flexibility and understanding. If sitting down to write dozens of notes feels emotionally or physically impossible, that's okay.

If you're up for it, though, a simple thank-you note or message is always appreciated:

- "Thank you so much for your kind words during this difficult time. Your support means more than I can say."
- "I truly appreciate you reaching out. Knowing I have people like you in my corner has been such a comfort."

A heartfelt thank-you in person, a short call when you're ready, or even a general message shared at a later date can be just as meaningful. And please don't feel pressured to respond to every message individually. Most people understand that grief takes up a tremendous amount of emotional space—and the people who love you aren't keeping score.

The most important thing? Be kind to yourself. Acknowledging condolences is less about following formalities and more about connecting with the people who've shown you love during a tough time. Do what feels right for you, and remember—it's okay to let others support you when you need it most.

Breakups and Divorces: When Love Stories Take a Different Turn

There's something about a breakup that can send even the strongest of us into a tailspin. Suddenly, you're not just losing a partner—you're shifting your life's entire narrative. And as friends, we find ourselves wondering: How do we help without overstepping? How do we offer comfort without turning into the peanut gallery? Here's how to handle those delicate moments.

- **Offer compassion, not commentary.** No matter how much you may have been rooting for—or against—the relationship, this isn't the time to dig up old judgments. Skip the "I never liked them anyway" and instead go with, "I'm here for you, however you need." Your friend is going through enough without your opinions in the mix; they're looking for support, not a play-by-play on what went wrong.
- **Respect their privacy.** If they're not ready to spill every detail, respect that. It's natural to be curious, but give them the space to share what they're comfortable with, when they're comfortable with it. A simple "I'm here if you ever need to talk" is like a soft landing spot that lets them know you're there—no prying questions required.
- **Navigate mutual friends with care.** When you're friends with a couple who have split—whether it's a breakup, a falling-out, or something messier—it can feel like you're suddenly stuck in a rom-com love

triangle. But you don't have to pick a side to be a good friend. Think of yourself as a calm middle ground, not the referee. Avoid taking sides or playing mediator. If you're close with both people, your job isn't to fix it—it's to offer kindness without turning their split into a battlefield.

What that looks like in real life:

- **Avoid gossip.** If one person starts venting, gently redirect with something like, "I care about both of you, and I really want to stay neutral—I hope that's okay."
- **Be thoughtful about invitations.** If you're hosting a group event and both parties are invited, give each a heads-up. Try: "I wanted to let you know that I've invited [Name] as well. I completely understand if that's not comfortable, and there's no pressure either way."
- **Don't pry or pick at the story.** If one friend wants to open up, listen with empathy but avoid fishing for details or trying to solve it. For example, "I'm so sorry this has been hard. I'm here to support you in whatever way feels helpful."
- **Create emotional boundaries.** If you're feeling caught in the middle, it's okay to say so: "I really want to be a good friend to both of you, and I'm trying to stay out of the details so I don't make things harder."

  It's possible—and kind—to hold space for both people without becoming a go-between. People will remember how you made them feel during hard times. Let that memory be one of compassion and quiet strength, not sides taken or gossip repeated.
- **Save the advice for when they ask.** They've probably already heard it all, from "you're better off" to "get back out there," and chances are, they're not looking for a pep talk. Instead of playing life coach, just listen. Let them know, "I'm here for whatever you need—no advice required." Trust that they'll find their way in their own time, without you steering the ship.
- **Suggest small, uplifting activities.** Breakups are exhausting, so help them unwind with something simple and low-key. Invite them for a coffee run, a movie night, or a quiet walk. These easy outings

remind them there's more to life than heartbreak, and help them reconnect with themselves, one small step at a time.

- **Check in, again and again.** Breakups don't have expiration dates, and sometimes the hardest part comes weeks or months after the fact. A quick message or a casual "thinking of you" can mean a great deal, even after the dust settles. A well-timed text can be the reminder that they're still surrounded by love, even when they're feeling lonely.
- **Let them heal on their own timeline.** Everyone has their own way of processing a breakup, so let them go at their own pace. Whether they need a few quiet months or are back out there the next week, trust that they know what's best for themselves. Remind yourself: The best support is the kind that empowers, not pressures.

Supporting a friend through a breakup or divorce means letting them take center stage in their own story while standing by as a steady, caring presence. It's not about offering answers—it's about showing up, over and over, in whatever way they need. And sometimes, just being there to help them write a new chapter is the most powerful thing you can do.

Q: *I was in a serious relationship where we posted a lot of our lives on social media, and after it ended, knowing what to do with all of our posts together was one of the hardest parts. I wasn't ready to tell the world that we were separating yet, but I also wanted to take down every picture of our past together. Am I terrible for thinking that? I'm not sure about the best approach.*

A: Social media post-breakup can feel like rewriting a very public love story—one that you're not quite sure how to edit yet. And no, you're not terrible for wanting to clear the slate. Each picture, every shared memory, is a snapshot of a life you're no longer living. The question isn't whether you should take down the photos; it's about when you're ready and what feels healthiest for you.

One option? Start with a "soft archive." Most platforms let you hide posts without deleting them forever, giving you some time to adjust before making any permanent moves. This way, you're not erasing history, just tucking it away until you're ready to decide what to keep, if anything. Or, if there are posts that still feel meaningful—like moments of friendship or personal milestones—consider leaving those. They can stand as reminders of your own journey, separate from the relationship.

The most important thing is to honor what feels right for you. Breakups are about reclaiming your space and story, and sometimes that means clearing out old snapshots to make room for new ones.

The Takeaway: When Words Fall Short, Kindness Doesn't

I still think about that night when I came home from the Holy Land, bone-tired and craving silence—only to find myself pulled into one of the most painful moments a dear friend had ever experienced. I didn't have the perfect words. I wasn't the perfect friend. But I wanted to show up for her. So I listened. I brought biscuits. And sometimes, that's what love looks like.

This chapter isn't a checklist of how to get it right during hard times. It's a reminder that even in grief, illness, heartbreak, or loss, what people most often need is to feel acknowledged and supported. They need someone to notice, to care, and to stand quietly beside them when the world has gone sideways.

Whether you're helping a friend through a breakup, writing a condolence card, visiting someone in the hospital, or gently sharing difficult news, etiquette in these moments isn't about formality—it's about humanity. It's about soft landings. Thoughtful boundaries. Knowing when to sit in silence and when to bring paper towels.

CHAPTER 10

MANNERS ON THE MOVE

My very first job was working for the *Bunny Clark*, a deep-sea fishing boat based out of Perkins Cove in Ogunquit, Maine. I was in high school at the time, and my days were spent perched in an Adirondack chair in the back of a pickup truck (it makes more sense if you've been there, I promise). I answered phones, sold tickets and merchandise, and had hours upon hours to simply sit and observe visitors, tourists, and locals.

That summer was a master class in people-watching—and, as I later realized, in etiquette.

There were the visitors who handled travel hiccups with patience and the ones who argued loudly over parking spots. The locals who welcomed tourists with kindness, and the ones who looked down on anyone who didn't know the ropes. There were guests who monopolized my attention with long-winded stories I didn't have the heart to interrupt, and frazzled parents doing their best to manage a toddler melting down after an hours-long car ride. And through it all, I quietly took note.

I decided over these summers that when I'm out and about, whether at home or traveling, I never want to be the person who picks a fight over a parking space, talks endlessly to someone who can't step away, or sneers at visitors who are simply figuring it out as they go. I never want to judge a parent for a child's outburst without knowing what kind of week—or year—they've had.

Travel etiquette isn't just for glamorous hotels in Dubai, gallery openings in Paris, or temples in Kyoto. It's just as important in the small fishing villages of Maine too. Wherever we go—whether it's down the street or across the ocean—how we carry ourselves in shared spaces is a reflection of our values, our awareness, and our care for others.

Flying with Finesse: The Etiquette of Air Travel

Air travel: It's equal parts adventure and test of patience, where you're contending with cramped spaces, unspoken rules, and the occasional overzealous recliner. While it might not always be glamorous, how you carry yourself in the skies says a lot about your grace under pressure. Here's how to jet-set with poise, charm, and consideration for your fellow passengers:

Don't Dillydally

Or at the very least, don't get in others' way. Delays, cancellations, flight changes, and tight connections are becoming more and more common. When moving about the airport, don't block escalators, moving walkways, and the like, and be considerate of others and their schedules.

A Smooth Start: Boarding Etiquette

Boarding isn't a race—it's a process. If your group hasn't been called yet, hang back and let those ahead of you board first. Hovering at the gate like it's the starting line of a marathon only adds to the chaos. Once it's your turn, have your boarding pass ready and your carry-on organized. Nothing says "I don't fly often" like digging through your bag while holding up the line.

Respect Overhead Bin Space

Carry-ons go in the overhead bin above your seat, not three rows back or in someone else's space. If you've got multiple bags, stow the smaller one under the seat in front of you. Remember, the overhead bin isn't your personal closet—it's shared real estate.

The Recline Debate

The great seat-recline debate. Yes, it's your right to recline, but consider the person behind you. Is their tray table covered in snacks, or are they clearly trying to work? A polite glance back and a slow recline shows you're aware that your comfort shouldn't come at their expense.

Armrest Etiquette

The middle seat gets both armrests. Period. If you're in the aisle or window, you already have an edge—either extra legroom or the view—so let the middle passenger have their moment of comfort.

Keep It Clean

Treat the airplane like a shared living room, not your personal den. Take your trash with you when you leave, avoid draping your long hair over the seatback (it's not a curtain), and please, no bare feet and no clipping your nails.

Be Mindful of Volume

Whether it's chatting with your seatmate, watching a movie, or playing music, keep the volume in check. Use earbuds, keep conversations low, and avoid turning the row into your personal stage.

Bathroom Boundaries

If you're in the aisle seat, be gracious about letting others out to use the restroom. If you're in the window or middle, try to time your trips strategically. And please, for the love of all things travel, wear shoes when you walk to the bathroom.

Be Gracious with Kids (and Their Parents)

Let's be real: Traveling with kids is a high-stakes game for parents. Between wrangling snacks, keeping little ones entertained, and navigating new surroundings, they're already working overtime to keep their family (and the cabin) calm. So, when you see a parent struggling, channel your inner grace and patience.

Parents have every right to buy tickets for their children anywhere on the plane, including in first or business class. There's no such thing as a designated "family section" on most airlines, and while a crying baby or a restless toddler might disrupt your peace, no one is more aware of the disruption than the parent. Trust me—they're not enjoying it either.

Instead of sighing loudly or throwing side-eye, try offering a smile or even a helping hand if it feels appropriate—whether it's assisting with a stroller at security or helping lift a bag during boarding. One mom once told me the best advice she got was, "At the airport, always accept the help!" After flying solo with a little one, she was deeply grateful for the strangers who stepped up. Even a simple "You're doing great" can mean the world to a parent who's balancing in-flight chaos while trying to keep it together themselves.

And if you're concerned about noise, come prepared—with headphones or earbuds, a playlist, or a good book. It's a small investment in your own comfort and a much better alternative to passive-aggressive glares.

Kindness Is Key

Travel can bring out the worst in people, but that's no excuse to be rude. Be polite to flight attendants (they're working hard for you), smile at your seatmate, and roll with the punches. A little compassion at thirty thousand feet never hurts.

Q: *How do I set boundaries around personal space on a crowded flight without seeming overly sensitive or rude? I don't want to be "that person," but I also value my space.*

A: Personal space on a crowded flight can feel like a silent negotiation, especially when everyone's crammed in shoulder to shoulder. To keep your boundaries politely, start with your posture: Sit comfortably, using your armrest in a relaxed but definite way—this signals that you're mindful of your space.

If a neighbor's elbow or leg begins to drift over, a subtle shift or repositioning can remind them without needing to say a word. And if things get too close for comfort, a simple "Excuse me, could I have a little more room?" with a quick smile is usually all it takes. You'll stay gracious, protect your space, and keep the peace.

Visiting Houses of Worship: Grace, Respect, and Cultural Awareness

Walking into a house of worship is more than stepping into a building—it's entering a sacred space where centuries of tradition, faith, and community converge. Whether you're marveling at Angkor Wat in Cambodia, kneeling at the Western Wall in Jerusalem, or exploring a Gothic cathedral in Italy, how you conduct yourself matters. The etiquette of visiting these places varies, but the universal rule is simple: Respect the space, its traditions, and its people. Here's your guide to visiting houses of worship with poise and cultural sensitivity.

General Dos and Don'ts for Any House of Worship

TURN OFF THE ELECTRONICS

Silence your phone, smartwatch, and any other devices. A beep or buzz during a service or quiet moment can disrupt the sacred atmosphere.

DRESS MODESTLY

Cover your shoulders and knees unless you know for sure the dress code is more relaxed. Bringing a scarf, shawl, or sweater is always a good idea—it's a stylish and practical way to ensure you're prepared, and yes, this even applies at major tourist-destination churches in the sweltering summer heat across Europe.

My husband learned this the hard way at a church in Israel, where he didn't quite believe me about the no-shorts dress code. Needless to say, he wasn't thrilled when my purple fringe shawl had to double as a makeshift sarong over his khaki shorts. It wasn't his most stylish moment, but at least he made it through the door.

REFRAIN FROM LOUD CONVERSATIONS

Whisper if you must speak, but better yet, soak in the silence. Loud chatter in a sacred space is not only disrespectful but also jarring to others seeking peace or prayer.

ASK BEFORE TAKING PHOTOS

Some sites forbid photography altogether, while others allow it but with restrictions like no flash. Always check before snapping, and remember that your camera doesn't need to capture every moment. If photos aren't allowed, signs will typically say so, and when in doubt ask a docent or other staff member for help and watch for signage at or near the entrance indicating an event in progress.

BE MINDFUL OF TIMING

Avoid visiting during services, ceremonies, or prayer times unless you're invited to observe. Research the best times to visit or ask staff upon arrival.

Buddhist Temples: Serenity and Reverence

SHOES OFF, PLEASE

Leave your shoes and hats at the designated area before entering. A pile of sandals and sneakers is your first clue.

COVER UP

Shoulders and legs should be covered. Light layers and a shawl are your best friends in the often hot and humid climates where temples are found.

NO TOUCHING

Don't touch or climb on Buddha statues. Resist the urge to snap a selfie up close or, worse, drape yourself over a statue for a photo.

STAND FOR MONKS AND NUNS

Show respect by standing when monks or nuns enter a room.

MIND YOUR MANNERS

Use your right hand for giving or receiving items, and don't point with your fingers—gesture with an open hand instead.

Hindu Temples: Vibrant and Sacred

SHOES AND LEATHER STAY OUTSIDE

In addition to removing shoes, it's polite to leave leather items like belts or jackets outside the temple.

DRESS MODESTLY

Avoid sleeveless tops or short skirts and shorts. Long pants or skirts paired with a scarf or shawl show respect.

PHOTOGRAPHY WITH PERMISSION

Always ask before photographing statues or deities. A small donation is a thoughtful gesture when taking photos.

Muslim Mosques: Modesty and Respect

Visiting the Al-Aqsa Mosque compound in Jerusalem was one of the most memorable and humbling moments of our time in the Holy Land. The space is sacred to millions and carries deep historical, spiritual, and political significance. I remember wearing a long coat that day—ankle-length and loose—so I was appropriately dressed. But several other women in our group, wearing tighter pants or shorter jackets, were kindly but firmly handed long skirts to wear over their clothes before we could proceed as we went through security at the entrance. These were available on-site for visitors, and while the moment was a little uncomfortable, it was also a reminder that we were entering a holy place—one that deserved our humility and respect.

When we paused to take a group photo, someone instinctively put an arm around a friend's shoulder in a standard American pose. But before the camera could even click, a staff member firmly called out, "No touching! This is a holy place!" The message was clear: This wasn't just a place for sightseeing or social media moments. Even small gestures that might seem completely normal elsewhere—like the casual half-hug photo pose Americans are so accustomed to—were out of place there.

The environment felt tense at times, and I'd be lying if I said I wasn't nervous. This is a place that has, tragically, been the site of conflict and violence over the years. I didn't want to do anything—knowingly or unknowingly—that might escalate tension or show disrespect. That experience reminded me that etiquette in sacred spaces isn't about rules for the sake of rules. It's about reverence, awareness, and taking the posture of a guest in someone else's spiritual home.

Here are a few things every visitor should know before entering a mosque—especially one as significant as Al-Aqsa:

COVER UP COMPLETELY

Women should bring a scarf to cover their hair, and all visitors—men and women—should wear ankle-length clothing with long sleeves. Avoid tight, sheer, or flashy clothing. Even if your outfit seems "modest enough" by your own standards, be prepared to adapt if asked. It's not personal—it's cultural and spiritual.

SEPARATE ENTRANCES AND SPACES

Many mosques have designated areas for men and women, including separate entrances and prayer spaces. If you're unsure, watch for signs or follow the flow of other visitors. It's always okay to ask a staff member quietly and respectfully.

SHOES OFF

Remove your shoes before entering any prayer hall and leave them in the designated area. It's a good idea to wear socks and bring a bag to carry your shoes if you're moving between spaces.

Christian Churches: Tradition and Variety

SHOES OFF IN SOME CASES

In places like Ethiopia, shoes should be removed before entering. This isn't the norm in most Western churches, but always check local customs.

COVER SHOULDERS AND KNEES

Especially in Catholic or Orthodox churches, modest dress is a sign of respect.

DON'T CROSS YOUR LEGS

In Greek Orthodox churches, crossing your legs is considered disrespectful.

SILENCE DURING SERVICES

If you happen to visit during a service, stay quiet, observe respectfully, and stand toward the back to avoid disruption.

Jewish Synagogues: Tradition and Reverence

YARMULKES FOR MEN

Men, and even young boys, should wear a yarmulke (available at most entrances) as a sign of respect.

DRESS CONSERVATIVELY

Women often wear dresses or skirts, and men typically wear suits or business casual attire. Long sleeves are encouraged for both.

NO PHOTOGRAPHY ON SHABBAT

During Shabbat (from Friday evening to Saturday evening), photography is prohibited.

AT THE WESTERN WALL IN JERUSALEM

Never turn your back on the wall when leaving. Walk backward a few steps before turning around, as a sign of reverence.

Key Takeaways for Any House of Worship

- **When in doubt, ask.** If you're unsure about a custom, ask a guide or someone who works at the site. Most will be happy to help you avoid an unintentional faux pas.
- **Observe before acting.** Watch how locals behave and follow their lead.

- **Bring layers.** A scarf or sweater can save the day when modesty is required.
- **Respect the sacred.** Whether it's a statue, a religious leader, or a quiet space, treat everything and everyone with care.

Visiting a house of worship is more than just seeing beautiful architecture—it's about experiencing the heart of a culture. A little awareness and a lot of respect will leave you feeling not just like a traveler, but an ambassador of kindness and grace. Ultimately, the most meaningful souvenirs are the connections you make along the way.

Exploring Museums with Courtesy and Care

Museums are magical spaces where history, art, and culture come to life. Whether you're admiring a Monet, exploring ancient artifacts, or marveling at interactive exhibits, how you conduct yourself is part of the experience. In a world eager to rediscover its treasures, it's essential to remember that museums, like any other sacred space, come with unspoken (and spoken) rules. Here's your guide to moving through them with thoughtfulness, respect, and quiet appreciation.

The Flash Dilemma: Ask Before You Snap

Museums may feel like social media gold mines, but not every exhibit is camera-friendly. Visible and invisible light from flashes can damage delicate artifacts, which is why many institutions ban flash photography. Always check the rules before snapping a shot, and when in doubt, ask permission from a museum staff member. Think of your phone as a polite guest—it's there to document, not disrupt.

Check Your Bags at the Door

Your oversized tote might complete your outfit, but it's a hazard in a gallery. Large bags, backpacks, and coats usually need to be left at the coat check or in lockers near the entrance. A baggage-free visit is not only more comfortable but also less likely to end with a knocked-over sculpture.

Look, Don't Touch

That Grecian urn may be beautiful, but your fingerprints don't belong on it. The oils from your hands can cause irreversible damage, which is why touching is generally forbidden. The exception? Interactive exhibits, which are made for curious fingers—but even then, check for posted guidelines before diving in. Remember, "fingerprints are forever," and not in a good way.

Keep It Calm and Collected

Museums are not the place for impromptu games of tag. Running, shoving, and other forms of horseplay can not only ruin artifacts but also disturb other visitors. If you're visiting with children, explore family-friendly areas and keep a watchful eye on those little hands.

Use Your Inside Voice

Channel your inner country-club member and keep your voice low and measured. Museums are places of quiet reflection, not Broadway auditions. Turn your phone to silent, avoid loud conversations, and step outside if you must take a call. And while you're at it, leave the whistling and singing for the car ride home.

Sketch, but Follow the Rules

If the art inspires you to grab a sketchpad, check the museum's policies first. Many allow only pencil use in galleries to prevent accidental damage. Be prepared with the proper materials and follow any restrictions to avoid trouble with security.

Snacks Stay in the Café

No one wants to see crumbs near a priceless painting. Eating and drinking in galleries is strictly prohibited, so plan your visit after a meal or take advantage of the museum's café. Even gum and candy can be frowned upon—when in doubt, ask before you chew.

The Golden Rule: Respect the Space

Every museum has its own unique set of rules, and following them ensures a meaningful visit for everyone. From being mindful of others to safeguarding priceless artifacts, practicing good etiquette shows respect for the experience. Museums are about more than just the past—they're about preserving beauty for future generations. Step lightly, speak softly, and let the art do the talking.

Theater Etiquette: How to Be a Class Act

Going to a live performance is like stepping into another world—one where the magic of storytelling, music, or dance comes alive before your eyes. But no matter how dazzling the stage is, the audience plays a role too. Knowing how to conduct yourself not only enhances your experience but also shows respect for the performers and fellow attendees.

Style Is Timeless—Your Arrival Shouldn't Be

There's nothing chic about stumbling into the theater after the lights have dimmed. Plan your arrival with time to spare—account for traffic, parking, or that last-minute dash to the restroom. Many venues won't seat latecomers, and showing up late means disrupting the experience for everyone else. Aim to be in your seat at least fifteen minutes before showtime.

Silence Is Golden

Phones are wonderful, but not during a performance. Turn off all devices—or at the very least, silence them (and consider switching to airplane mode). A rogue ringtone during a dramatic pause is a faux pas you won't recover from. If you must take an emergency call, quietly excuse yourself and step outside.

The most meaningful souvenirs are the connections you make along the way.

Watch, Don't Chatter

Even the juiciest plot twist in a play isn't an invitation to discuss it with your neighbor mid-show. Talking—even in whispers—is distracting for both the audience and the performers. Save your commentary for intermission or the ride home.

No Unscheduled Duets

Yes, you know all the words to "Defying Gravity," but that doesn't mean the rest of the theater wants to hear your rendition. Unless the performers explicitly invite audience participation, keep your vocal stylings to yourself.

The Performer Is the Star, Not Your Camera

Most productions strictly prohibit photography and recording for good reason—it's distracting, disruptive, and often illegal. Leave the flash off and focus on enjoying the moment.

Stay Seated, Stay Engaged

While it may be tempting to beat the crowd, leaving your seat before the final bow is a major no-no. The performers have poured their hearts into the production; the least you can do is stay to applaud their efforts. When the house lights come up, that's your cue to gather your things and exit gracefully.

Respect the Performers' Space

If you're lucky enough to meet the artists at a stage door or post-performance event, be gracious and respectful. Compliments are welcome, but don't cross boundaries by asking for personal information or lingering too long. A heartfelt "Thank you for such a wonderful performance" will always be well-received.

Dress the Part

While dress codes vary by venue, it's always better to be slightly over-dressed than underdressed. Think smart casual at a minimum or something elegant for a formal event. Your outfit should show respect for the occasion and the effort that went into the production.

Keep Snacks in the Lobby

While some modern theaters allow food and drinks, it's best to consume anything noisy or aromatic before you take your seat. The sound of crunching popcorn can compete with even the best orchestra. Use your best judgment on whether your snacks will distract.

Show Gratitude

If you loved the performance—whether it was a play, a symphony, a solo recital, or something in between—show your appreciation with warm, enthusiastic applause at the appropriate time. If there's a curtain call or final bow, that's your cue to let the performers know their work resonated. Standing ovations are a powerful gesture, but they're most meaningful when reserved for truly extraordinary moments, not every single performance.

The Curtain Call: Why Etiquette Matters

Attending a performance is a shared experience—it's about everyone in the room. By following these guidelines, you help create an atmosphere where the magic of live entertainment can shine. The beauty of a night at the theater lies in its ability to transport us, and being a thoughtful audience member ensures everyone gets to enjoy the show.

Moving with Manners: Elevators, Escalators, and Stairs Made Simple

Navigating elevators, escalators, and stairs might not seem like the stage for etiquette, but these small, everyday moments can say a lot about who you are. Whether you're rushing to a meeting, riding with strangers, or gracefully descending a grand staircase, the way you handle yourself in tight spaces shows how much you value those around you. Here's how to keep it classy, whether you're headed up, down, or in between:

Elevator Etiquette: Rising to the Occasion

Elevators may be small, but they're big on opportunities to show kindness.

DON'T CROWD THE DOORS

Hovering at the elevator like it's Black Friday at a department store is a no-go. Stand to the side, let others exit first, and enter when it's your turn—smooth and simple.

BE THE BUTTON HERO

If you're closest to the panel, congratulations—you're in charge of the buttons. Hold the "door open" button for others, especially if they're juggling strollers, luggage, or just moving a little slower. This small gesture leaves a big impression.

MIND THE PERSONAL BUBBLE

In crowded elevators, space is at a premium. Face forward, keep your bag close, and save the life updates for when you're out of the box. If your phone rings, it can wait.

EXIT GRACEFULLY

Heading out? A polite "excuse me" works wonders. If someone behind you needs to leave first, step aside and let them through—no dramatic exits required.

Escalator Etiquette: Keep the Flow Moving

Escalators are like highways—there's a fast lane and a slow lane, and knowing which is which keeps everyone happy.

STAND RIGHT, WALK LEFT

If you're just along for the ride, stand on the right. Leave the left side clear for those who prefer to power-walk their way to the top.

STEP ON AND OFF LIKE A PRO

No sudden stops, no second guesses. Keep a steady pace as you step on and off. If you're wrangling kids or luggage, make sure everything is secure before you hop on.

USE A LIGHT TOUCH ON HANDRAILS

Leaning on a handrail might feel casual, but it's there for balance, not lounging. And sliding down the rail? It's a hard no—it's unsafe and, let's be honest, a little ridiculous.

KEEP CONVERSATIONS IN CHECK

Escalator rides are brief. Keep chats low and don't hold up traffic—save the TED Talk for coffee later.

Stair Etiquette: Steps to Success

Stairs might be the oldest mode of transportation, but they're still ripe for etiquette opportunities.

KEEP TO THE RIGHT

Whether it's a grand staircase or a subway entrance, stay to the right and leave the left side open for people in a hurry. It's traffic flow 101.

PACE YOURSELF

Moving slow? Stick to the edge so faster climbers can pass. Feeling energetic? Power up or down with care—nobody's impressed by a near-miss collision.

DON'T HOG THE RAIL

The handrail isn't just for decoration. Keep it clear for those who need extra support, and if you're carrying bulky items, stay mindful of the space you take up.

NO MID-STEP STOPPING

Need to check your phone or fix your bag? Move to a landing or step aside. Stopping in the middle of a staircase is a surefire way to create a domino effect of frustration.

Awareness Is Everything

Whether you're riding an elevator, gliding on an escalator, or taking the stairs two at a time, the key to good etiquette is simple: Stay aware.

Hold the door, step aside, keep the flow moving, and remember that even small acts of courtesy can make someone's day a little brighter.

Because everyday moments aren't just about getting from point A to point B—they're about how we go through life, with a little more grace and a lot more consideration.

The Etiquette of Public Transportation: Moving Through the World with Class

Public transportation—it's a place where the boundaries of personal space shrink, the pace of life speeds up, and humanity, in all its forms, comes together. Whether you're catching the subway, riding the bus, or hopping on a train, how you handle yourself in these shared spaces says a lot about who you are. Public transit is a little like a social contract: We're all in this together, so let's make the ride pleasant for everyone.

Here's how to approach public transportation with courtesy, awareness, and the right amount of urgency:

- **Respect the Line—It's Not a Free-for-All**

  Whether you're boarding a bus or waiting for the next train, there's an unspoken rule: Lines exist for a reason. Cutting the line or rushing ahead isn't just rude—it's a recipe for eye rolls and passive-aggressive sighs. Wait your turn, and when the doors open, let people exit before you board. Patience and awareness make public spaces more pleasant for everyone.
- **Personal Space and Boundaries in Shared Spaces**

  Public transportation doesn't exactly offer roomy seating arrangements, but respecting what little personal space exists is a must.
- **On a Packed Ride**

  Stand tall, hold on to a pole or handle, and avoid leaning on others.
- **Seated Next to Someone**

  Keep your bags, elbows, and knees within your designated bubble. Nobody likes an accidental nudge from a stranger's shoulder.

- **Offer Your Seat—and Do It Graciously**

  If you're sitting and someone who clearly needs a seat more than you enters—pregnant individuals, elderly passengers, or someone with a disability—offer your spot without hesitation. And do it without making a scene. A simple smile and a polite gesture say everything.
- **Mind the Volume**
  - Public transit isn't your personal concert venue or phone booth, so keep the noise to a minimum.
  - Headphones or Earbuds Are a Must: If you're to music or a podcast, keep the volume low. Nobody else needs to know you're revisiting your high school playlist.
  - Keep Calls Brief: If you absolutely must take a call, make it quick and keep your voice down. Public transit isn't the place for a detailed breakdown of your weekend plans.

International Etiquette Tip: In some parts of the world, like Japan, Finland, and Switzerland, public transit is a quiet zone. Conversations are kept to a whisper—if they happen at all. Phones are often silenced, and even answering a call might be considered rude. If you're traveling internationally, look for posted signs or take a cue from the locals. If they're silent, it's your sign to enjoy the ride in peace.

- **Bags Belong on You, Not the Seat**

  Seats are for people, not your tote bag, gym gear, or shopping haul. If the bus or train fills up, place your belongings on your lap or the floor in front of you, or on overhead racks if available. Taking up extra space while others stand? Not a good look.
- **Don't Be the Aisle Blocker**

  If you're standing near the doors, step aside to let others board or exit. Being the person who blocks the flow of traffic because you're distracted by your phone or too stubborn to move is a fast track to commuter infamy.

- **Food and Drinks? Keep It Clean**

  While a coffee or water bottle is fine on most public transit, think twice before bringing a full-on meal. No one wants to smell your takeout first thing in the morning, and spills are not a good way to make new friends.
- **Eye Contact? Keep It Light**

  Public transit is a shared space, but it's also an oddly personal one. You're close enough to count someone's freckles—but staring? That's a hard no. If you accidentally lock eyes with someone, a quick smile is fine, but keep it casual.
- **Mind Your Mess**

  Trash doesn't belong on the floor of the subway, and gum definitely doesn't belong stuck under the seat. Be responsible for your own mess—carry your trash until you find a bin, and leave your space as clean as it was when you arrived.
- **Know When to Hustle and When to Pause**

  Public transit runs on a schedule, and nobody likes to be held up by someone who's taking their sweet time. Move quickly when boarding or exiting. But, if you're early, don't crowd the doors or rush past others—find a balance between urgency and consideration.

The Takeaway: We're All in This Together

Public transportation is the ultimate shared experience, and how you behave on the ride reflects how much you respect those around you. By being considerate, patient, and just a little bit charming, you'll not only make the ride better for everyone, you'll also show the world that even in the chaos of rush hour, good manners never go out of style.

Q: *What if I spot someone I know on the metro—do I need to say hello, or can I keep my AirPods in and avoid a conversation?*

A: This is one of those tricky, in-the-moment decisions, but the short answer is, it's up to you. The one rule? Don't pretend you didn't see them. If your eyes meet or it's clear you've recognized each other, a quick smile or a polite "Hi, how are you?" is the gracious thing to do.

That said, you're not obligated to turn your commute into an impromptu catch-up session. A brief acknowledgment—like "So great to see you!"—is often enough to be polite without committing to a long conversation.

But what if they're really eager to connect?

If they seem ready to dive into a full conversation and you're not up for it, set a kind but clear boundary. For example:

- "It's so nice to see you! I'm catching up on a podcast I've been meaning to finish, but let's find a time to connect soon."
- Or: "I'd love to chat more, but I've got some reading I need to get through. Let's catch up another time!"

  If you sense their excitement and don't want to brush them off entirely, offer something actionable:
- "I'd love to hear more about what you're up to! Let's grab coffee sometime soon—what's your schedule like?"

This lets them know you value the connection while still keeping your commute your own. Remember, it's all about finding the balance between being gracious and honoring your own space. Every ride doesn't need to turn into a reunion tour.

The Etiquette of Getting In and Out of a Car: Channeling Your Inner Princess Diana

Sliding into or stepping out of a vehicle may seem like a mundane act, but with a touch of elegance, it can become a moment of effortless grace. Princess Diana, the queen of poised entrances and exits, knew this all too well. Inspired by her timeless style, here's how to master the art of car etiquette.

Entering a Car: Glide, Don't Stumble

1. **Face Away First**

   As you approach the car, turn your body so that you're facing away from the seat. Think of it as leading with your poise—your focus is on sliding in smoothly, not flopping down like a bag of groceries.

2. **Sit Sideways**

   Lower yourself onto the seat with your body still facing outward. This way, you're seated neatly before making any adjustments. Bonus: This position is far more elegant than fumbling forward.

3. **Swing Both Legs Together**

   Once you're seated, keep your knees together and swing both legs into the car in one graceful motion. Princess Diana's signature move avoided both awkward angles and unflattering paparazzi shots.

4. **Watch Your Head**

   Always be mindful of the door jamb as you slide in—there's nothing chic about bumping your head.

Exiting a Car

1. **Hold On for Balance**

   Use the steering wheel, door frame, or seat to steady yourself as you prepare to step out. A poised exit starts with stability.

2. **Knees Together, Legs Swing Out**

   Just as you entered, keep your knees together and swing both legs out simultaneously. This not only looks polished but also prevents any unwanted mishaps.

3. **Check Your Surroundings**

   Before stepping out fully, glance around for passing cars, bicycles, or motorcycles. Even the most graceful exit won't impress if it causes a traffic incident.

4. **Mind the Door**

   Gently close the door behind you—slamming it disrupts the tranquility of your exit and can come across as careless.

The Diana Effect: Add a Little Clutch to Your Routine

If you want to channel the Princess of Wales's style, consider adding a clutch to your car etiquette arsenal. Diana famously used her "cleavage bags" to discreetly shield her neckline from prying cameras as she stepped out of vehicles. Not only was this clever, but it also became an iconic part of her look. The lesson? A small, stylish accessory can double as a practical tool for maintaining composure in tricky moments.

Emerging from a car gracefully may not always be headline-worthy, but it's these small acts of poise that elevate your everyday life. Whether you're stepping into a gala or just running errands, remember: It's not only about where you're going but how you get there. And if you're holding a clutch, even better.

Shopping Etiquette: How to Shop with Style and Kindness

Shopping might seem like a routine errand, but how you navigate the aisles, interact with staff, and carry yourself in a store says a lot about your character. Whether you're browsing for groceries, clothes, or beauty products, a little etiquette transforms the experience into an act of kindness—for yourself, fellow shoppers, and the employees working hard to keep things running smoothly.

I think we could all benefit from taking a page out of the shopping experience found in the bucolic communities of Europe. When my husband and I were wandering (and, let's be honest, getting a little lost) along the winding pedestrian streets of Saint-Paul de Vence in the South of France, I witnessed something lovely: the subtle, almost choreographed rhythm between shopkeeper and shopper. There was no rush. No one was barking questions from across the store or juggling five items while talking on the phone. Instead, there was eye contact. Conversation. A sense of mutual respect. The shopper gave the shopkeeper their full attention, and in return, the shopkeeper offered thoughtful suggestions and warm hospitality.

It was a kind of social dance—and one I think we often forget in our rush-through-it, grab-and-go culture.

Shopping doesn't have to feel chaotic or transactional. With a little more mindfulness, it can be a small but meaningful moment of connection. Whether you're in a bustling American department store or a quiet artisan shop in a hilltop village, treating people with patience, courtesy, and awareness makes the experience more pleasant for everyone.

Aisle Jams: Keep the Flow Going

- **Yield to Courtesy**

  Parking your cart smack in the middle of the aisle at the supermarket? A rookie move. Instead, treat the aisle like a road and pull over to the side. Bonus points for ensuring that others can still easily pass while you debate which brand of pasta sauce to grab.
- **Don't Be a Statue**

  Standing in the middle of an aisle scrolling on your phone or analyzing ingredient labels like you're solving a mystery? Step aside! Keeping the aisles clear shows respect for everyone trying to get their shopping done.

Family Affairs: Control the Chaos

- **Wrangle the Little Shoppers**

  Bringing the kids along? Make it a family outing, not a free-for-all. Letting them run wild in the cereal aisle like it's recess can annoy other shoppers and create unnecessary hazards. Keep them close, and turn the outing into a chance to teach them about thoughtful choices.

Health and Safety: Keep It Clean

- **Pets Stay Home**

  Unless you have a service animal or you're at a pet store, your furry friend doesn't belong in a shopping cart—or the store. Doggie drool and public spaces don't mix, and neither do food safety rules and pets.
- **It's Not a Free Buffet**

  Sampling grapes or popping open a container of berries might seem harmless, but it's unsanitary, messy, and, frankly, stealing. Inspect your produce, buy it, and save the nibbling for after checkout.

Basic Manners: Think of Others

- **The Power of Polite Words**

  Whether you're squeezing past someone in a tight aisle or asking for help finding an item, polite words show thoughtfulness. A simple "excuse me" or "thank you" makes the shopping experience more pleasant for everyone.
- **Don't Phone It In**

  Loud phone calls on speaker in a busy store? It's not a good look. If you must take a call, step aside, lower your voice, and keep it brief. You're shopping, not hosting a podcast.

Change Your Mind? Put Items Back Properly

If you decide against that sweater or jar of sauce, don't abandon it on a random shelf. Either return it to its original spot or let a cashier or sales associate know. They'll appreciate the effort, and the store will stay organized for others.

Beauty and Retail Etiquette: Know the Rules

- **Free Services Aren't Entirely Free**

  If you're taking advantage of a complimentary beauty consultation or a personal shopper service, remember there's an unspoken agreement to purchase at least one product. These services take time and effort, and supporting the employee's work is part of good manners and good faith.
- **Don't Be a DIY Sample Taster**

  Makeup counters may look tempting, but resist dipping your fingers into product jars. Use provided applicators or ask for assistance. You wouldn't want someone else's germs in your favorite shade—extend the same courtesy.

Shopping doesn't happen in a vacuum—you're sharing the space with employees and other customers. From keeping aisles clear to showing gratitude, small acts of mindfulness make a big difference. Because grace and kindness? That's always in style—at home and abroad.

Tipping Traditions Around the World: Your Global Guide to Gratitude

When, where, and how do you tip? It's a recurring question during international travel. Tipping customs vary widely across the globe, and understanding them can make or break your experience as a traveler. What's seen as a gesture of appreciation in one country might be considered unnecessary—or even rude—in another. This curated guide is designed to help you approach tipping thoughtfully and appropriately, wherever your travels may lead.

Key Takeaways for Savvy Travelers

- **Research before you go.** Always learn the tipping customs of your destination to avoid offending locals or overpaying unnecessarily. Check online and consider making notes on your phone's note app to remind you while you're on the go.
- **Carry local currency.** Keeping small bills and change in the local currency ensures you're prepared to tip appropriately.
- **Ask when unsure.** Hotel concierges or guides can help clarify what's customary in their region.
- **Be discreet.** In some cultures, tipping is better left subtle or done indirectly, like leaving money in an envelope, so you might consider bringing some with you or asking the concierge at your hotel.
- **Think beyond cash.** A kind word, heartfelt compliment, or even a smile can be as meaningful as money in certain cultures.

Cultural Etiquette Around the World: A Traveler's Guide to Grace

Etiquette isn't just about knowing which fork to use—it's a language of respect, a way to connect, and, often, a mirror of a culture's values. Around the world, what's considered polite in one place might be shocking in another. For travelers eager to experience the world with poise, understanding these differences is the ultimate passport to meaningful and respectful connections.

Asia: Subtle Gestures and Thoughtful Silence

JAPAN: THE QUIET LIFE

Japan's etiquette is rooted in harmony and respect. Loud voices in public, eating while walking, and pointing with fingers or chopsticks are seen as rude. Bowing is a common way to greet, thank, or apologize, and learning this nuance shows cultural awareness and care. And remember, when exchanging business cards, always use two hands, and take a moment to admire the card before putting it away—it's a sign of respect for the person you're meeting.

CHINA: SAVING FACE

Public disagreements or overt displays of emotion are frowned upon in China, where maintaining "face" (dignity and respect) is paramount. Accepting gifts or business cards with both hands is a must, but opening a gift in front of the giver can be seen as greedy. And if you're at a banquet, never start eating before the host invites everyone to begin.

INDIA: RIGHT HAND RULES

In India, the right hand is used for eating, passing items, and greeting, as the left hand is considered unclean. Feet are also seen as impure, so avoid pointing your feet at people or sacred objects. If you're invited to someone's home, it's customary to bring a small gift, like sweets or flowers, as a token of appreciation.

Middle East: Hospitality and Modesty

UNITED ARAB EMIRATES: RESPECT THE CUSTOMS

In the UAE, modesty in dress and behavior is crucial. Avoid public displays of affection and dress conservatively, especially at religious sites or in traditional areas. When greeting, men should wait for women to extend their hand first, as not all women will shake hands. Hospitality is a cornerstone of Middle Eastern culture, and refusing an offer of tea or coffee can be considered impolite.

EGYPT: GENEROSITY IN INTERACTION

Egyptians are known for their warmth and hospitality, but there are a few unspoken rules. Avoid discussing politics or religion unless you know the person well. When invited to someone's home, bringing sweets or pastries is a thoughtful gesture. In conversation, direct eye contact can sometimes feel intense, so keep eye contact friendly but not overly prolonged.

Europe: Traditions with a Twist

FRANCE: KEEP IT FORMAL

In France, greetings are formal and important—start with a polite "bonjour" (hello) or "bonsoir" (good evening) before launching into conversation. Don't rush through a meal; dining is an art form there. Splitting the bill evenly isn't common—typically, each person pays their share, or the host foots the bill. And punctuality? Fashionably late (by ten to fifteen minutes) is often the norm for social gatherings.

ITALY: LA BELLA FIGURA

Italians value making a good impression, so dress stylishly and maintain a warm, approachable demeanor. When dining, never cut pasta with a knife—it's practically a sin! And remember: Espresso and espresso drinks are for mornings; ordering a cappuccino after lunch has long been a tourist giveaway, though this is changing as the world is becoming increasingly smaller and more international.

GERMANY: PRECISION AND RESPECT

Germans appreciate punctuality, whether for a business meeting or a dinner invitation. If you're invited to someone's home, bring flowers—just make sure they add up to an odd number, as even numbers are reserved for funerals. And don't cross the street unless the pedestrian light is green; jaywalking can earn you stern glares.

The Americas: Warm and Open, with a Few Exceptions

UNITED STATES: PERSONAL SPACE MATTERS

Americans value their personal space—standing too close can make people uncomfortable. Tipping culture, as mentioned, is nonnegotiable, and punctuality is generally expected. Small talk is a hallmark of friendliness, but steer clear of polarizing topics like politics or religion unless you know your audience well.

MEXICO: FAMILY FIRST

In Mexico, relationships and personal connections come first, so take the time to greet everyone individually in a group setting. If you're invited to a meal, arriving thirty minutes late is considered polite—it gives the host time to prepare. And while gifts are appreciated, avoid giving marigolds, as they're associated with funerals.

Oceania: Easygoing Elegance

AUSTRALIA: RELAX, BUT BE RESPECTFUL

Aussies are famously laid-back, but respect for others is deeply ingrained. First names are used almost immediately, but don't mistake this casualness for a lack of manners. Avoid talking about money or boasting, and remember that honesty and humility are valued.

NEW ZEALAND: RESPECT THE LAND

Kiwis take pride in their pristine environment and indigenous Māori culture. If visiting sacred Māori sites, listen to your guide's instructions and treat the area with reverence. And if you're invited to a barbecue, it's common to bring a bottle of wine or a plate of food to share.

Key Takeaways for Cultured Travelers

- **Observe before acting.** Watch how locals behave to pick up on unspoken rules.
- **Learn a few phrases.** Saying hello or thank you in the local language can open doors and hearts.

- **Dress the part.** Research what's appropriate for your destination to avoid sticking out or offending.
- **Keep an open mind.** Customs might feel unfamiliar, but embracing them enriches your travel experience.

By understanding cultural etiquette, you don't just avoid faux pas—you become a more thoughtful, connected traveler. Whether it's bowing in Japan, sharing a toast in Mexico, or respecting sacred spaces in New Zealand, these gestures of respect make every journey more meaningful.

The Takeaway: Grace Belongs Far Beyond Your Front Door

Whether we're ordering coffee, navigating a crowded sidewalk, or riding public transportation, how we carry ourselves in public says so much—often more than we realize. Etiquette on the go means carrying our consideration with us—through crowds, coffee lines, and commutes.

Throughout this chapter, I've shared stories of moments where a little kindness, patience, or situational awareness shifted the dynamic in a meaningful way. I hope those snapshots reminded you that etiquette isn't reserved for fancy dinners or formal events—it lives in the everyday. It's the stranger who holds the elevator, the visitor who makes the effort to embrace local customs, the commuter who gives up their seat with a smile.

What I hope you take from here into your travels is simple: When in doubt, lead with consideration. Let your presence bring a bit more calm, a bit more warmth, and a bit more grace to the world around you.

CONCLUSION

SHINING AS THE MORE CONSIDERATE, CONFIDENT YOU

You made it to the end of the book! You've opened yourself up to a new world of etiquette, picking up tips and tools along the way. I'm proud of you!

Despite all the details we've discussed, the one thing I want to leave you with is this: Diving into the world of etiquette isn't about memorizing rules or perfecting napkin folds (though those are nice touches). It's about choosing kindness, showing respect, and moving through life with intention.

Let's be real: While knowing some etiquette is definitely useful—how to write a tricky thank-you note or gracefully handle an awkward social situation—most of these concepts aren't life or death. What is serious, though, is kindness, respect, and integrity. That's what etiquette is really about. It's not about following rules for the sake of it; it's about showing others that they matter.

Remember what we talked about in the introduction ("Before We Begin, Don't Ask if She's Pregnant")? Etiquette matters because people matter. The way you treat others, even in the most mundane interactions, speaks volumes about who you are. Kindness is the great equalizer—it transcends titles, backgrounds, and even awkward first impressions. And the best part? You don't need a degree in diplomacy or a silver spoon to show it.

So go ahead—smile at the barista who gets your complicated coffee order just right. Write that thank-you note that's been on your to-do list. Ask your neighbor how they're really doing. These tiny gestures may seem small, but trust me, they're the kind of things people remember.

And if you're ever worried about getting it wrong, here's your permission slip to let go of the pressure. Nobody is perfect—not me, not you, not even the most polished among us. What matters is the effort, the intention, and the heart you bring to every interaction.

So go out there and be your lovely, kind, and thoughtful self. Sprinkle a little grace wherever you go. And if you ever need a refresher, you have this book, and you know where to find me: probably adjusting my posture, tweaking my thank-you note wording, or telling another story about the power of a good handshake.

Let's Stay in Touch

After you close this book, I'd love for you to continue this journey with me through Elevate Etiquette, my platform dedicated to modern manners, meaningful connections, and the kind of personal growth that feels both elegant and approachable. Whether you're preparing for a big job interview, hosting your first dinner party, or sending a tricky text, my goal is to help you move through life with warmth, clarity, and confidence.

You're always welcome in our online community, where we talk about real-life etiquette dilemmas, share behind-the-scenes stories, and answer your most pressing questions. You can find free resources, courses, and more at elevateetiquette.com, and follow along on social media @elevateetiquette for daily insights and a bit of fun.

Have a question I didn't answer here? Curious about a particular scenario? I love hearing from readers—your questions and stories inspire so much of what I do and write. Pop into the Q&A on Instagram or send me a message anytime.

Here's to thoughtful living, gracious connection, and always finding a kinder way to say (and do) things. I'm so glad we're on this journey together.

ACKNOWLEDGMENTS

You didn't think I'd end this book without saying thank you, did you? Writing may be a solo act, but creating a book—especially this one—has taken the love, insight, and generosity of so many people. I am deeply grateful.

To my extraordinary team at W Publishing—Damon Reiss, Caren Wolfe, Kerri Daly, Elizabeth Hawkins, and Rachel Buller—thank you for your encouragement, wisdom, and true spirit of teamwork. Working with you has been such a joy. To my editor, Carrie Marrs, your kind, uplifting edits, and suggestions felt more like gentle conversation than critique. You have such a magical way of making every page better, and I couldn't have asked for a more thoughtful partner in this process.

To Ruth Samsel, the first person in publishing to believe in me—thank you for your faith, your honesty, and your generosity.

To my agent, Rebekah Von Lintel, thank you for your steady professionalism and thoughtful advocacy every step of the way.

To Arianne Minks, thank you for planting the seed that the quiet passion I held for etiquette could one day become a vibrant, purposeful business.

To Madison Porter, thank you for advocating for me and encouraging me to take a leap of faith at a pivotal moment in my career. Accepting the job you championed changed the course of my life in ways I never could have imagined.

To Valeria and Gary Lipovetsky, thank you for your mentorship and support in helping me take my business to the next level. I'm so grateful for your encouragement and wisdom.

To my family and friends, thank you for your patience and cheerleading during the long stretches of writing and for letting me test-drive countless etiquette principles and party-hosting ideas in real time. I appreciate you more than you know. I'm especially grateful to Linsey and Donald Crowell, Gloria and Bob Burkett, Mary Margaret and Matt Bush, Danielle Fillion, Hope Harvard, Lauren Stimpert Leonard and Josh Leonard, Caroline Nabity, Megan and Forrest Parker, Kaitlyn Roberts, and Hannah Zakaria for showing up in every way that matters. And to Jane Kennedy, thank you for the prayers, the long walks, and the conversations that always left me feeling calmer and clearer.

To Robb Austin, thank you for your endless generosity, mentorship, and friendship. You shaped the professional I am today, and I will always be grateful.

To Amelia Brown, thank you for capturing the essence of my work—and my heart—so beautifully through your photography. You've taught me so much about confidence and presence over the years. Working with you is always a gift, and I'm so grateful for your friendship and creative eye.

To Lauren Stimpert Leonard, your illustrations brought this book to life with beauty and timeless charm. Your wide-ranging talents never cease to amaze me.

To the team of people who keep me grounded and help me perform at my best—Shelby Anderson Booth, Kaylee Ann Barber, Kelly Bechen, Claudia Díaz, and Alvin Hinton—thank you for sharing your talent and care so consistently.

To my Nana, who inspired my love of books before I even knew how to read, and to Papa, for teaching me work ethic—something I definitely needed to finish this book! To my parents, Tom and Paula Carey, for being phenomenal examples of kindness and generosity. And to my siblings, Carolyn, Ryan, and TJ, for always cheering me on—and lovingly keeping me humble.

To Jason—for listening to more excerpts of this book than anyone ever should, for giving me space when I needed to retreat and write, and for never, ever doubting all that this book could become. Your steady belief in me means more than I can say (and that's saying something—I wrote a whole book!).

And to anyone who has ever trusted me to help you become a more confident, polished, and respectful version of yourself, asked a vulnerable question, or taken etiquette seriously not because you "had to," but because you wanted to—you're the reason I wrote this book. I appreciate you more than you know.

NOTES

Introduction

1. *Cambridge Dictionary*, "etiquette," accessed December 1, 2025, https://dictionary.cambridge.org/us/dictionary/english/etiquette.

Chapter 1: Greetings and Introductions

1. Eric Wargo, "How Many Seconds to a First Impression?," Association for Psychological Science, July 1, 2006, https://www.psychologicalscience.org/observer/how-many-seconds-to-a-first-impression; Serenity Gibbons, "You and Your Business Have 7 Seconds to Make a First Impression: Here's How to Succeed," *Forbes*, updated December 10, 2021, https://www.forbes.com/sites/serenitygibbons/2018/06/19/you-have-7-seconds-to-make-a-first-impression-heres-how-to-succeed/.
2. Researchers have long emphasized the power of body language in shaping perception; in fact, Vanessa Van Edwards notes that "nonverbal signals account for 60 to 90% of our total communication." Vanessa Van Edwards, "Researchers Find that Nonverbal Signals Account for 60 to 90% of Our Total Communication," LinkedIn, November 15, 2023, https://www.linkedin.com/posts/vanessavanedwards_bodylanguage-recoveringawkwardperson-activity-7241536326938849280-MZXX?utm_source=share&utm_medium=member_desktop&rcm=ACoAAAi9_fIBTGzzqTiKbFzTKcNSr8R6baePZ7I.
3. See generally Albert Mehrabian, *Silent Messages: Implicit Communication of Emotions and Attitudes* (Wadsworth, 1971), https://e-edu.nbu.bg/pluginfile.php/855150/mod_resource/content/1/Albert-Mehrabian%20-%20Silent%20Messages%201971%20-%20red.size.pdf; see generally Mehrabian,

Silent Messages, 2nd ed. (Wadsworth, 1980/1981), https://archive.org/details/silentmessagesim00mehr.

4. Dana R. Carney, Amy J. C. Cuddy, and Andy J. Yap, "Power Posing: Brief Nonverbal Displays Affect Neuroendocrine Levels and Risk Tolerance," *Psychological Science* 21, no. 10 (2010): 1363–68, https://doi.10.1177/0956797610383437.
5. Erik Peper and I-Mei Lin, "Increase or Decrease Depression: How Body Postures Influence Your Energy Level," *Biofeedback* 40, no. 3 (2012): 125–30, https://www.researchgate.net/publication/279348439_Increase_or_Decrease_Depression_How_Body_Postures_Influence_Your_Energy_Level. (This study investigates how body posture during movement affects subjective energy levels, indicating that slouched postures are associated with decreased energy and increased feelings of depression.); and Shwetha Nair et al., "Do Slumped and Upright Postures Affect Stress Responses? A Randomized Trial," *Health Psychology* 34, no. 6 (2015): 632–41, https://pubmed.ncbi.nlm.nih.gov/25222091. (This research explores the effects of upright versus slumped postures on stress responses, finding that upright participants reported higher self-esteem and better mood compared to those in slumped positions.)
6. Peper and Lin, "Increase or Decrease Depression"; Nair et al., "Do Slumped and Upright Postures Affect Stress Responses?"
7. CareerBuilder, "More Than Half of Employers Have Found Content on Social Media That Caused Them NOT to Hire a Candidate," PR Newswire, August 9, 2018, https://www.prnewswire.com/news-releases/more-than-half-of-employers-have-found-content-on-social-media-that-caused-them-not-to-hire-a-candidate-according-to-recent-careerbuilder-survey-300694437.html?utm_source=chatgpt.com.
8. "Don't Post That! Why Half of Americans Regret Their Social Media Posts," Social Media Today, July 28, 2015, https://www.socialmediatoday.com/social-networks/sarah-snow/2015-07-28/dont-post-why-half-americans-regret-their-social-media-posts; Yevgeniy Reznik, "Study: Americans' Privacy May Be at Risk as People Overshare About Politics, Kids, and Bodily Functions," Secure Data Recovery, updated October 3, 2023, https://www.securedatarecovery.com/blog/americans-overshare-social-media#:~:text=The%20majority%20of%20Americans%20(53,and%20your%20latest%20gardening%20escapades.

Chapter 2: Small Talk, Big Impact

1. In *How to Win Friends and Influence People* (Simon & Schuster, 1936), Dale Carnegie famously wrote: "A person's name is to that person the sweetest and most important sound in any language." Although it's anecdotal, this principle is widely supported in modern interpersonal communication and sales psychology for building trust and emotional connection; Han Bao et al., "Specificity in the Processing of a Subject's Own Name," *Social Cognitive and Affective Neuroscience* 18, no. 1 (2023): nsad066, https://doi.org/10.1093/scan/nsad066. (This study supports the idea that hearing one's own name triggers unique brain responses, underscoring the personal significance and potential positive emotional impact of one's name in social interactions.)
2. When it comes to building your financial knowledge, trusted resources are key. Two thought leaders I highly recommend for honest, relatable advice are Professor Scott Galloway (https://profgmedia.com) and Vivian Tu from Your Rich BFF (https://www.yourrichbff.com). Both provide valuable insights on personal finance and wealth building, empowering you to make informed financial decisions without needing to compare salary details with colleagues.

Chapter 3: Main Character Energy: Job Search Edition

1. "Title VII of the Civil Rights Act of 1964," US Equal Employment Opportunity Commission, accessed June 7, 2025, https://www.eeoc.gov/statutes/title-vii-civil-rights-act-1964; "Age Discrimination in Employment Act of 1967," US Equal Employment Opportunity Commission, accessed June 7, 2025, https://www.eeoc.gov/statutes/age-discrimination-employment-act-1967; "What Shouldn't I Ask When Hiring?," US Equal Employment Opportunity Commission, accessed June 7, 2025, https://www.eeoc.gov/employers/small-business/what-shouldnt-i-ask-when-hiring; and "Americans with Disabilities Act of 1990, as Amended," ADA.gov, accessed June 7, 2025, https://www.ada.gov/law-and-regs/ada/.

Chapter 5: Relationships in Love and Life

1. University of California, Irvine, "Teens' Online Friendships Just as Meaningful as Face-to-Face Ones," *ScienceDaily*, September 27, 2017, https://www.sciencedaily.com/releases/2017/09/170927105416.htm.

2. "#BrandsGetReal: Social Media & the Evolution of Transparency," Sprout Social (blog), accessed June 7, 2025, https://sproutsocial.com/insights/data/social-media-transparency/.
3. Emily A. Vogels and Colleen McClain, "Key Findings About Online Dating in the U.S.," Pew Research Center, February 2, 2023, https://www.pewresearch.org/short-reads/2023/02/02/key-findings-about-online-dating-in-the-u-s/.

Chapter 8: Dining Out with Decorum

1. "All About Scones," last modified September 1, 2022, https://savannahsconecompany.com/all-about-scones/.

INDEX

C

D

E

Q

R

S

T

V

W

Y

ABOUT THE AUTHOR

Alison M. Cheperdak, JD, is the founder of Elevate Etiquette, a distinguished consultancy offering social, business, and dining etiquette courses as well as international protocol training.

From private coaching to keynoting conferences, Alison teaches etiquette and executive presence to individuals and organizations around the world. She has led trainings at the White House, Harvard Law School, the US Congress, and Fortune 100 companies. Her insights are frequently featured in national and international media, and she shares daily etiquette tips with millions across social media.

Her passion for etiquette began while planning her wedding in 2012. Curious about the finer points of tradition, she purchased her first etiquette book—and never stopped reading. Since then, she has studied etiquette, protocol, and emotional intelligence extensively and graduated with merit from The English Manner and Beaumont Etiquette's Train the Trainer Grade One and Grade Two Programs.

Alison's professional background profoundly influences her thoughtful, contemporary approach to modern manners. After graduating magna cum laude and Phi Beta Kappa from Villanova University, she worked as a TV news reporter for an NBC station in New York. She then moved to Washington, DC, where she earned her law degree from The George Washington University Law School and was recognized with the President's Volunteer Service Award for pro bono legal work. Her legal career has included roles in a large corporate law firm as well as in the legislative, judicial, and executive branches of the federal government, including the West Wing of the White House. She also served as executive director of a leading national nonprofit.

Learn more at elevateetiquette.com.

The journey doesn't end here!

Discover Alison Cheperdak's signature etiquette tips to help you navigate life with poise and confidence. From tricky situations to everyday elegance, her advice is your go-to for living gracefully.

STAY INSPIRED. STAY POISED.

Follow **@elevateetiquette** for daily tips, exclusive content, and practical advice!

ELEVATE YOUR PRESENCE WITH ALISON M. CHEPERDAK

Discover the art of modern manners and executive presence with Alison M. Cheperdak, J.D., founder of Elevate Etiquette.

Whether you're looking to refine your professional presence, master social etiquette, or simply elevate your everyday interactions, Alison is here to guide you.

Visit ElevateEtiquette.com to learn more and join a community dedicated to living with elegance and intention.

ElevateEtiquette.com